GARETH

CW01496322

Eyewitness to th

"The historian does not simply come in to replenish the gaps of memory. He constantly challenges even those memories that have survived intact.... No subject is potentially unworthy of his interest, no document, no artifact beneath his attention."
Zakhor, Yosef Khaim Yerushalmi,

"Where can that life have gone? And that suffering, that terrible suffering? Can there really be nothing left? Is it really true that no one will be held to account for it all? That it will all just be forgotten without a trace?"
Everything Flows, Vasily Grossman

"... even so rich and commanding a newspaper as the [*New York*] *Times* does not take seriously enough the equipment of the correspondent. For extraordinarily difficult posts in extraordinary times, something more than routine correspondents are required. Reporting is one of the most difficult professions, requiring much expert knowledge and serious education. The old contention that properly trained men lack the 'news sense' will not stand against the fact that improperly trained men have seriously misled a whole nation."
Walter Lippmann and Charles Merz, "A Test of the News,"
The New Republic, August 4, 1920

"Journalists are a wonderful community everywhere and there is a fine feeling of cooperation and hospitality among them."
Letter dated March 24, 1935, Gareth Jones

GARETH JONES

Eyewitness to the *Holodomor*

Ray Gamache

Welsh Academic Press

Published in Wales by Welsh Academic Press, an imprint of

Ashley Drake Publishing Ltd
PO Box 733
Cardiff
CF14 7ZY

www.welsh-academic-press.wales

First edition published in hardback 2013
First edition published in paperback 2016
Second edition published in paperback 2018

ISBN
978-1-86057-128-2

British Library Cataloguing-in-Publication Data.
A CIP catalogue for this book is available from the British Library.

Typeset by Replika Press Pvt Ltd, India

Contents

List of Illustrations

1. *Evening Standard*, 31 March 1933.
2. Graphic representation of the relation between text, supra-text, and context.
3. Annie Gwen Jones with the Hughes family.
4. *Bezbozhnik (The Godless)* newspaper, 22 April 1923.
5. Postcard to Mr. Edgar Jones from Gareth Jones, August 1930.
6. Letter from Gareth Jones depicting the location of Ivy Lee and Associates.
7. Jack Heinz II, "On the eve of your departure...".
8. Soviet propaganda poster about eliminating illiteracy.
9. Gareth Jones' diary entry drawing of the "Hoover" propaganda poster
10. The "Hoover" propaganda poster, from the archives of Gareth Jones.
11. Gareth Jones' diary entry with 'See Hamlet'.
12. Postcard to Margaret Stewart, 7 March 1933.
13. Gareth Jones' letter to his family sent from Kharkov, 14 March 1933.
14. *New York Evening Post*, 30 March 1933.
15. Gareth Jones' passport, March 1933.
16. Gareth Jones' diary entry, 'I don't trust Duranty'.
17. Picture of an orphanage, from the archives of Gareth Jones.
18. A poster advertising Gareth Jones' 'The Enigma of Bolshevik Russia' travelogue.
19. Gareth Jones in the KFWB radio station, January 1935.
20. The plaque commemorating Gareth Jones at the Old College building, Aberystwyth University.
21. Memorandum by A. W. Kliefoth, dated 4 June 1931.

Acknowledgements

I could not have written this book without the love and support of my wife, Jane Margaret Benesch, who guides and nurtures every one of my projects. Additional support comes from my mother, Rachel Gamache; sister Aline Gamache; and sisters-in-law, Amy and Sarah Benesch.

I owe a debt of gratitude to our dear friends in Wales, John Clark and Mary Ward-Jackson, who opened up their home, and served as gracious hosts, bird finders, and tour guides during our trip to Wales.

Dr. Margaret Siriol Colley (1925-2011), niece and biographer of Gareth Jones, graciously answered my initial inquiries and encouraged me to pursue my work.

Mr. Nigel Linsan Colley, great-nephew of Gareth Jones, not only provided me with a tremendous amount of archival material as well as his thoughts, feelings, and discoveries about Jones, but he also took me on a delightful walking tour of London one fine June day, fed me home-made sandwiches, and answered all of my questions.

Dr. Graham Jones, political archivist at the National Library of Wales, took time from his busy schedule to make sure I had access to all the archives in the Gareth Vaughan Jones Papers. He and his competent staff made my time at the Library a pleasurable experience, one I'll always treasure.

A special thank you goes out to Thomas Ruddy and Kenya Flash, at the D. Leonard Corgan Library, King's College, who expedited and filled every one of my requests for Interlibrary Loans with professional aplomb.

The King's College administration for awarding me a Summer Research Grant, which enabled me to travel to Wales, Princeton University, and Washington, D.C., to conduct my research.

Mrs. Eirionedd Baskerville and Mr. Nick Cole assisted me in locating newspaper citations. Without their able assistance, I could not have finished this project on time.

Author's Note

To simplify the problems of presenting Russian names and terms, I have retained the spellings and transliterations used in the source materials. In the 1930s, journalists often employed the generic name "Russia" to mean the USSR—the Union of Soviet Socialist Republics. I have endeavored to refrain from using "Russia" interchangeably with the USSR, although I have used "Russian" as a qualifier for nouns like language, culture, etc. Most Russian terms are retained in their original form and italicized, accompanied with an explanation in the text. Others that are more familiar to the reader of English have been rendered as English words, kulak for example. Newspapers like *Pravda (Truth)* and *Izvestia (News)*, well known in English, have not been translated in the text; those less known have been translated. The term "peasant" has been used to refer to those villagers who lived and worked in the countryside; when referring to a specific class, the word *batrak, bednyak*, etc., was used.

My purpose in writing this book was to offer a close reading of Gareth Jones's articles about the USSR and its Five-Year Plan. I alone bear responsibility for the interpretations of those articles, diaries and personal correspondence, as well as the significance of the *Holodomor* and its meanings. I do not offer assertions of fact about demographic losses related to the famine or its causes, other than those offered by Jones in his work.

1

'Famine Rules Russia'

'Hero of Ukraine'

On March 31, 1933, the London *Evening Standard* published an article (Illustration 1) titled "Famine Rules Russia" by Gareth Jones, a young Welsh journalist who had recently returned from an unescorted walking tour through several of the grain growing districts in the Soviet Union. In his article, the first of twenty-one that he wrote over the next few weeks, Jones asserts that "the present state of Russian agriculture is already catastrophic but that in a year's time its condition will have worsened tenfold."[1] On the very same day, the *New York Times* published an article titled "Russians Hungry, But Not Starving," by Walter Duranty, an Englishman who had been the Moscow correspondent for the *New York Times* since 1921. In his lead paragraph, Duranty calls Jones' claims "a big scare story…with 'thousands already dead and millions menaced by death and starvation.' Its author is Gareth Jones."[2] By denigrating Jones by name, Duranty, the Pulitzer Prize winner in 1932, not only denied that a famine was raging across the USSR, but he also ignited a controversy that has persisted for more than eighty years.

The contrast between the two articles and the authors is striking beyond the obvious difference in their headlines. A graduate of Cambridge fluent in Russian, German, and French, Jones was twenty-seven years old and a part-time journalist, known mainly as the foreign affairs adviser to the former Prime Minister, David Lloyd George. Nonetheless, Jones' article merits consideration for its forthright presentation of testimony from peasants gathered during a difficult and dangerous walking tour through fourteen villages across more than forty miles within Russia and Ukraine at a time when travel within these regions was banned. For his part, Duranty was a forty-seven-year-old seasoned journalist at the height of his fame, considered the most important Western journalist in Moscow. His article, written while en route to Berlin, was pieced together by making inquiries "in Soviet commissariats and in foreign embassies...and from my personal connections, Russian and foreign."[3] Jones' reporting represents journalism at its best, bold and assertive in chronicling a disaster of catastrophic proportions; Duranty's article uses biased sources and euphemisms to conceal the grim realities of a famine.

The Duranty-initiated controversy, which was chronicled by a number of journalists who were stationed in Moscow at the time and aware of the famine and its cover-up, as well as by numerous scholars, represents what Sally J. Taylor, in *Stalin's Apologist: Walter Duranty— The New York Times's Man in Moscow*, calls "one of the sorriest periods of reportage in the history of the free press."[4] Unfortunately, the controversy came to overshadow Jones' reporting of the Five-Year Plan and the famine of 1932-33. However, on the day that both of their articles were published, Jones was jubilant about what he had already accomplished, most likely unaware of Duranty's criticism of his reporting. Jones writes to his family:

> I have never had two such days in my life. Yesterday the N.Y. Times, the Associated Press, the Allied Newspapers, the Press Association all wanted interviews! Then I went to tell L.G. [Lloyd George] about my visit. Then was called to the Daily Express to the Editor and offered £250 to write a series of articles...[5]

While scholarship has focused a harsh light on Duranty's role in denying the famine, these studies have given scant attention to Jones' reporting, which began in 1930 after the first of three trips to the USSR. Jones' reporting was further eclipsed after journals like the Ukrainian-language *Svoboda (Freedom)* and its English-language subsidiary, the *Ukrainian Weekly*, took over the primary reporting of the famine in October 1933, when they launched a campaign asserting that Soviet policy had distinctly targeted Ukrainians, in the process murdering millions of innocent people in a genocide.[6] A campaign by Ukrainians to have that genocide rightfully recognized by governments across the globe continues to this day.

Stunned by the Duranty-orchestrated denials and shunned by some of the people who had supported him, Gareth Jones fell from his brief stay in the international spotlight during his tenure as a reporter with the *Western Mail*. However, on one assignment in 1934 he interviewed newspaper magnate William Randolph Hearst at his Welsh estate of St. Donat's Castle at Llantwit Major, a few miles southwest of Cardiff. Hearst was impressed enough with Jones' understanding of world affairs to invite him to his ranch in San Simeon, California, when Jones traveled to the United States on his way to the Far East. Arriving on

January 1, 1935, Jones supplied Hearst with three short articles that were syndicated in Hearst newspapers from January 12-14, part of an anti-Communist campaign focused on the Soviet famine of 1932-33. While the articles' anti-Communist perspective resonated with Hearst, Jones' reputation was further tarnished when Hearst newspapers published several fabricated articles and faked photographs supplied by Thomas Walker, alias of Robert Green, an escaped convict. Furnished with Green's travel dates by Soviet authorities, Louis Fischer of *The Nation* exposed the Walker fraud, in the process sowing seeds of doubt on all reporting about the Soviet famine.[7] Without ever mentioning Jones by name, Fischer finished what Duranty had begun two years earlier, casting aspersions on Jones' honest reporting. For the next seventy years, Gareth Jones was effectively airbrushed from journalism history.

Jones emerged from obscurity with the publication of *Gareth Jones—A Manchukuo Incident* by Dr. Margaret Siriol Colley, Jones' niece, a thoroughly researched investigation into Gareth's untimely death at the hands of Chinese bandits. Jones' death, one day before he would have turned thirty, has engendered considerable speculation, in part because the two men who helped him arrange his trip—Dr. Herbert Mueller and Adam Purpiss—both had connections with the NKVD [Soviet secret police] and the driver was a Russian. Dr. Colley, in collaboration with her son Nigel Linsan Colley, then published a biography in 2005, titled *More than a Grain of Truth: The Biography of Gareth Richard Vaughan Jones*. The legacy of Gareth Jones has undergone a remarkable surge since those works as well as his articles, diaries, and correspondence were released. Since that time, the number of conference papers, newspaper articles, radio reports, documentaries, and awards has proliferated. Having witnessed and documented the famine, Jones has become the key journalist for Ukrainians worldwide in their quest to legitimate the *Holodomor*[8] as a genocide perpetrated by the USSR. In numerous articles, Jones is referred to as a "Hero of Ukraine."

Holodomor as 'Critical Incident'

The famine of 1932-33 constitutes what journalism historian Barbie Zelizer refers to as a "critical incident."[9] When employed analytically, the term refers to those moments in which the people within a nation collectively formulate and articulate their cultural identity. As a journalist, Jones provided independent eyewitness testimony about what happened to Ukrainians during this critical incident, providing them with the necessary documentation to shape collective memory around it. As Zelizer explains, "In this view, collective memories pivot on discussions of some kind of critical incident…. Critical incidents uphold the importance of discourse and narrative in shaping the community over time."[10] That narrative of genocide was articulated by Professor Raphael Lemkin of Harvard University and author of the United Nations Convention against genocide, who in 1953 addressed a rally of largely American-Ukrainian protestors in New York City marking the twentieth anniversary of the famine. As reported in *The Ukrainian Weekly* Section of *Svoboda*, Lemkin reviewed the fate of millions of Ukrainians who died "victims to the Soviet Russian plan to exterminate as many of them as possible in order to break the heroic Ukrainian national resistance to Soviet Russian rule and occupation and to Communism."[11] In his analysis of Stalin's genocidal intent against the Ukrainians, Lemkin delineated a four-prong attack on Ukrainian sovereignty: (1) destruction of the intelligentsia; (2) destruction of Ukrainian churches; (3) destruction of the peasantry by starvation through dekulakization, forced collectivization, murderous procurements, and the exporting of grain; and (4) the destruction of Ukrainian people through a process of dispersion, deportation, exile, and repopulation by the addition of foreign peoples.[12] Following along these lines, Dr. Alexander Motyl argues that the famine must be seen as one of a number of Soviet mass killings perpetrated by a genocidal regime.

To be sure, the *Holodomor* was the result of a brutal agricultural policy called forced collectivization. But, more important, the death of millions of Ukrainian peasants was the direct consequence of the Soviet regime's unwillingness to alleviate the massive famine that collectivization had unleashed in Ukraine and of its adoption of closed-border policies that intensified the *Holodomor*'s impact and permitted it to run its deathly course.[13]

In the years since the famine, that narrative has also, in one small part, become focused around two attendant campaigns related to the reporting of the famine—to elevate Jones to the status of hero and to strip Duranty of his 1932 Pulitzer Prize.

Jones has rightfully become the linchpin journalist of the *Holodomor*, which means literally "to kill by hunger," even though that term and the term genocide had yet to be used to describe what happened in the USSR from 1931-1933. By invoking his reporting of the famine, Ukrainians frame distant memories in a more current context. Memories, as Kansteiner suggests, "are at their most collective when they transcend time and space of the events' original occurrence. As such, they take on a powerful life of their own...."[14] This project argues that collective memory is more powerful when it is constituted on the basis of interpretations of specific texts, in this case the articles and diaries Jones wrote about the Soviet Union. How we make meaning of past events and the journalists who covered them represents an important component of historical inquiry, one that calls for interpretations that challenge established, tacit assumptions. This is not to suggest that Jones' status as "hero of Ukraine" is not deserved; rather, an analysis of Jones' reporting clearly illustrates why he is so deserving.

Estimations of Jones' importance as a journalist are based on a detailed analysis of his reporting. As such, this analysis draws upon the intertextuality of his newspaper articles, diaries, and personal correspondence within the context of the time period. This project interprets primary source evidence rather than recollections "that assume a collective authority derived from their assembled presence."[15] A tremendous amount of Jones' primary source material is available to scholars—both at the National Library of Wales and at the garethjones. org website, thanks to the tireless work of Nigel Linsan Colley, his great-nephew. Additionally, Mr. Colley has made available relevant materials from a number of the other journalists like Duranty, Lyons, and Malcolm Muggeridge, who were key figures in the reporting of the famine or its cover-up. Another important primary source of information comes from agricultural experts like Otto Schiller and Andrew Cairns, both of whom travelled through the USSR in the summer of 1932 and wrote extensive reports on their findings.

In his 2010 seminal work *Bloodlands*, Timothy Snyder posits that the history of the bloodlands[16] has largely been maintained by dividing the European past into national interests while keeping them separate and distinct. He notes, "Yet attention to any single persecuted group, no matter how well executed as history, will fail as an account of what happened in Europe between 1933 and 1945. Perfect knowledge of the Ukrainian past will not produce the causes of the famine...."[17] The work of Gareth Jones is very important not only because it explains the horrible experiences of one nation, but also because it so compellingly and compassionately documents what happened to many different groups of people having to endure "the taste of hunger, or a tyrant's reign."[18]

The Journalist as Eyewitness

Significantly, Jones' reporting provided eyewitness testimony to the famine. Eyewitnessing has special significance in journalism mythology, for to have been there, to preserve for posterity something of the individual human experience within historical events and conditions gives journalists an authority that no training can impart. Barbie Zelizer has noted that eyewitnessing "offers members of the journalistic community a way to reference what journalists do, should do and ought not do."[19] In this way, it governs norms, setting boundaries around which kinds of practice are appropriate and preferred. Equally important, eyewitness evidence is crucial to establish journalistic authority, for as British critic John Carey has observed, "eyewitness evidence makes for authenticity.... Eyewitness accounts have the feel of truth, because they are quick, subjective and incomplete."[20] Indeed, Jones was criticized by Duranty in the *New York Times* for his limited sample. Duranty writes, "It appeared that he [Jones] had made a forty-mile walk through villages in the neighborhood of Kharkov and had found conditions sad. I suggested that that was a rather inadequate cross-section of a big country, but nothing could shake his conviction of impending doom."[21] On the surface, Duranty's criticism might seem valid. But eyewitnessing cannot merely be measured by the distance covered; in fact, as John Locke explained, the witness' proximity to the event should be the relevant barometer. Jones got as close as he could to the people: he slept on the floor of their huts, he talked directly to them, recording them in his reporter's notebooks/diaries, and he shared with them the little food he had packed in his rucksack.

Most importantly, Jones gave voice to people who in all likelihood would not survive the famine. Only by keeping their experiences alive through the discursive act of writing his newspaper articles did Jones assure access to the truth and authenticity of their experiences. The eyewitness' account distinguishes the real world from the world of fiction. John Durham Peters explains this important distinction. "In tragedy, the representation of pain (and pain is definitional for the genre) is not supposed to excite the spectator to humanitarian service but to clarify through representation what is possible in life. The drama offers terror without danger, pity without duty.... Factual distress calls for our aid, not our appreciation; our duty, not our pleasure."[22] The boundary between fact and fiction is an ethical one; it demands respect, or bearing witness, to the pain of victims. While courts of law favor the objective witness, offering only the facts, bearing witness requires more than a dispassionate reporting of what happened.

Similarly, journalism's desire for objectivity and impartiality reflects a paradigm in which the reporter's subjectivity does not adulterate the public record of events as they really happened. However, when it comes to witnessing the distant suffering of others, Jones' reporting reminds us that objectively rendering what happened, attempting to present a fair and balanced report, giving voice to all constituencies, and seeking authoritative sources is ultimately inadequate. Rather, Jones' reporting offers an exemplar of what Martin Bell, BBC correspondent before becoming a member of the British parliament, called the "journalism of attachment," a journalism "that cares as well as knows; that is aware of its responsibilities; that will not stand neutrally between good and evil, right and wrong, the victim and the oppressor."[23] Another characteristic of the "journalism of attachment" is the injunction to care. A care ethic gives priority to the problems, concerns and suffering of marginalized or oppressed people. For journalists, this involves moving care from the personal to the social. As Peters notes, "Witnessing in this sense suggests a morally justified individual who speaks out against unjust power."[24] However, journalistic reporting on human tragedies such as famine can be exploited for commercial and ideological purposes.[25] In order for the journalist to move from merely witnessing death and dying to bearing witness "in a morally infused sense underpinned by a cosmopolitan outlook and sense of responsibility to others."[26]

It is worth noting that Gareth Jones financed this third trip to the USSR by himself. And though he was part of the comfortable world of privilege, he risked arrest, deportation or worse when he detrained and began walking through the villages. Rather than accessing authoritative sources, as Duranty claimed to do, Jones crafted his news stories with the "deliberate use of visceral images and embodied in the evocation of bodily sense of sight, sound, smell, taste and touch."[27] This invocation of the senses rather than gratuitous or base sensationalism formed the core of his famine reporting, which was anything but impartial and detached journalism.

The privileged role and articulated sense of responsibility comes with a price, however. According to the journalists' own accounts, it can produce ambivalent ideas about professionalism and personal responsibility. Unfortunately, Jones never had the chance to reflect on his coverage. While many others from this time period produced memoirs, including Duranty, Lyons, Chamberlin and Muggeridge, Jones did not offer very much in the way of self-reflexivity. If he had lived into his thirties and beyond, perhaps we would have a greater understanding of his motivations and what he thought about reporting on this catastrophic famine. Jones' reporting of the famine anticipates today's "journalism of attachment," the ontology of witnessing a disaster and bearing witness to it through the act of writing a series of newspaper articles that satisfy the injunction to care for people who had almost no way to communicate what was happening to them, whose voices were being muffled by the official Soviet denials that were subsequently echoed by journalists like Duranty, and whose only recourse was through personal correspondence.

Sources

In addition to analyzing primary source material, this project is informed by a considerable number of books and articles that can be placed into three distinct categories—works about the Five-Year Plan and the famine of 1932-33, works about the journalists who covered the famine, and works that shed light on the ethical and psychological dimensions of journalists covering disasters. Those secondary sources were not selected on the basis of whether or not they interpret the famine as artificial and organized, or the result of natural causes, or bureaucratic malfeasance. Given the complexity of the famine, no single narrative completely explains the famine or its causes. As Motyl pointed out, the *Holodomor* must be viewed "as a complex and multi-layered phenomenon produced by, and comprehensible only in terms of, an exceedingly complex ideological, political and imperial context."[28] That context was comprised of class warfare, forced collectivization, dekulakization, and a famine exacerbated by natural and man-made factors, including exports, murderous grain quotas, passportization, and decrees like the one issued on January 22, 1933, in which Stalin and Molotov ordered the OGPU to stop the exodus from Ukraine and the Kuban region of starving peasants attempting to secure food. This and other decrees exacerbated an already dire situation and resulted in the genocidal murder of more than four million Ukrainians.

One of the key early works from the first category was Moshe Lewin's *Russian Peasants and Soviet Power: A Study of Collectivization*, in which Lewin explains how Stalin seized upon the grain crisis of 1927-28 to move agriculture from the market principles of NEP to large collectivized farms in the form of *kolkhozy* [collective farms] and *sovkhozy* [state farms]. Lewin argues that collectivization of the peasants "constituted a social upheaval of a totally unprecedented nature..." which along with the creation of a *kolkhoz* and *sovkhoz* sector provided a means of solving "both the formidable problem of grain and the whole 'accursed problem' of relations between the Soviet authorities and the peasants."[29] Over the course of the Five-Year Plan those relations proved to be considerably more problematic than the authorities imagined. Published before the collapse of the Soviet Union and the opening of Soviet archives, Robert Conquest's *Harvest of Sorrow* in 1986 offers a comprehensive history of the class warfare that in part characterized the Five-Year Plan's drive for the collectivization of Soviet agriculture and the rapid increase in industrialization, spurred by the export of grain. Conquest argues that the 1932-33 "terror-famine"[30] was used by Stalin and the Politburo to punish peasants in Ukraine, Lower Volga and North Caucasus for resisting collectivization and to blunt nationalist ambitions as non-Bolshevik. Based on official sources available at the time, reports in the Soviet press, testimony of former Party activists, and first-hand reports by survivors, Conquest's work argues that an estimated 14.5 million deaths resulted directly and indirectly from the famine, forced collectivization, and the process of dekulakization.[31] Conquest devotes a chapter to Western press accounts of the famine, asserting that Jones' "honourable and honest report was subject to gross libel, not only by Soviet officialdom, but also by Walter Duranty, and by other correspondents wishing to stay on in order to cover the forthcoming 'Metro-Vic' faked trial, then major news."[32] The arrest and trial of six British engineers employed in the USSR by the Metropolitan-Vickers firm strained relations between the USSR and Great Britain. The six engineers went on trial on 12 April 1933; four of them—Gregory, Monkhouse, Cushny and Nordwall—were expelled from the USSR at the trial's conclusion on April 19, 1933. The two men who had made confessions, Leslie Thornton and W. H. MacDonald, were sentenced to three- and two-year sentences respectively. Those sentences were commuted, and the two men were released in July.[33]

A second wave of scholarship emerged after 1990 and the opening of the former Soviet Union's archives, including secret reports about the famine written at the time. *The Years of Hunger: Soviet Agriculture, 1931-1933* by R. W. Davies and Stephen G. Wheatcroft is a work that devotes particular attention to the economic and social background of the famine. The book is particularly instructive in providing official Politburo decisions, including top-secret special papers, private letters, and telegrams exchanged between members of the Politburo and between the Politburo and key government departments and regional authorities.[34] The book does not, however, consider the work of Jones or other journalists, although it does quote from Soviet newspapers and agricultural journals. At least one scholar, Mark B. Tauger, has argued that the environmental context of the famine deserves greater emphasis. In articles like "Natural Disaster and Human Actions in the Soviet Famine of 1931-1933" and "The 1932 Harvest and the Famine of 1933," Tauger argues that environmental conditions reduced the Soviet grain harvest in 1932 and that "Soviet leadership did not fully understand the crisis and out of ignorance acted inconsistently in response to it."[35] Using Soviet archival data that show the 1932 harvest was much smaller than has been previously assumed, Tauger posits that the genocide interpretation cannot be supported; rather, the low harvest, and famine, "resulted from a complex of human and environmental factors, an interaction of man and nature, much as most previous famines in history."[36] Tauger draws on the accounts of

Cairns, Schiller, and agricultural specialists as well as the economic implications of grain exports; he explores dimensions that enhance an understanding of the famine and its causes, despite mentioning almost nothing about the role of journalists in chronicling the famine.

Two books offer contrasting views of the famine in the context of Ukrainian national aspirations and the Soviet policies of *korenizatsiia* [indigenization]. In *The Affirmative Action Empire: Nations and Nationalism in the Soviet Union 1923-1939*, Terry Martin argues that nationality was not the most important factor in the two-pronged terror campaign—a grain requisitions terror and a nationalities terror—that the Politburo unleashed in 1932-1933. Rather, he posits that the grain requisitions terror was the culmination of a campaign begun in 1927-1928 to extract the maximum possible amount of grain from a hostile peasantry. The nationalities terror resulted from a hardline critique of *korenizatsiia*, formalized in decrees that linked Ukrainian cultural and educational institutions to the infiltration by counter-revolutionary elements, e.g., kulaks and Petliurites, which sought to undermine grain requisitions in Ukraine. Martin concludes, "The famine was not an intentional act of genocide specifically targeting the Ukrainian nation. It is equally false, however, to assert that nationality played no role whatsoever in the famine."[37] In *Soviet Nationality policy, Urban Growth, and Identity Change in the Ukrainian SSR 1923-1934*, George O. Liber argues that the complex interplay among industrialization, urbanization, and *korenizatsiia* threatened to replace Stalin's nationalities policy "national in form, socialist in content," with "socialist in form, national in content." This threat led to a hardening of political will by Stalin's closest supporters to abandon compromises associated with the NEP and *korenizatsiia* and replace them with a version of war communism that dealt harshly with any perceived nationalist deviation. In this way, national identity was replaced with a Bolshevik Ukrainization that depended on Stalin's Russocentrism. As Liber notes, "By starving millions of peasants to death, traumatizing the famine's survivors, and by purging those who could best define and articulate this new Ukrainian identity, these interventions left an indelible imprint on the psychology of the new city dwellers and their descendants."[38]

The second category, the role of Western journalists in reporting the famine, is comprised, in part, of works by the journalists themselves. Memoirs by Lyons, Duranty, Muggeridge, and Chamberlin document the working conditions faced by Western journalists forced to satisfy the censors.[39] Of the memoirs, *Assignment in Utopia*, published by Eugene Lyons in 1937, offers the most complete, albeit flawed, explanation of how Western correspondents conspired to repudiate Jones' reporting of the famine upon his arrival in Berlin after leaving the USSR. The following description has served as the basis for almost every interpretation of how Jones was branded a liar.

> The scene in which the American press corps combined to repudiate Jones is fresh in my mind. It was in the evening and Comrade [Konstantin] Umansky, the soul of graciousness, consented to meet us in the hotel room of a correspondent. He knew that he had a strategic advantage over us because of the Metro-Vickers story.... There was much bargaining in a spirit of gentlemanly give-and-take, under the effulgence of Umansky's gilded smile, before a formula of denial was worked out.
>
> We admitted enough to soothe our consciences, but in round-about phrases that damned Jones as a liar. The filthy business having been disposed of, someone ordered vodka and *zakuski*, Umansky joined the celebration, and the party did not break up until the early morning hours.[40]

This passage constitutes the only first-hand account regarding Jones' reporting of the famine and the immediate repudiation of that reporting. Until recently, many scholars accepted this version of events uncritically. Casting Jones in the role of the victim served a dual role: On the one hand, it purportedly absolved those journalists who, barred from travelling to the famine-stricken areas, were forced to conceal the famine in order to gain access to the Metro-Vickers trial. On the other hand, the victimization of Jones adds a mythological dimension that sustains the professional practices of all journalists. As Lyons recounts, "Jones had a conscientious streak in his make-up which took him on a secret journey into the Ukraine.... That same streak was to take him a few years later into the interior of China during political disturbances, and was to cost him his life at the hands of Chinese military bandits."[41] Perpetuating a mythology of courage under duress is part of journalism's overall narrative. This particular narrative also has a duplicitous, even willing, villain in the person of Walter Duranty, on whom so much of the scholarship has been focused.

Marco Carynnyk's "Making the News Fit to Print: Walter Duranty, the *New York Times* and the Ukrainian Famine of 1933" offers a compelling account of the sordid affair, focusing primarily on Duranty's role in orchestrating attempts to discredit Jones' reports in March 1933. However, Carynnyk devotes a mere handful of paragraphs to Jones' first-hand accounts.[42] In "A Blanket of Silence: The Response of the Western Press Corps in Moscow to the Ukraine Famine of 1932-33," Sally J. Taylor, one of Duranty's biographers, distills the lengths to which Duranty went to appease Soviet authorities in order to maintain his standing as the doyen of Western journalists based in the USSR. Taylor considers accounts of the famine by Muggeridge, William Henry Chamberlin, and Ralph Barnes, all of whom published articles before Jones returned from the area. She even quotes from the Duranty article of March 31, but curiously never mentions Jones by name in this article, though he is mentioned in the biography.

In *Angels in Stalin's Paradise: Western Reporters in Soviet Russia, 1917 to 1937, a Case Study of Louis Fischer and Walter Duranty,* James William Crowl devotes the better part of two chapters to the famine cover-up, detailing the inadequacies of many correspondents' reporting but mentioning little about Jones' reporting, other than to say that Jones, like Muggeridge and Barnes, learned that he could slip onto trains and spend days or weeks in stricken areas despite the travel ban on reporters. Crowl asserts that the stories Jones wrote caused such a stir in the West that "the Kremlin was eager for the foreign press in Moscow to deny its claims."[43] Jones himself corroborated that point in personal correspondence.

A number of works provides context within economic, historical, political, and religious spheres that impacted the USSR's rapid industrialization and collectivization of agriculture. In "Modernization from the Other Shore: American Observers and the Costs of Soviet Economic Development," David C. Engerman argues that even though Chamberlin, Lyons, Fischer, and Duranty held distinctly different views about the famine, they shared many common assumptions about the need for modernization in the USSR as well as notions of what constituted the Russian national character. Engerman describes Jones not as a journalist but as "a Russian-speaking assistant to former British Prime Minister David Lloyd George, [who] obtained his information during brief travels through Ukraine."[44] Engerman's description does not contextualize Jones' work within a journalistic framework, never noting his previous publications related to agricultural conditions, forced collectivization, the Five-Year Plan, or Jones' astute understanding of political situation in the USSR.

Whitman Bassow's *The Moscow Correspondents* provides a history of the journalists who reported from Russia since the Revolution in 1917. Bassow explains that Western journalists gained access to the USSR as a result of the famine of 1921 when the Bolsheviks were forced to plead for help. One of the provisos attached to humanitarian aid was that American correspondents be permitted to enter the USSR and travel freely to report on food distribution by the American Relief Agency (ARA), which was headed by Herbert Hoover. In his chapter focused on coverage of the 1932-33 famine, Bassow identifies Jones as "an enterprising reporter for Britain's *Manchester Guardian*... [whose]

eyewitness reports in the *Guardian* created a furor."[45] Bassow also uses Lyons' account of the Umansky-ordered famine denials to explain the concealment.

Several works detail the political backdrop in which the famine occurred. Marco Carynnyk has edited a volume titled *The Foreign Office and the Famine*, which offers firsthand reports by diplomats, journalists, agricultural experts, as well as by the victims themselves, delineating what the British government knew about the famine, what it knew about the causes, what it knew about Moscow's response to the famine, and its own response or lack thereof. While the British Foreign Office was aware of Jones' unescorted tramp through the Soviet countryside in March 1933, there is almost no mention of his articles that appeared in British and Welsh newspapers. In "The Politics of Famine: American Government and Press Response to the Ukrainian Famine, 1932-33," James E. Mace argues that the establishment of diplomatic relations between the United States and the USSR in November 1933 was a critical factor in explaining why the U.S. government chose not to acknowledge the famine publicly and why leading members of the American press corps stationed in Moscow deliberately covered up the famine. Mace actually quotes some of the information Jones provided reporters during his Berlin press conference on March 29; however, he then suggests Jones "had actually based his account primarily on what he had been told by Western correspondents and diplomats in Moscow."[46] Finally, Richard Ellman's "Stalin and the Soviet Famine of 1932-33" considers Stalin's role in the famine by delineating the policies he pursued against various populations, including judicial and extra-judicial repression.

Drawing on Communist Party and state archives in Moscow and two provincial outposts, Daniel Peris, in *Storming the Heavens: The Soviet League of the Militant Godless*, provides a comprehensive account of the League's antireligious propaganda activities, its membership, organization and the functioning of local councils. Peris explores the importance of atheism within the Bolshevik leadership's propaganda agenda and how antireligious efforts "complemented the effects of rapid industrialization, urbanization, and the collectivization of agriculture beginning in the late 1920s."[47] Joan Delaney's narrowly focused article, "The Origins of Soviet Antireligious Organizations," argues that the development of antireligious organizations occurred at the same time that Stalin was consolidating his position within the Communist Party between 1923-1929. Delaney posits that Yemelyan Yaroslavsky, under Stalin's direction, took charge of the antireligious apparatus in 1922, directed its methodology, and published two important publications, the weekly newspaper *Bezbozhnik* (*The Godless*) and the journal *Antireligioznik*. As Delaney notes, "... the story of this organization's rise and success is, to a significant degree, a paradigm and a function of what was happening in the larger arena of the party: bureaucratization and the centralization of power under Stalin."[48] Jones was particularly concerned with antireligious propaganda and its impact on the peasants, which he details in one article, "Easter in Godless Russia."

The third category of works helps to explain Jones' development as a journalist and the ethical dimensions of his reporting on the famine. By the time Jones made his initial foray into journalism with a one-month trial at *The [London] Times* in August 1929, applicants had to show more than just education; in fact, *The Times* policy was to take only those men who had previous experience, so Jones was advised to spend a year on a provincial newspaper. However, that was not the route Jones took at all. Rather, it was during his employment with Lloyd George that he met Lord Lothian [Philip Kerr], who put him in touch with Geoffrey Dawson, editor of *The Times*, after hearing Jones describe his trip to the Soviet Union in August 1930.[49]

Even though his parents wanted him to have an academic career, Jones wanted anything but that. Significantly, from the time he graduated from Cambridge, Jones justified his desire to do more than accept the safety of a university position by pointing out that he wanted adventure rather than security. In a letter to his family, he writes:

No man ever got on or did the slightest bit of good by putting the L.S.D. [pound, shillings and pence] he will receive at the age of 60 before considerations of public good, love of work, overwhelming interest and to think of myself spending my life talking about German literature in which I have not the slightest interest saying the same thing every week, every year, makes me prefer any kind of adventure with a little excitement into how the world moves.[50]

Jones entered journalism because he had a genuine interest in the USSR and a sense of purpose in wanting to communicate what he discovered on his trips there. In several ways, he was already exhibiting many of the characteristics—necessary ego strength, intellectual curiosity, and creative capacity—that allow journalists to endure considerable emotional stress without succumbing to "compassion fatigue."[51] Once Jones began writing about the Soviet Union in 1930, he became increasingly impacted by what he saw happening on subsequent trips. In reporting on famine, forced collectivization, and the exiling of kulaks, Jones believed that his work had a profound moral dimension.

This is particularly relevant for Jones and his reporting of the famine of 1932-33, and it explains why he put himself into such dangerous situations, including his fateful trip to China in 1935 that resulted in his murder.

Coverage of famine and other disasters invariably involves ethical dimensions, even though there was no code of ethics in Great Britain at the time of Jones' reporting. Scholars have explored a number of those ethical dimensions from various viewpoints. In *Media Ethics: A Philosophical Approach*, Matthew Kieran debunks the arguments that would exempt media institutions and journalistic practices from ethical obligations, positing that philosophical ethics involves "not just understanding ethical theories but critically modifying ethical principles and their application, principles that, since they are both normative and practical, have a direct bearing on the deliberations and decisions of everyday life."[52] In addition to those works that delineate the importance of the journalist as eyewitness previously noted (Zelizer, 2007; Cottle, 2013; Steiner and Okrusch, 2006; and Hoijer, 2004), this work considers the norms utilized by Jones in his reporting of the 1932-33 famine.

Because Jones' reporting made ample use of quotations from peasants and workers, it is important to understand the dimensions of a journalist's relationship with sources. Almost all of the quotations Jones uses in his stories are anonymous; he rigidly protected the confidentiality of his sources, knowing full well that anyone speaking out against the Communist Party, the Five-Year Plan or collectivization would have suffered severe reprisals. Not having been trained as a journalist in school and having only one month's experience before being invited to write his first series of articles about the Soviet Union, Jones did not have a ready-made repertoire of story forms upon which to draw. His articles "combine cold fact and personal event, in the author's humane company,"[53] which is how Mark Kramer defines literary journalism in "Breakable Rules for Literary Journalists." While the term literary journalism is relatively new, following the contentious "New Journalism" coined by Tom Wolfe in the 1960s, the sort of nonfiction "in which arts of style and narrative construction long associated with fiction help pierce to the quick of what's happening—the essence of journalism."[54] Kramer also believes that there is something inherently political and democratic in the common practices of the form, cutting through creeds, countries and bureaucracies. One of the goals of this project is to show through analysis and interpretation that Jones created enduring narratives of the felt lives of everyday people, contesting the idealization of the Five-Year Plan against its actualities.

Methodology

As a work of media history, this project makes use of a methodology suggested by Jan Ifversen in "Text, Discourse, Concept: Approaches to Textual Analysis." Ifversen's methodology involves combining the advantages of source criticism with textual analysis. Source criticism attempts to come to grips with "the representational chain that links memory to testimony and testimony to writing."[55] As a means of analyzing the work of Gareth Jones, source criticism delineates how he gathered and recorded source information and then incorporated that information into his texts. Illustrating the correspondence between the diaries and the newspaper articles constitutes one of the principle goals of this research. Facsimiles of the diaries (without transcriptions) from Jones' 1931 and 1933 trips to the USSR were first made available to the public at the GarethJones.org website by Nigel Linsan Colley in November 2007, and they are now archived at the National Library of Wales in Aberystwyth.

In addition to answering questions related to the sources, this project investigates how Jones' texts produce meaning. Ifversen offers a model (Illustration 2) that illustrates the triangular relation between text [newspaper articles], supra-text [diaries and correspondence], and context [Five-Year Plan]. Journalism texts are linguistic representations of reality; they serve as a first draft of history. Briefly, a text can be defined as a semantic unit containing specific textual components that give it internal cohesion and functionality within an information system.[56] More specifically, the textual components (i.e., headline, lead, cutline, etc.) give the text its form (e.g., newspaper article); that material form of the text is important to render cohesion, and it tells us that we have textual unity.

While textual analysis is interested in describing the production of meaning in single texts, it is also important to consider the way specific discourse, themes and concepts are produced and reproduced in a body of work comprised of several texts. The historical situation confronting Gareth Jones was a Global Depression brought on by a number of economic, social and political factors; an ideological battle between socialism and capitalism occupied a significant position within this situation, attracting unemployed and disenfranchised workers from around the world to the USSR's workers' paradise. To suggest that Jones was only responding to this historical context would be overly simplistic; this project argues that Jones' texts operate around the interplay of intention, genre, and historical situation.

To illustrate, Jones generated an analysis of the Five-Year Plan and the resulting famine through five series of newspaper articles starting in 1930 and ending in 1935 that increasingly focused on a discourse on famine. A discourse on famine—a discourse that makes famine and those suffering from famine an object—is different from concepts Duranty used like "food shortages" or "death from malnutrition."[57] Jones specifies what the object is about: Stalin's Five-Year Plan forced collectivization on more than eighty percent of the peasantry to spur rapid industrialization and socialize agriculture. To accomplish this, Stalin waged class warfare on the kulaks as well as other nationalist movements by imposing punitive grain procurements and by purging the intelligentsia. Additionally, Jones focuses on political, economic, and agricultural decisions that led to destabilization of the economy resulting in the loss of credit from foreign powers and the devaluation of Soviet currency. When environmental conditions led to poor harvests in 1931 and 1932, the peasants were left to starve in large numbers. A textual analysis of Gareth Jones' reporting of the tragedy in the Soviet countryside between 1930 and 1933 has heretofore been missing from almost all scholarship related to press coverage of the famine.

Précis of Chapters

This analysis of Jones' coverage of the Soviet Union is based on a close reading of five series of newspaper articles that Jones wrote between 1930-1935, corresponding to trips he made to the Soviet Union in 1930, 1931 and 1933. Chapter Two provides biographical information on his family, his education, and his early travels. It considers the importance of his mother, née Annie Gwen Jones, who travelled to Russia in 1889 and served as the governess to John Hughes's granddaughters for three years. Her unpublished manuscript, "Impressions of Life on the Steppes," offers insights into several of the themes that can be found in Gareth's newspaper articles, especially those related to class warfare, intolerance of religious beliefs, and the squalid living conditions of Russia's peasantry. After graduating from Cambridge with Honors in 1929, Jones considered various career options before finding employment with Lloyd George in August 1929. It explains his motivation for travelling to the USSR in August 1930 and analyzes the correspondence related to the trip, which serves as a vehicle to explore his development as a newspaper correspondent.

Chapter Three chronicles Jones' entrance into newspaper writing, which was dramatic by any standard; he produced fourteen articles for five different newspapers. These articles provide considerable insight into not only how Jones worked, but also his attitudes about the Five-Year Plan and its two cornerstones, forced collectivization and dekulakization. Jones' concern for the peasants and workers become distinguishing characteristics of his reporting, as well as his criticism of Stalin, the Politburo, and the OGPU.

The second series of three articles for *The Times*, based largely on Jones' trip to the Soviet Union with Jack Heinz II, heir to the manufacturing empire, is analyzed in Chapter Four. In their travels across Russia, Ukraine, and the Volga regions, they personally witnessed and recorded testimony from peasants that documents cases of starvation. Chapter Five focuses on Jones' move back to Great Britain after leaving the employ of Ivy Lee during a period of time when world financial collapse was a distinct possibility. Jones secured employment with Lloyd George, and as autumn approached, he began researching the deteriorating agricultural situation in the USSR; he read newspapers from the USSR on a daily basis. By mid-October Jones completed two articles that were published in the *Western Mail* on October 15 and 17 under the title "Will There Be Soup?"

Chapter Six details the events from the time Jones arrived in Berlin on March 29, when he announced to the world during a press conference what he had personally witnessed during his trip. Several articles were published in American and British newspapers the next day. Several other key incidents occurred over the next forty-eight hours, including the purported meeting arranged by Umansky to brand Jones as a liar, Jones' speech at the Royal Institute for International Affairs on March 30, the publication of Jones' first by-lined article on the famine in the *London Evening Standard* and Duranty's famine-denying story in the *New York Times* on March 31. These events constitute the most important yet most often misunderstood aspects of this crucial time.

Chapters Seven and Eight analyze the twenty-one articles that Jones published about his trip to the USSR, which appeared between March 31 and April 20, 1933. In addition to the initial article published in the London *Evening Standard*, these include seven articles for the *Daily Express*, ten for the *Western Mail*, and a three-part series for the *Financial News*. Over the next several months, Jones wrote two important Letters to the Editor. Additionally, two articles about the famine were syndicated in Hearst-owned newspapers in June. By this time, Jones had begun his tenure with the *Western Mail*, and while he primarily covered events in Wales and Ireland, he gave a number of lectures about the USSR throughout Great Britain. Finally, after Jones left the *Western Mail* in autumn 1934, he turned his attention to the Far East with the intention of doing a "Round the World Fact-Finding Tour." In addition to covering the U.S. election in November 1934, Jones visited William Randolph Hearst in January 1935 and furnished him with three highly anti-Communist articles that were syndicated in Hearst newspapers. These letters, articles and lectures are analyzed in Chapter Nine.

In the final chapter, Jones' legacy as a reporter is considered in light of his death at the hands of Chinese bandits after exposing Japanese military maneuvers along the Manchukuo border. Additionally, evidence suggesting Soviet involvement in his murder is considered. More recent articles commemorating him as a hero of the Ukraine are analyzed to illustrate how Jones has been rehabilitated as one of the most important journalists of the twentieth century. Finally, the chapter addresses the campaign to strip Duranty of his Pulitzer Prize and argues that the *New York Times* should voluntarily return the prize.

In addition to giving a close reading to his published articles, notebook diaries and personal correspondence, this project provides context for Jones' work by delineating those personal, professional, and academic influences that prepared him for his journalistic endeavors, arguing Jones was superbly prepared to report on the Soviet Union's Five-Year Plan and the resulting famine. Additional context related to the economic, ideological, agricultural, and social policies that precipitated and exacerbated the famine are also discussed. The goal is to shed light on Jones' work, which could have, and should have, been acclaimed, not dismissed and covered up in what Eugene Lyons calls "the whole shabby episode of our failure to report honestly the gruesome Russian famine of 1932-33."[58] Only by fully examining Jones' work, contextualized in light of the Duranty-orchestrated controversy, can we begin to appreciate this man's contributions to journalism.

Notes

1. Gareth Jones, "Famine Rules Russia," *Evening Standard*, March 31, 1933, 7.
2. Walter Duranty, "Russians Hungry But Not Starving," *New York Times*, March 31, 1933, 13.
3. Ibid.
4. Sally J. Taylor, in *Stalin's Apologist: Walter Duranty*—The New York Times's *Man in Moscow* (New York: Oxford University Press, 1990), 209.
5. Gareth Jones, Letter dated March 31, 1933. Gareth Vaughan Jones Papers, National Library of Wales. File B6/7.
6. For a definition of genocide and its applicability to the Soviet famine of 1932-33, see Frank Chalk and Kurt Jonassohn, "Conceptualizations of Genocide and Ethnocide," in *Famine in Ukraine 1932-1933*, eds. Roman Serbyn and Bohdan Krawchenko, (Edmonton, Alberta: Canadian Institute of Ukrainian Studies, 1986), 179-190.
7. For a discussion of Fischer's exposing the reporting of Walker, see Douglas Tottle, *Fraud, Famine and Fascism* (Toronto: Progress Books, 1987), 5-12.

8. Literally, *holodomor* means "to kill by starving"; *holod* is the cognate for the Ukrainian word *golod*, which means "hunger," but more properly translated idiomatically as "starvation."

9. Barbie Zelizer, *Covering the Body: The Kennedy Assassination, the Media, and the Shaping of Collective Memory* (Chicago and London:University of Chicago Press, 1992), 4.

10. Ibid. See also Claude Levi-Strauss, *The Savage Mind* (Chicago: University of Chicago Press, 1966), 259. Michel de Certeau, *The Writing of History* (New York: Columbia University Press, 1978). Levi-Strauss described "hot moments" as events through which a society assesses its own significance. Michel de Certau explains in *The Writing of History* that these incidents constitute projections by the individuals or groups who give them meaning in discourse.

11. "Over 15,000 N.Y. Ukrainian Americans March in Protest Parade Marking Anniversary of Soviet Fostered 1932-33 Famine in Ukraine," *Svoboda-Ukrainian Weekly Section*, 26 September 1953, 1. See also Raphael Lemkin, *Soviet Genocide in the Ukraine* (Kingston, Ontario: Kashtan Press, 2014).

12. Roman Serbyn, "What was the Holodomor and Why did it Happen? Conceptualizing the Ukrainian Genocide," Conference Paper, Taking Measures of the Holodomor, New York, November 5-6, 2013.

13. Alexander J. Motyl, "Looking at the Holodomor through the Lens of the Holocaust," *The Ukrainian Weekly*, 27 July 2008, 7.

14. Wulf Kansteiner, "Finding Meaning in Memory: A Methodological Critique of Collective Memory Studies," *History and Theory*, 41 (May 2002), 189.

15. Barbie Zelizer, "Reading the Past Against the Grain: The Shape of Memory Studies," *Critical Studies in Mass Communication* vol. 12, no. 2, (June 1995), 226.

16. Snyder defines the bloodlands geographically as the area that extends from central Poland to western Russia, through Ukraine, Belarus, and the Baltic States.

17. Timothy Snyder, *Bloodlands: Europe between Hitler and Stalin* (New York: Basic Books, 2010), xix.

18. The line appears in the First Quarto version of *Hamlet* in 1603, published by Nicholas Ling and John Trundell, but not in the Second Quarto edition of 1604, nor in the First Folio version of 1623, both of which are attributed to William Shakespeare.

19. Barbie Zelizer, "On Having Been There: Eyewitnessing as a Journalistic Key Word," *Critical Studies in Media Communication*, 24 (5), 410.

20. Quoted in B. Zelizer, "On Having Been There: Eyewitnessing as a Journalistic Key Word," *Critical Studies in Media Communication*, 24 (5), 411.

21. Walter Duranty, "Russians Hungry, But Not Starving," *New York Times*, 31 March 1933, 13.

22. John Dunham Peters, "Witnessing," in *Media Witnessing: Testimony in the Age of Mass Communication*. Eds. Paul Frosh and Amit Pinchevski. Houndmills, (UK: Palgrave Macmillan, 2008), 39.

23. Quoted in Birgitta Hoijer, "The Discourse of Global Compassion: The Audience and Media Reporting of Human Suffering," *Media, Culture & Society*, Vol. 26(4), 516.

24. Peters, "Witnessing," 30.

25. See Susan Moeller, *Compassion Fatigue: How the Media Sell Disease, Famine, War and Death* (New York: Routledge, 1999). See also Snyder, *Bloodlands*, 59-71.

26. Simon Cottle, "Journalists Witnessing Disaster: From the Calculus of Death to the Injunction to Care," *Journalism Studies*, 2013, Vol. 14 (2), 233.

27. Ibid., 239.

28. Motyl, "Looking at the Holodomor," 7.

29. Moshe Lewin, *Russian Peasants and Soviet Power: A Study of Collectivization*, trans. Irene Nove (New York: Norton, 1968), 19.

30. Robert Conquest, *Harvest of Sorrow: Soviet Collectivization and the Terror-Famine* (New York: Oxford University Press, 1986), 4.

31. Ibid., 306.

32. Ibid., 309.

33. Dr. Margaret Siriol Colley, *More Than a Grain of Truth: The Biography of Gareth Richard Vaughan Jones* (Newark, Nottinghamshire: N. L. Colley, Margaret Colley, 2005), 256-57.

34. R. W. Davies and Stephen G. Wheatcroft, *The Years of Hunger: Soviet Agriculture, 1931-1933* (New York: Palgrave Macmillan, 2004), xiv.

35. Mark B. Tauger, "Natural Disaster and Human Actions in the Soviet Famine 1931-1933," *The Carl Beck Papers in Russian & East European Studies*, Number 1506 (Pittsburgh: Center for Russian and East European Studies, 2001), 6.

36. Ibid., 6.

37. Terry Martin, *The Affirmative Action Empire: Nations and Nationalism in the Soviet Union, 1923-1939* (Ithaca: Cornell University Press, 2001), 305.

38. George O. Liber, *Soviet Nationality Policy, Urban Growth, and Identity Change in the Ukrainian SSR 1923-1934* (Cambridge: Cambridge University Press), 1992, 182-183.

39. See Walter Duranty, *I Write as I Please* (New York: Simon & Schuster, 1935). Malcolm Muggeridge, *Chronicles of Wasted Time* (New York: William Morrow & Company, 1973). W. H. Chamberlin, *Russia's Iron Age* (Boston: Little, Brown, 1934).

40. Eugene Lyons, *Assignment in Utopia* (New York: Harcourt, Brace and Company, 1937), 575-576.

41. Ibid., 575.

42. Marco Carynnyk, "Making the News Fit to Print: Walter Duranty, the *New York Times* and the Ukrainian Famine of 1933," in *Famine in Ukraine 1932-1933*, eds. Roman Serbyn and Bohdan Krawchenko, (Edmonton, Alberta: Canadian Institute of Ukrainian Studies, 1986), 77.

43. James William Crowl, *Angels in Stalin's Paradise* (Lanham, Maryland: University Press of America, 1982), 160.

44. David C. Engerman, "Modernization from the Other Shore: American Observers and the Costs of Soviet Economic Development," *The American Historical Review*, Vol. 105, No. 2 (April 2000), 393.

45. Whitman Bassow, *The Moscow Correspondents: Reporting on Russia from the Revolution to Glasnost* (New York: Morrow, 1988), 68. Jones was not employed at the *Manchester Guardian* at this time, but a story based on Jones' Berlin press conference was published in the *Guardian* on March 30.

46. James E. Mace, "The Politics of Famine: American Government and Press Response to the Ukrainian Famine, 1932-1933," *Holocaust and Genocide Studies*, Vol. 3, No. 1 (1988), 79.

47. Daniel Peris, *Storming the Heavens: The Soviet League of the Militant Godless*, (Ithaca: Cornell University Press, 1998), 6.

48. Joan Delaney, "The Origins of Soviet Antireligious Organizations," in *Aspects of Religion in the Soviet Union 1917-1967*, ed. Richard H. Marshall, Jr. (Chicago: The University of Chicago Press, 1971), 103.

49. Colley, *More than a Grain*, 86-89.

50. Letter dated February 5, 1930. Gareth Vaughan Jones Papers, National Library of Wales, Aberystwyth, Folder B6/2: Letters from Cambridge University, London, and the Continent, 1929-1930. Quoted in Colley, *More Than a Grain*, 67.

51. Keith Tester, *Compassion, Morality and the Media* (Buckingham: Open University Press, 2001), 41.

52. Matthew Kieran, *Media Ethics: A Philosophical Approach* (London: Praeger, 1997), 17.

53. Mark Kramer, "Breakable Rules for Literary Journalists," in *Literary Journalism*, eds. Norman Sims and Mark Kramer (New York: Ballantine Books, 1995), 34.

54. Ibid., 21.

55. Jan Ifversen, "Text, Discourse, Concept: Approaches to Textual Analysis," *Kontur*, nr. 7 (2003), 60.

56. Ibid., 61.

57. Duranty, "Russians Hungry, But Not Starving," 13.

58. Lyons, *Assignment in Utopia*, 572.

2

'Alone in an Unknown Country'

From Barry to Aberystwyth

Long before Gareth Jones began his formal studies of the Russian language and culture, he was introduced to both by his mother, whose maiden name was Annie Gwen Jones (Illustration 3). As a young woman of twenty, she traveled to Russia in 1889 and tutored the grandchildren of John Hughes, the steel industrialist and founder of Hughesovka in Ukraine, until forced to leave in 1892 during the cholera riots.[1] Annie Gwen Jones was one of the first women to attend University College of Wales in Aberystwyth where she met and became engaged to Edgar Jones, who was appointed headmaster of the Llandeilo Secondary School in 1894 and the Barry County School in 1899. Annie and Edgar settled down in Barry in a house called "Eryl." Gareth was taught at home by his mother until the age of seven when he began attending his father's school.[2]

In addition to hearing about his mother's travels to Hughesovka, Gareth certainly listened to many adventure stories from sailors down at the Barry docks where he allowed his imagination to roam freely. Adventure and travel became the cornerstones in the formation of his character. With two parents having attended the university in Aberystwyth, there was little question that Gareth would be afforded a university education, and in 1922 he earned a County Scholarship, intending to study modern languages, particularly Russian, "so that he might follow in his mother's footsteps to the land of the Tsars."[3] In addition to his formal study of Russia, Gareth may very well have read her unpublished personal essay, "Impressions of Life on the Steppes of Russia," which contains her reminiscences of the three-year period spent there. In chronicling her journey to Russia, Annie Gwen Jones describes becoming lost after wandering alone from a hotel at which her party was staying outside Warsaw, Poland.

I had gone for a walk in the afternoon to get my first idea of the city, the novelty of the countryside, the strangeness of the inhabitants, the beauty of the buildings and of the park, the wide fine peculiarly paved streets led me to prolong my walk somewhat beyond what was prudent. I kept, as I had imagined, a sharp lookout at the way I went thinking of returning along the same route. I retraced my steps, but after trudging for what appeared to me to be an age, I did not seem to be getting any nearer to the Hotel we were staying at. I did not know Polish; I had not a single coin in my pocket except English money that was of no use to me....

It was an uncanny feeling being stranded in a strange city, but it taught me not to wander forth again alone in an unknown country without efficient escort.[4]

Finding a sense of wonder in the surroundings, journeying beyond what was prudent and wandering alone in an unknown country without escort also became characteristics of her son's wanderlust when he set off on his journeys to a much different Russia in the 1930s.

Jones' love of life at the college in Aberystwyth was well documented in letters to his family. He fully enjoyed not only the academics, but also the social activities, regularly playing nine holes of golf at the local course and attending rugby matches. That sense of enjoyment carried over to his studies, and he won several academic prizes. Thanks to his Methodist upbringing, Jones attended Welsh tabernacle, occasionally twice on Sunday, where he heard the Reverend Principal Preece preach.[5] Significantly, one of the things that appears in many of his newspaper articles and diaries was a discussion of religion, which remained strong in the older generation of Russians and Ukrainians, but was gradually being squelched by atheism among the young communists.

Jones' formal study of languages was enhanced by a requirement that he spend two years studying abroad in Alsace, at the University of Strasbourg, where he studied from 1923-1925. Jones graduated with distinction and was awarded the *Diplôme Supérieur des Études Françaises*. Despite his love of the French language, Jones did not become enamored with France, nor did he travel extensively in the country. In September 1924, Jones travelled to Warsaw, Poland, as a delegate to the Congress of the International Students. After the conference, the delegates could take an excursion to either Posen (Poznan) or Vilna (Vilnius), and Jones chose the latter because it was only 120 miles from the USSR. In Vilna's town square, Jones noticed that the walls of the cathedral, its towers, and other buildings were riddled with bullet holes, evidence of the carnage the city had endured as control passed among the Germans, Poles, and Bolsheviks during World War I and the Bolshevik Revolution. He met many students who had lost property in Russia following the Revolution and had settled in Vilna. They described the terror enacted by the Bolsheviks, estates confiscated, and executions of their friends.[6]

In 1926 Jones graduated from University College of Wales with First-Class Honors in French, and by that time he had already received an Entrance Exhibition at Trinity College, Cambridge, where he planned to continue his education in French, German, and Russian. During the summer after his first year at Trinity College, Jones decided to return to the Baltics, on this occasion to Riga, in Latvia, to improve his Russian. Intending to earn living expenses by teaching English, Jones covered his travelling expenses by finding work aboard the *S.S. Vesta* bound for Stavanger, Norway, with a load of coal. From there, he caught a train to Oslo, another train the following evening to Stockholm, Sweden, where he continued his journey in third class across the Baltic Sea aboard the *S.S. Angermanland*. Arriving in Riga, he met his host, Pastor Fetler, who offered him board in the Mission until he found other accommodations.[7] Conditions in Riga were considerably more dismal than what he had seen in the Scandinavian cities.

> There are lots of tiny dirty wooden houses and ramshackle buildings.... Everything in the streets seems uncared for; no proper gutters.... I have never seen so many disabled, deformed, ragged dirty people.[8]

Furnished with a recommendation by the British Consulate, Jones found accommodations with Madame Krzyzanovki, a Russian émigré whose husband had been killed in World War I, and her daughter Olga. The Krzyzanovkis were effective teachers of Russian, even though they looked down on Latvians as a race of peasants.[9] Jones supplemented their instruction by buying a daily Russian newspaper, and in one letter to his family he reported that the situation in Russia was very bad.

> Every leader is calling on every citizen to arm. There is quite a panic in some parts of Russia. But here in Riga people are quite calm. It seems a political move on the part of the Communist leaders. There will probably be a bust up between the two sections before long. It is interesting to see detailed speeches from Russia instead of the snippets in English newspapers.[10]

Jones' analysis of the situation in the USSR was particularly astute. After their defeat by Stalin at the Fourteenth Party Congress in December 1925,

Grigory Zinoviev and Lev Kamenev joined forces with Trotsky's Left Opposition in what became known as the United Opposition. Between July–October 1926, the United Opposition again lost out to Stalin, and its leaders were expelled from the ruling Politburo.[11] While Jones was in Riga, the last Opposition members were about to be expelled from the Communist Party Central Committee, and in November 1927 Trotsky and Zinoviev were expelled from the Party itself. In December 1927, the Fifteenth Party Congress declared Left Opposition and Trotskyist views to be incompatible with Party membership and expelled all leading oppositionists from the Party. The crisis worsened when grain procurements in the fall of 1927 yielded only 300 million poods, or sixty percent of the 500 million poods that were expected. By the end of January 1928, the leadership was faced with imminent disaster. As Lewin notes, "They might have to face discontent among the troops, and among the workers who were short of food, with the added prospect of a drop in wages and a rise in prices, the inevitable failure to supply bread to the regions producing industrial crops, the collapse of all their economic plans, in short a situation which imperiled the very existence of the regime."[12] The Central Committee subsequently ordered emergency measures by the local committees to spearhead the procurement by setting up troikas to take charge of the offensive. Despite what Stalin was saying in speeches, he had already begun appropriating the Left's policies, especially as he seized upon the idea to forestall another grain crisis by collectivizing agriculture and liquidating the kulak. Class warfare against the kulak was the beginning of the New Economic Policy's death knell.[13]

Despite advertising in the *Riga Times*, Jones was unable to find anyone interested in taking English lessons, and he apologized to his parents for the expenses he was incurring. Part of that expense was spent buying Russian books. "I bought a large number of Russian books in Riga 2nd hand and had them sent to Cambridge, quite a foundation to a small Russian library. All the books are essential for the Tripos [exams]. I got them very cheaply."[14] The books came in handy as Jones finished his last two years at Cambridge, a time marked by his continued fascination with world affairs, evidenced by his being elected chief secretary of the Cambridge League of Nations. His affiliation with that group as well as the Trinity Madrigal Society widened his circle of friends considerably, and he was especially open to befriending students from Germany and Russia.[15]

As graduation approached, Jones was fully confident going into exams, and that confidence was reflected in his achieving First-Class Honors in German and Russian in the Medieval and Modern Language Tripos, Part II, with distinction in the oral examinations. His references were nothing short of glowing. The first was from Dr. Stewart, a Fellow of Trinity College.

> With nimbleness of mind and rapidity, he reached a high first class standard in every language he studied. His grasp of history and principles of literature is remarkable. He has a clever head and a retentive memory and I have no doubt that whichever way he turns his intellectual attention he will succeed and reach a commanding position.

The second was from his German professor, Dr. Breul, Fellow of King's College.

> Apart from his proficiency in German, he speaks French and Russian, and besides his travels in German speaking countries, he has visited France, Switzerland, Poland, Czecho-Slovakia, Latvia and the Scandinavian countries and made a study of the conditions and characteristic features of these countries. I am convinced that either as Foreign Correspondent to a leading newspaper or as a member of the Consular Service, or working on the staff of the League of Nations, Mr. Jones would be sure to do most valuable work, and I strongly recommend him for any post of this or a similar nature.[16]

Dr. Breul's assessment of Jones' journalistic potential was particularly astute, given that at the time Jones did not seem to be headed for a career in journalism. Despite being told by an adviser of the Civil Service that he had an excellent chance of being selected, Jones, like the other students who applied for the Consular or Diplomatic Service in 1929, was not offered a position. However, Jones had options, one of which included a month's trial at *The Times* in London during the month of August. It constituted his introduction, albeit a brief one, into journalism.

A Trial at *The Times* and a Breakthrough

As he did with almost all of his noteworthy experiences, Jones recorded his first night at *The Times*, on August 27, 1929, in considerable detail, offering a snapshot of what it was like to work at the prestigious newspaper. Not only does he describe one of the main work rooms with its guide-books, reference books, cutting books, *Atlases* and *Who's Who*, but he also offers insight into how the Imperial and Foreign

Department, to which he was assigned, handled the flow of news. His very first assignment was, coincidentally, to edit a long telephone message from the correspondent in Riga. As Jones explains in a letter to his family, Mr. Cana, his temporary supervisor, told him, "Our Riga correspondent has an abominable style. Just lick that into respectable English."[17] In addition to Jones and Mr. Cana, three others worked in room number one, which was "furnished in a very old-fashioned way, like a dining-room in a commercial travelers hotel. The room was not big, but the table in the middle was round and vast."[18] The walls were adorned with old photographs and caricatures. Taking his place with the other men, Jones was told, "You must begin from the principle that all our foreign correspondents, except one, write abominably."[19]

What Jones licked into respectable English for the Riga correspondent was a story titled "A New Working Week," which appeared the next day under the "Imperial and Foreign News" section of *The Times*. The story described a resolution passed by the Council of People's Commissars of the USSR to abolish Sunday as the general day of rest. Significantly, the story explains that this change in the work week would have an impact on religion by destroying Sunday as a day of worship even though this was merely a by-product of the resolution, its main goal being to support the Five-Year Plan's drive to develop the economy. Additionally, the story mentions that the Plan was regarded as dogma, and anyone who opposed it was a heretic. The story names Alexi Rykov, Mikhail Tomsky, and Nikolai Bukharin as members of the Right-Wing Opposition who opposed parts of the Plan and were repressed and degraded as a result. They were forced to admit their mistakes in November 1929 for taking a moderate stance in regards to collectivization. On December 19, 1930, after admitting another round of mistakes, Rykov was replaced by Vyacheslav Molotov as both Soviet Premier and Chairman of the Council of Labor and Defense. Two days later, Rykov was expelled from the Politburo, nullifying any chance of political advancement. Finally, in 1938 he was arrested and charged with treason. At the Trial of the Twenty-One on March 13, another of the show trials, Rykov was found guilty, and two days later he was executed.[20]

Jones' trial period at *The Times* ended on September 20, 1929, and on that night he was informed that while he showed potential, he lacked the necessary journalistic experience to secure full-time employment. Spending a year on a provincial newspaper was recommended to improve his chances of being accepted. For Jones, however, that route was not especially viable since he needed income. As would often be his fortune, Jones rebounded from the setback when only a few days later Dr. Stewart, who had written one of the laudatory reference letters, offered him a position at Trinity College, Cambridge, as a coach. The remuneration was a scholarship worth £100 with the opportunity to make more by coaching students at Newnham, the women's college; he accepted the offer, despite having professed on several occasions that he had little interest in an academic career. Jones interviewed with Sir Bernard Pares of the Slavonic and East European Studies program, who provided Jones with a subject for his doctoral thesis, "The Russian Press during the Revolution."[21]

Armed with a bibliography and a stack of Russian newspapers, Jones settled into his room at Trinity College, Cambridge, furnished with a picture of Queen Victoria and several etchings from home. However, no sooner had he begun the next phase of an academic career, he received an urgent letter from the Civil Service Commission summoning him for a medical examination on October 7. He replied that he would not attend for the medical because he had accepted another position. In declining an existing vacancy in the Consular Service, he was removing himself from the list of that service.[22] Two weeks later, however, Jones' fate took another momentous turn.

Jones was introduced to former Prime Minister David Lloyd George by Dr. Tomas Jones, who had served as deputy cabinet secretary for Lloyd George during World War I and was a neighbor and friend of Gareth's father, Major Edgar Jones. Jones was invited to prepare notes on the present political situation in Germany as part of the interview process. Impressed with what Jones had prepared, Lloyd George offered Jones a twelve-month or six-month position with a salary of £400 per year. The position involved being stationed in London and preparing notes for debates, articles, and speeches by the former prime minister as well as some travel abroad. Jones writes to his family that Lloyd George was telling him the experience would be invaluable. "I feel therefore very keen on trying for six months, but I do not want to decide anything before getting your advice. So will you please write and let me know everything you think."[23] Despite reservations from his parents about venturing into a career in politics, Jones informed them that he had definitely decided to accept the offer, as everybody at Cambridge advised him to do. On October 30, he received a telegram informing him that his salary would be £500 and the position was to commence on January 1, 1930. "It is funny to think so, but I would have an influence on Foreign Affairs through Lloyd George,"[24] he writes his family. Little did he know just how great an influence he would, indeed, have on world events.

In the same month that Jones began working for Lloyd George, diplomatic relations between Great Britain and the Soviet Union were restored, and travel to the Soviet Union was again permitted. Additionally, developments in the Soviet Union warranted Lloyd George's attention. For example, in a December 1929 speech, Stalin announced that the socialization of agriculture had to include liquidating the kulaks as a class.

> To launch an offensive against the kulaks means that we must smash the kulaks, eliminate them as a class. Unless we set ourselves these aims, an offensive would be mere declamation, pinpricks, phrase-mongering, anything but a real Bolshevik offensive. To launch an offensive against the kulaks means that we must prepare for it and then strike at the kulaks, strike so hard as to prevent them from rising to their feet again. That is what we Bolsheviks call a real offensive.[25]

The kulaks were characterized as those successful farmers who systematically used hired labor, rented out implements and horses, and had their own workshops.[26] On her tour of the countryside, Anna Louise Strong noted, "With Stalin's statement of December 27th a million families suddenly found themselves pariahs, without any rights which need be respected, and without any knowledge as to what they might do to be saved."[27] Liquidation was a means of destroying leadership of the villagers, which might then diminish the resistance to the ongoing policy of forced collectivization. In February 1930, the OGPU put the Politburo policy into action by establishing a nationwide network of troikas (triumvirates) to implement the process of dekulakization. The policy organized three categories of kulaks to be targeted; the first category included those to be shot or imprisoned, the second category included those families of the first group to be exiled to Siberia, the Urals or Kazakhstan, and the third included those to be moved out of the *kolkhoz* to land elsewhere in the district. The number of death sentences approved by OGPU troikas for Category I kulaks reached more than 18,000 by October, and more than a quarter million additional people were arrested under this category, including former White officers, emigrants, members of religious and sectarian groups, rich peasants, usurers, speculators, and former landowners. In all more than a million people were exiled under Category II, and another 200,000 kulak families were dekulakized but had not been exiled under Category III. It's important to remember that this was only the first phase of dekulakization; a second, more brutal drive took place in 1931 during which seventy percent of all exiles—268,000 households, including 1,252,000 people—were exiled.[28]

Briefs

Not surprisingly, one of the first briefs Jones wrote for Lloyd George was on developments of the Soviet Union's first Five-Year Plan, which had been officially approved in spring 1929. He met with, among others, Nicolai Yemshikov from the Soviet embassy, who spoke to Jones about the Five-Year Plan, the Chekists' [secret police] presence in London, and the possibility of Civil War in Ukraine, Turkestan, and the Caucasus. Jones notes in his diary what Yemshikov told him: "The standard of life in Russia was being reduced in order to get money to buy exports; that there was great suffering; only children were allowed milk; a grownup was allowed two eggs per week. A peasant revolt was possible, but the Soviet Government had aeroplanes, troops, and guns; everything to crush it."[29] Jones noted after another meeting with Yemshikov that in most aspects of everyday life preference was being given to members of the Communist Party and that the peasants were only willing to join the *kolkhoz* to get grain; as soon as the crops were harvested, they resisted handing over the crops.

Domination by the Communist Party, which was composed of no more than ten percent of the population, became a major theme in Jones' reporting on the USSR. That theme of domination by a minority can be traced back to his mother's manuscript essay.

> What strikes me immensely is the wide, enormous, unbridged gulf between the upper and lower classes of Russia. Unfortunately there are only two real classes; there is no middle class, the chief mainstay and backbone of a country.[30]

Almost forty years after Annie Gwen Jones wrote this, the gulf was no longer between the nobility and the peasants but between members of the Communist Party and practically everyone else in the USSR.

During another meeting with Yemshikov, this one held in St. James Park to protect his confidentiality, Yemshikov expressed concern that because he was not a communist, he might lose his job to a member of the Communist Party. He also told Jones that England was encouraging separatist movements in Ukraine, Turkestan, and the Caucasus. Jones notes in his diary what Yemshikov told him:

> There will be Civil War in Russia if this continues. There is a rumour that the Foreign Secretary is giving money to Ukraine and Caucasian separatists. The Ukrainian propaganda is far cleverer than Russian propaganda and is much more active. I hate the

Bolsheviks, but if there were a War between the Bolsheviks and the Ukrainians I would fight for the Bolsheviks.[31]

Throughout his reporting on the USSR, Jones held the view that nationalist movements were strong and might result in insurrections. Shortly after this meeting with Yemshikov, Jones attended a lecture at the Royal Institute of International Affairs (RIIA) about American trade policy with the Soviet Union and the likely success of the Five-Year Plan. During the discussion following the presentation, one man spoke about the need for export credits, and Jones believed the man was Mr. Metcalf, a director of the Metropolitan-Vickers engineering firm, which three years later would be accused of espionage; access to the trial of the British engineers was purportedly used to goad Western correspondents into defaming Jones. The following morning Jones interviewed the head of the Vickers firm, who confirmed the loss of a significant amount of trade with the USSR because the British government was unwilling to guarantee sixty to eighty percent credit. Jones also interviewed Mr. Somerville, head of the Russian Department in the office of the American Commercial Attaché, who was decidedly not optimistic about trade between the United States and the USSR. Somerville did not believe the Five-Year Plan would succeed and questioned the stability of the current regime.[32]

While composing his brief on the Plan for Lloyd George, Jones met regularly with Sir Bernard Pares at the School of Slavonic and East European Studies. Pares was greatly concerned about Stalin's oppression of the kulaks, a policy which he characterized as the reintroduction of serfdom. Pares advocated for a public protest by Lloyd George decrying the persecution of the kulaks as well as the persecution of religion throughout the Soviet Union.[33] In February, Jones began work on a brief about the persecution of religion in the USSR in anticipation of Lloyd George's meeting with the Soviet ambassador to Great Britain, perhaps having read the statement issued by Pope Pius XI that same month condemning the religious persecution in the USSR.

Once again, it is possible to trace Jones' attitudes concerning religion back to what his mother had written about the strong religious belief among the peasants. "Every Russian house whether rich or poor had an icon or an image of Christ or the Virgin Mary in a top corner of the room; it is before the image that they pray."[34] Annie Gwen Jones also wrote about the persecution of the Jews. "The Russian persecution of the Jews stands apart from other anti-Semitic movements on account of its unparalleled magnitude and ferocity and also because it is the direct act of a Government deliberately and systematically, remorsefully seeking to reduce to utter misery about four and one half million of its own subjects."[35]

For his brief, Jones was asked to interview Dr. Rushbrooke, the secretary of the Baptist World Alliance, who showed him a letter written by a Baptist within the USSR that described the sufferings of the Russian Baptist population. The following day Jones interviewed the chief Rabbi in Great Britain, who shared with him a telegram from Vilna that stated the Rabbi in Minsk was in mortal danger. Finally, he met with Dr. Jochelmann, who conveyed that the persecution of the Jews was moral rather than physical. Until the Revolution, Jews had not been allowed to hold any official office, not allowed to work in the railways or in their construction. While anti-Semitism became the official Soviet policy, the Bolsheviks regarded all religious activity as counter-scientific superstition and a remnant of the old pre-communist order.

By the time Jones began working for Lloyd George, antireligious activity had become intertwined with the Party's policy toward the countryside in that the increased pressure to collectivize agriculture provided an opportunity for the League of the Militant Godless, headed up by Yemelyan Yaroslavsky, to increase antireligious agitation. After several years of dispute between Yaroslavsky's League and Mariia M. Kostelovskaia's Moscow Society of Godless over methodology, a conference on antireligious propaganda had been organized in connection with the Central Committee in April 1926 to settle on which methods should be employed. The theses accepted at the meeting were prepared for publication by the editorial staffs of *Bezbozhnik* (Illustration 4) and the journal *Antireligioznik*, both of which were overseen by Yaroslavsky. The theses included principles Yaroslavsky had been articulating throughout the decade and included denunciations of both right and left deviations—the do-nothing approach of the rightists who asserted that religion would gradually fade away and the leftist approach that attacked all forms of religion as class enemies. Both were condemned as deviations from the party line.[36] Interestingly, the League's response to Pope Pius XI's denunciation included a collection of funds for a tank that was to be called "Our Answer to the Pope in Rome." as well as numerous condemnations in *Bezbozhnik* and other publications. If nothing else, it launched a campaign for subscriptions to League periodicals and buttressed the League financially and politically.[37]

At the very last moment, Lloyd George decided not to write about religion in the USSR and instead assigned Jones to write a biographical sketch of Admiral Reinhard Scheer and General Hoffmann. Nonetheless, Jones continued researching aspects of the Five-Year Plan, and in May he visited a Soviet ship, the *Felix Dzerzhinsky*, with Miss Gellan, who was also working for Lloyd George. In his diary he writes that the sailors tried to convince him how excellent everything was in the USSR; he also summarizes the gist of a conversation he had with two men from Mayfair House.

> Russia is now in a state of war, but in a state of a war of construction, not of destruction. We are to evolve a new collectivist psychology. We are battling for the Five-Year Plan, which is sure to succeed because the whole country is in exactly the same state as Great Britain during the last War. Of course we cannot tolerate defeatists; that is why we oppose any counter-revolutionary force. The spirit between factories increases the production in a 'spirit of war'. Russians are being asked to sacrifice for the present to gain in the future.[38]

Jones continued working on the brief, and having arranged an interview with Professor A. Onou, assistant to cabinet secretary Vladimir Nabokov in the Kerensky Provisional Government, Jones kept the appointment as scheduled. His diary notes reveal his empathy for the man. "Poor old Professor Onou! He is a funny, nervy man with a goatee beard. I was sorry for him. Nobody seems to consult him about Russia, although he once played an important part. He feels himself neglected, and I was glad I went to ask him for his opinion."[39]

Pilgrimage

Other than his family connection, it is not altogether clear exactly why Jones decided to go to the Soviet Union in August 1930. Jones obtained a Soviet visa shortly after relations were restored and began making plans to visit the town of Hughesovka [Donetsk, Ukraine], where his mother had been tutor to the granddaughters of John Hughes, the Welsh engineer. Before leaving for the Soviet Union, Jones attended a lecture at the RIIA where he met Dr. Gerald Merton, Chairman of the Executive of the Air League. Merton put him in touch with a Colonel Thwaites, who had served in British Intelligence during World War I and was interested in learning more about Soviet aviation. Dr. Colley posits that it is doubtful Jones undertook any espionage for Thwaites since there are no references to him in his diaries other than the one referencing their first, and apparently, only meeting, and there are no papers relating to any covert actions in the records of the British Government or Foreign Office.[40] However, upon his return from the USSR, during which he enjoyed a plane ride from Rostov to Moscow,

Jones did write an article, titled "Civil Aviation in Soviet Russia," for the December 1930 issue of *Air*, an aviation journal. It would not be his last notable plane ride, and Jones came to see aviation being employed to impact military operations.

On the train journey east into Soviet Russia, Jones met Saul Bron, the Soviet trade representative for Great Britain, who accurately surmised from reports that there was a campaign against the kulaks and the implementation of a second round of forced collectivization was being planned "as soon as the harvest was in."[41] In a letter to his family written while in Warsaw, Poland, Jones recounts that, in addition to meeting Bron, he also met a man from Hughesovka, who had been studying engineering in America. The man told him that the Five-Year Plan was moving too quickly. Jones records the man asking, "What on earth was the government exporting food to buy machines when there was not enough to eat in the country?"[42] The use of food exports to finance industrial modernization continued unabated, even after it was clear that famine conditions were beginning to ravage Ukraine, Lower Volga, and North Caucasus after drought diminished the harvest of 1931-32 and was followed by another dismal harvest in 1932-33.

Jones spent approximately three weeks in the Soviet Union, arriving on August 6 and departing on August 26. He spent the first part of the trip in Moscow where he got to see the newspaper offices of *Pravda* and *Izvestia*, and he met with Party officials, including the Head of the Press Department at the foreign office and the Minister of Agriculture, who granted him a two-hour interview and arranged for him to visit *sovkhozy* and *kolkhozy* in Ukraine. Jones sent his family several postcards and letters during the course of his travels, often from railway stations. Jones knew that anything he wrote would be carefully scrutinized by the OGPU Press Office, so his letters from within the Soviet Union are deliberately vague or complimentary. For example, on August 15, he sent a postcard (Illustration 5) featuring a picture of Stalin from Kupk Station, and the following day he sent a letter from Kharkov Station that focuses on creature comforts.

> Here I am halfway to Rostov. The time passes very quickly in Russian trains, and I slept excellently on my hired mattress, clean sheets and pillow, lying full-length. The train left Moscow at 4 o'clock yesterday afternoon and in Tula station, I had a real treat, cheese sandwiches, cakes and lemonade. A Cossack Communist with the 'Order of the Red Flag' told me a lot of things about present day Russia, and I listened to a discussion about factories and engineers.[43]

Finally, on August 17, he arrived in Hughesovka after a very long journey.

> Here I am in Hughesovka! It's taken a long time to get here, but I did not want to miss it. I am sitting in the gardens just near the church…. I am delighted to be here where you lived. It would be hard to find someone you knew. So all I can do is to send you my Sunday letter from here.[44]

He wrote again from Rostov-on-Don on August 20, detailing his remaining itinerary, and in a carefully worded manner let his family know just how strenuous the trip had been and how much he was looking forward to getting back. He makes sure to add more details about Soviet accomplishments. "Yesterday I went in a car to a State Farm, Gigant No. 2. It is amazing to see how they have converted the desert steppes into a vast farm covering a hundred thousand acres and run by the most modern agricultural implements."[45]

Once Jones departed the Soviet Union and arrived in Berlin, however, he provided a completely different picture of what he had seen and heard. On August 26, he writes to his family from Berlin, "Russia is in a very bad state; rotten, no food, only bread; oppression, injustice, misery among the workers and 90% discontented…. The winter is going to be one of great suffering there and there is starvation. The government is the most brutal in the world. The peasants hate the Communists."[46] Significantly, this mention of starvation was not something that he developed more fully in the newspaper articles, suggesting that in all likelihood it was not widespread but occurring in isolated areas that he visited. He mentions in the August 20 letter that he had excellent meals at the state farm; by specifying that the meals there were excellent, Jones was implying that elsewhere food was almost non-existent in many areas, Hughesovka included. "One reason why I left Hughesovka so quickly was that all I could get to eat was a roll of bread—and that is all I had up to seven o'clock. Many Russians are too weak to work. I am terribly sorry for them."[47]

Reporting Methods

Before analyzing the first set of articles Jones wrote about the Soviet Union beginning in September 1930, a description of his reporting methods is warranted. In an introduction to the very first article he published upon his return, "Glimpses of Soviet Russia," which was for the *Liberal Woman's News* on September 18, 1930, he is described as speaking "Russian fluently, and as an unaccompanied observer went to Moscow, the South of Russia, Caucasia, and flew from Rostov to Moscow as the guest of the Soviet Civil Air Fleet."[48] In a *News Chronicle* article, he is described as "an Englishman recently returned from Moscow,"[49] and *The Times* prefaces its series by noting, "The brief series of articles begun below records impressions recently gathered by an unshepherded visitor to Russia who was able to collect at first hand some rank-and-file opinion on the regime and its policies."[50] Jones was not yet recognized as a practicing journalist, and only the *Liberal Woman's News* carried his by-line, which doubtlessly protected his anonymity and his ability to gain entrance to the USSR on subsequent visits. By late December when he published two articles in the *Western Mail* and later his series of five articles for them in April 1931, all were by-lined, but there is no evidence that they drew the notice of anyone in the Soviet Embassy in London or in Moscow, for he was granted a visa for his 1931 visit.

Jones articulated his reporting methods in the first *Times* article, clearly distinguishing groups of tourists led around by "competent and charming guides the façade of Soviet Russia" from someone like Jones, who knew the language, read the Bolshevist Press (i.e., *Pravda* and *Izvestia*) and had contacts with "peasants, miners, nobles, restaurant workers, private traders, priests, civil servants, and engineers."[51] Jones recognized that the aim of Party officials was to impress visitors, "disarm criticism and leave the foreign delegations blissfully ignorant of the hunger, discontent, opposition, and hatred"[52] then spreading throughout the USSR. Significantly, this resembles his criticism of people like George Bernard Shaw and Western journalists after Duranty attacked his reporting in late March 1933. Jones, however, was astute in recognizing that the advantages he had could also be manipulated by his sources.

> In estimating the importance of the opinion expressed by Russians the character and position of the speakers should be taken into consideration on the presumption that a miner escaping from the Donetz Basin, where there has been a serious breakdown in food supplies, is far more likely to exaggerate the gravity of the situation than a well-paid specialist working in the electrical industry, which is making great progress.[53]

Jones even explains how he recorded conversations. "The following estimate of the state of affairs in Russia has been made on these methods during a recent visit to the Soviet Union, and the conversations quoted in the following articles were written down at the earliest possible moment after the Russian had left the writer's presence."[54] Jones' description of how he recorded these conversations after the speaker had left is significant in at least two ways. For one, while the speaker might know that Jones was not a Russian, s/he would not have any reason to suppose that Jones was a reporter or that what they were saying would be recorded and used in a newspaper article. This might certainly result in the source being more candid, and more openly critical. Secondly, if the speaker knew that Jones was a foreigner, and there is evidence that was known, s/he might, as Jones notes, exaggerate conditions in the hope that his/her plight might reach a wider audience. Based on the number of conversations Jones recorded, what is clear is that a great number of people risked censure or worse to express their views about conditions in the USSR at the time even when they knew, as they often did, that he was from the West, something Jones did not attempt to hide. Jones' articles make ample use of these conversations to substantiate his views of what conditions were like.

That Jones was a meticulous reporter and note-taker was also documented by Eugene Lyons in his 1937 book *Assignment in Utopia*. "An earnest and meticulous little man, Gareth Jones was the sort who carries a note-book and unashamedly records your words as you talk. Patiently he went from one correspondent to the next, asking questions and writing down the answers."[55] While Lyons' description verges on caricature, the volume of material Jones compiled in his diaries and personal correspondence testify to his meticulous note-taking. Jones' diaries contain not only the conversations he engaged in with both officials and everyday people, but they also include random notes not intended to be used later in his writings. As Nigel Colley notes:

> This complete publication of his diary pages are now being published online for academic completeness & thereby proving credibility as to their provenance—and are by no means, either an easy read (due in part to deciphering his hand writing), nor though fascinating, always an interesting one—as they document almost everything he experienced of note on his trips, from his conversations with the highest in the land to the lowliest Ukrainian peasant, and were never actually tended for publication today.[56]

The articles are not solely based on first-hand conversations, for Jones also based them on information he gleaned from reading newspapers and journals, the opinions of foreign experts whom he interviewed, and his own observations.

What becomes immediately obvious is that Jones always wrote with his readers in mind. His focus in "Glimpses of Soviet Russia" was most obviously women. Some of the articles make use of a first-person or "I" narrator, while others, like *The Times* series, are more analytical. Doubtlessly, his trial at *The Times* and whatever editorial advice he received shaped his reporting and news writing style. Jones knew the difference between a leader, a feature, and an editorial. A comparison of his famine articles and those written by Ralph Barnes, Malcolm Muggeridge, and William H. Chamberlin reveals many similarities. Moreover, news writing in the 1930s was not predicated on the cult of objectivity; rather, these reporters wrote interpretive articles, characterized by analysis, first-hand observation, and recorded conversations. In short, they are neither straight hard-news stories nor travelogues. Jones was attempting to communicate what he found—unabashedly honest and perhaps somewhat naïve in that he did not couch his criticisms in euphemisms that might escape the notice of Communist Party censors because he was not based in Moscow; additionally, he was identified as an adviser to Lloyd George, not a journalist.

Another characteristic was Jones' almost complete disregard for his own comfort. Shortly after he started working for Lloyd George he wrote to his parents, who, despite his lucrative employment, were concerned about him. In February 1930, he writes:

> I should consider myself a flabby little coward if I ever gave up the chance of a good and interesting career for the mere thought of safety. I have no respect for any man whose acceptance or judgment of a post depends on the answer to the question: Will it give me a pension? ... I have come to the conclusion that the only life I can live with interest and which I can really be of use is one connected with foreign affairs and with men and women of today; not with the writers of two centuries ago.[57]

This disregard for safety not only allowed Jones to report one of the most horrible events in the twentieth century, but also resulted in his death five years later before the age of 30.

Notes

1. Annie Gwen Jones, "Impressions of Life on the Steppes of Russia." Unpublished manuscript. Gareth Vaughan Jones Papers. National Library of Wales. File A/2.
2. Colley, *More than a Grain*, 2-7.
3. Ibid., 6.

4. Annie Gwen Jones, "Impressions," 1.
5. Colley, *More than a Grain*, 7.
6. Ibid., 8-11.
7. Ibid., 23-27.
8. Gareth Jones, Letter dated July 21, 1927. Gareth Vaughan Jones Papers. National Library of Wales. File B6/1.
9. Colley, *More than a Grain*, 28.
10. Gareth Jones, Letter dated July 21, 1927. Gareth Vaughan Jones Papers. National Library of Wales. File B6/1.
11. See Fifteenth Congress of the CPSU (Bolshevik) in *The Great Soviet Encyclopedia, 3rd Ed.* (1970-1979). See also Lewis H. Siegelbaum, *Soviet State and Society between Revolutions, 1918–1929* (Cambridge: Cambridge University Press, 1992), 189-190.
12. Lewin, *Soviet Peasants*, 216.
13. Conquest, *The Harvest of Sorrow: Soviet Collectivization and the Terror-Famine*, 78-79.
14. Gareth Jones, Letter dated August 16, 1927. Gareth Vaughan Jones Papers. National Library of Wales. File B6/1.
15. Colley, *More than a Grain*, 32-37.
16. Quoted in Colley, *More than a Grain*, 45-46.
17. Gareth Jones, Letter dated August 27, 1929. Gareth Vaughan Jones Papers. National Library of Wales. File B6/2.
18. Ibid.
19. Ibid.
20. Helen Rappaport, *Joseph Stalin: A Biographical Companion* (Santa Barbara, Calif.: ABC-CLIO, 1999), 238.
21. Colley, *More than a Grain*, 49-50.
22. Ibid., 51.
23. Gareth Jones, Letter dated September 30, 1929. Gareth Vaughan Jones Papers. National Library of Wales. File B6/2.
24. Gareth Jones, Letter dated October 30, 1929. Gareth Vaughan Jones Papers. National Library of Wales. File B6/2.
25. J. V. Stalin, "Concerning Questions of Agrarian Policy in the USSR," *Works*, Volume 12 (Moscow: Foreign Languages Publishing House, 1954), 176. Originally published in *Pravda*, No. 309, December 29, 1929.
26. Conquest, *The Harvest of Sorrow*, 119-120.
27. Anna Louise Strong, *The Soviets Conquer Wheat* (New York: Henry Holt and Company, 1931), 81.
28. R. W. Davies and Stephen G. Wheatcroft, *The Years of Hunger: Soviet Agriculture, 1931-1933* 21-23, 46. Conquest's numbers are slightly higher; he estimates 7-7.5 million persons to have been dekulakized.
29. Gareth Jones, Diary of Service with Lloyd George, 1929-1930. Gareth Vaughan Jones Papers, National Library of Wales. File B1/3.
30. Annie Gwen Jones, "Impressions," 8.
31. Gareth Jones, Diary of Service with Lloyd George, 1929-1930. Gareth Vaughan Jones Papers, National Library of Wales. File B1/3.
32. Colley, *More than a Grain*, 65.
33. Ibid.
34. Annie Gwen Jones, "Impressions," 9.

35. Ibid., 15.
36. Delaney, "The Origins of Soviet Antireligious Organizations," 118-120.
37. Peris, *Storming the Heavens*, 106-109.
38. Gareth Jones, Diary of Service with Lloyd George, 1929-1930. Gareth Vaughan Jones Papers, National Library of Wales. File B1/3.
39. Ibid.
40. Colley, *More than a Grain*, 78.
41. Gareth Jones, Letter dated August 5, 1930. Gareth Vaughan Jones Papers, National Library of Wales. File 6/2.
42. Ibid.
43. Gareth Jones, Letter dated August 16, 1930. Gareth Vaughan Jones Papers. National Library of Wales. Folder 16.
44. Gareth Jones, Letter dated August 17, 1930. Gareth Vaughan Jones Papers. National Library of Wales. Folder 16.
45. Gareth Jones, Letter dated August 20, 1930. Gareth Vaughan Jones Papers. National Library of Wales. Folder 16.
46. Gareth Jones, Letter dated August 26, 1930. Gareth Vaughan Jones Papers. National Library of Wales. Folder 16.
47. Ibid.
48. Gareth Jones, "Glimpses of Soviet Russia," *The Liberal Woman's News*, 18 September 1930, 483.
49. An Englishman, [Gareth Jones], "The Snobbery of Soviet Russia," *News Chronicle*, 3 October 1930, n.p.
50. From a Correspondent, [Gareth Jones], "Rulers and Ruled," *The Times*, 13 October 1930, 13.
51. Ibid.
52. Ibid.
53. Ibid.
54. Ibid.
55. Lyons, *Assignment in Utopia*, 575.
56. Nigel Linsan Colley, "Unedited Photos of Gareth Jones' Entire Soviet Diaries." Accessed on 23 September 2011 from http://www.garethjones.org/soviet_articles/gareth_jones_diary.htm.
57. Gareth Jones, Letter dated February 5, 1930. Gareth Vaughan Jones Papers. National Library of Wales. Folder 16.

3

'The Two Russias'

'Small Coin'

It is reasonable to assume that Gareth Jones was honoring his mother by publishing his very first newspaper article in the *Liberal Woman's News*. Titled "Glimpses of Soviet Russia," the article begins with the words of a young, brown-eyed woman. "I'm terribly excited. I have never been in Moscow before and I've read so much about it. They're going to take us round and show us everything, and give us a fine week's holiday. I *am* glad I joined the young people's fighting brigade in our factory."[1] Jones effectively allows the young woman's enthusiasm to propel the reader into the article, and in a way she also speaks for him since he had never been in Moscow either. The scene is a simple one: Jones, the young woman, and two communists are drinking early morning coffee in the restaurant car of a train heading for the capital of the USSR. Jones offers a few details, describing her as "dark and clothed in a flimsy brown cotton dress..." before allowing her to complete her story about joining a brigade and improving the factory's production quotas. "We *did* work hard. Then I fell ill and I went to a Rest House in the country.... They are going to take us to cinemas and they say the Moscow cinemas are a thousand times better than our cinemas in Smolensk."[2] Jones allows the young woman to convey all that is good about this Workers' Paradise without commentary—the initiative and drive of the workers, gender equality, medical leave, and free entertainment.

Deftly, Jones changes the focus in the next paragraph when he tries to pay for the coffees and hands the waiter a five-ruble note for a bill of three rubles, fifty, and the waiter shouts about the lack of change. Jones creates a moment that is Kafkaesque. "I had struck one of Russia's serious problems, that of small coin, and I little imagined that a few weeks later I should hear newspaper boys rushing through the streets of a town in South Russia shouting 'Nine men shot for hoarding small coin! Nine men shot for hoarding small coin.'"[3] His understated tone belies the fact that on each successive trip to the USSR, Jones increasingly recognized the power of the OGPU to terrorize the citizenry. Jones then shifts attention to Moscow with its "profusion of propaganda posters on all sides."[4] That Jones was impressed by these colorful banners is evidenced by the fact he collected several propaganda posters on subsequent trips; the three he lists relate to messages about imperialist aggression, the dangers of alcohol and religion, and the need to abolish illiteracy.

In the article's final section, Jones documents a scene in front of a meat shop where women in a queue complain about having to stand in line for hours, yet no meat is available. Not having a ration card, Jones is told to go to the private traders where he finds "miserable and weak people offering their wares."[5] Butter was eight rubles a pound, and bad meat covered with flies was two rubles a pound. He leaves, feeling pity for the private traders "who are gradually being crushed out of existence by the State."[6] Jones concludes by contrasting the young Communist girl he met on the train with the vast majority of women who struggle to find meat and basic necessities.

> No wonder that they dread the months when Russia will be under snow, and no wonder they tell you on the trains: "What we want is a free market, and a chance of saying what we want to, and buying where we want to"; which indeed is an unconventional but apt way of describing Liberalism.[7]

Jones' first foray into journalism illustrates his ability to present real life situations, making use of techniques that anticipate literary journalism. Even though he is overly empathetic in places, he gradually learned to allow his reporting to convey the peasants' and workers' suffering.

'Snobbery'

By the time he published his next article in the *News Chronicle* on October 3, more executions provided the frame for his article, titled "The Snobbery of Russia." Significantly, this piece begins with a statement about "the repeated reports in the last few days of the 'execution' of 'specialists' on a charge of sabotaging the food supply of Soviet Russia."[8] In fact, nine prominent economists had been arrested in early September as counter-revolutionary conspirators, all of whom disappeared or were tried and confessed to working for foreign intervention. Later that month, forty-eight members of the People's

Commissariat of Trade were indicted for sabotaging food supplies. They were all shot. As Conquest notes in *The Harvest of Sorrow*, such acts "effectively silenced opponents, and made it clear that disagreement, or even failure to fulfill impossible plans, was a capital crime."[9]

In this article, Jones uses first-person narration to convey impressions of what he calls Soviet snobbery, personified in the town-worker, who is "the aristocrat of the Union of Socialist Soviet Republics."[10] This aristocrat, Jones asserts, receives all sorts of privileges—first place in the queue when meat is short, a far larger share of bread, and reduced prices in cinemas, theatres, concerts, gardens and restaurants. He uses phrases like "I shall never forget the shocked faces of the customers..." "One evening I went to a Moscow theatre, and was struck by the snobbishness..." and "I was chatting with a Russian caretaker and his wife..."[11] Jones' point is to articulate the differences between those who are workers or born to workers with those who are not. He does this by having the caretaker's wife describe "some dirty little children at play." When these children grow up, she says, they "will never be able to go to a university, and now they cannot have food until the workers' children have had their fill, poor, unhappy ones!"[12]

The three unsigned articles, published in mid-October in *The Times* under the title "The Two Russias," were the result of a meeting at Lloyd George's country residence in Surrey where Jones discussed his trip with Lloyd George, Wallace Steward, Seebohm Rowntree, and Lord Lothian [Philip Kerr]. Lord Lothian was so impressed by Jones' knowledge of Soviet affairs that he put him in touch with Geoffrey Dawson, editor of *The Times*.[13] A close reading of these articles reveals not only how astute Jones was in his assessment of Stalin, the Five-Year Plan, and the ruthlessness of the Communist Party, but also how greatly Jones benefitted from editorial guidance. Gone is the first-person narration. Each of the three parts has a clear focus about how the Communist Party has split the vast country into two Russias—the 10 percent who rule and the 90 percent who are ruled. Conversations with the people are used sparingly and balanced between party and non-party members.

After delineating his reporting methods in the first part of "Rulers and Ruled," Jones presents two views of what was happening under the "dictatorship of the proletariat." While the rulers "are filled with enthusiasm," the ruled "dread the return in the coming months of the conditions which reigned in 1918 and 1919."[14] Jones focuses on the youth of this active minority, many of whom had no conception of life in a capitalist country, having grown up in the communist training grounds of the Pioneers and the *Komsomol*. He describes them as being "impatient with...the slow progress of socialization in Russia."[15] These young people formed the basis of the shock brigades sent out to enforce collectivization in the villages "where they arouse the enmity of the peasants by their vigour and ruthlessness in forcing the households too rapidly into collective farms."[16]

In fact, 25,000 Communist workers were given a two-week course in January 1930 and then sent off to their assignments. Originally, they were to stay a year; then this order was extended to two years; finally, on December 5, 1930, the Central Committee made it permanent.[17] In addition, 72,204 workers, including many demobilized Red Army veterans, were sent to the countryside in the spring of 1930 on temporary assignment for the collectivization work. In Ukraine alone 23,500 officials in addition to more than 23,000 selected industrial workers appeared in the villages by February 1930. As Conquest notes, their task was threefold: first, beat down the kulak agents; second, fulfill the government's plan for grain delivery; third, complete the threshing of the grain, repair tools, plows, tractors, reapers, and other equipment.[18] Jones effectively captures the ruthlessness that characterized the methods used by these shock brigades when he quotes a Red Army commander: "We must be strong and show no mercy. We are not a tender-hearted set of people. We must not hesitate, for example, to crush the kulaks and send them to cut wood in the forests of the north."[19]

Jones then explains the threefold object of the Five-Year Plan—rapid industrialization, complete collectivization of agriculture, and the elimination of all capitalist elements in the country. Formally adopted on October 1, 1928, the Plan was to be executed through all national activities, and Jones asserts that one of main weapons used to accomplish the Plan's objective was propaganda. Interestingly, he reuses the same slogans that appeared in the *Liberal Woman's News* article and introduces others like "Art is a weapon of class warfare."[20] He also discusses the use of the film industry, the museums, and even minor institutions like a shooting range—where the targets are pictures of the Tsar, a priest, a kulak, a Chinaman, and a drunkard—to teach the overriding lesson that capitalism is evil and the revolution is glorious.

In the final section, Jones contrasts truth with statistics. While admitting that the Soviets had succeeded in some branches of industry, Jones asserts that statistics conceal poor materials, failure to provide factories with raw materials, and the destruction of expensive imported machinery through carelessness. Another wasteful tendency was evident in giving political keenness more importance than business acumen or education, causing experts to lose their jobs because of bourgeois parents. Jones asserts that Russia would remain a poor and discontented country because the Five-Year Plan was met with resistance, especially when collectivization of a village was coupled with closing of a church, arrest of the clergy, destruction of icons, and other excesses.

Food difficulties arising from the slaughter of animals which followed the violent collectivization campaign in January and February, and from the Soviet policy of exporting foodstuffs to obtain credit at all costs, are already putting a brake on the progress of industrialization, as is proved by the decision to postpone the beginning of the Third Year of the Plan from October to January.[21]

Jones recognized that despite all the optimism about the Plan, many difficulties were confronting its implementation, and the real truth could only be found in the views of the rank and file.

'A Dog's Life'

In the second part of the series "Fanaticism and Disillusion: Open Discontent," Jones shows the gulf that existed between the rulers and the ruled and how widely their expectations of the future differed. In this piece he quotes several miners and farmers from the Donetz Basin, who attributed the food shortage to two causes—forced collectivization of the farms and the absence of a free market. In the first letter he wrote after crossing the Soviet border, Jones writes, "In the Donetz Basin conditions are unbearable. Thousands are leaving. I shall never forget the night I spent in railway stations on the way to Hughesovka."[22] In his article, Jones uses eyewitness testimony to document conditions in the Basin. Two members of a collective farm offer a bleak picture. "It's a dog's life.... It would be better to live under the earth than to live now. They force us to join collective farms. The very best people... were sent to the Urals and Siberia, and their houses were taken from them. What is the use of living?"[23] Jones reused this quote in his *Western Mail* series in April 1931.

Jones notes in the first article that food difficulties were arising from the slaughter of animals which followed the violent collectivization campaign in January and February 1930 and from the exporting of foodstuffs to obtain credit. In fact, this widespread response by the peasants resulted in the loss of 42.6 percent of all cattle, 65.1 percent of sheep, and 47 percent of horses by 1934. This, Conquest asserts, "precipitated a vast economic disaster, which eventually worsened the famine of 1932-33."[24] So vehement was the response by the peasants that on March 2, 1930, Stalin published his "Dizzy from Success" article in *Pravda*, in which he warned that despite the Soviet government's successes in collectivizing more than fifty percent of all the peasant farms across the USSR and in fulfilling the Five-Year Plan's goal by more than 100 percent, such successes often had a negative side that might induce a spirit of vanity and conceit.

People not infrequently become intoxicated by such successes; they become dizzy with success, lose all sense of proportion and the capacity to understand realities; they show a tendency to overrate their own strength and to underrate the strength of the enemy; adventurist attempts are made to solve all questions of socialist construction "in a trice."

In such a case, there is no room for concern to consolidate the successes achieved and to utilise them systematically for further advancement.[25]

After explaining that the *artel* was the main link of the collective-farm movement because it consolidated the basic means of production, Stalin attacked attempts "to skip the *artel* framework and to leap straight away into the agricultural commune. The *artel* is still not consolidated, but they are already 'socialising' dwelling houses, small livestock and poultry; moreover, this 'socialisation' is degenerating into bureaucratic decreeing on paper, because the conditions which would make such socialisation necessary do not yet exist."[26] In explaining the over-zealous approach, Stalin shifted responsibility for the mistakes from the Central Committee of the Communist Party to local officials and sweepingly accused them of bungling the program through their over-zealousness. Stalin issued a similar correction in January 1933 after the harsh methods employed to collect grain in the late autumn of 1932, which left most of the grain growing regions with no seed and the prospect of certain starvation.

Jones clearly attributes the growing food shortage to the agricultural revolution begun the previous year and the absence of a free market, against which the peasants revolted by slaughtering their livestock, fleeing the collective farms, or simply destroying their property— usually by arson. Despite Stalin's article, the Communist Party did not completely abandon forced collectivization; rather, they forced many peasants back onto the farms by withholding food. Jones quotes a Cossack farmer:

I come here to the big town and I go to a shop to buy something. They say: "Show us your collective farm card." I reply: "But I have to no collective farm card." They say: "Then we cannot sell you anything." So in time I shall have to give up my land. Otherwise I shall not be able to buy a single thing and perhaps they will just take my house away and send me to Siberia.[27]

Jones was certainly not exaggerating how desperate conditions had become. On her trip through the Lower Volga and North Caucasus region in the spring of 1930, presented in the largely propagandistic *Soviets Conquer Wheat*, Anna Louise Strong documents similar over-zealousness. "Half-baked organizers uselessly violating village feelings; over-zealous small officials or even corrupt ones, persecuting the wrong people. Plenty of chaos."[28] In contrast, Jones concludes by pointing to the openness with which many peasants were expressing their dissatisfaction, leading him to question just how the Politburo could remain stable.

In the final part of the series "War Propaganda," Jones analyzes how the Communist Party used the threat of foreign intervention to justify its policies. He notes the strength of the OGPU [state political police], which "is a strong body, with powers of life and death, which can ruthlessly and immediately suppress any counter-revolutionary movement."[29] Similarly, he notes the Red Army was a class army, impregnated with Communist Party doctrines, which would ensure the continuance of the regime. Jones demonstrates his keen understanding of how Stalin was using *sovkhozy* and *kolkhozy* to supply the Red Army with food. He notes, "By these 'grain factories,' as they are called, the Government is guaranteed a stable supply of grain, and, if the Soviet plans for building 'pig and cattle factories' succeed, there will be a regular source of meat for the army and for the important factories."[30]

Jones was absolutely correct in his estimation of how Stalin planned on using agrarian policy to maintain the Red Army while growing the industrial sector. He explains that collective farming was helped by an excellent harvest in 1930 and warned that even though many who knew about conditions in the countryside were deriding the Party's boast that not a single individual farmer would be left within three years, "it would be unwise to underestimate the energy of the authorities, the advantages which are offered to the members of collective farms, and the deprivations which the individual farmers are made to suffer."[31]

Jones asserts that the foreign policy of the Bolsheviks was decidedly one of peace, especially in light of needing time to fulfill the objectives of the Five-Year Plan. In the years following, however, signs indicated a growing military threat, evidenced by a developing war industry, especially its nickel industry. If the Five-Year Plan was successful and the USSR could export enough materials to rival Great Britain and the United States, Jones reasons that a conflict between the capitalist system and communist system would become more likely. The fear of war was a rallying point for the communist régime, even among its critics. Jones quotes a bitter opponent of communism: "I hate the Bolsheviks, but if Russia were at war, whether the Bolsheviks were in power or not, I should fight at once and so would every good Russian."[32] That reasoning, fueled by Soviet war propaganda, led to increased membership in the *Osoaviakhim*, the Society for Air Defense and Chemical Warfare, especially among the young.

In his conclusion to the series, Jones asserts that war mongering helped the Bolsheviks to deflect attention away from the deficiencies in home policy, especially agrarian policy. Thanks to a bountiful harvest, large-scale agriculture would result in increased production all around. "More food will mean better work in the factories and although the Five-Year Plan is now tottering, and although a series of bad harvests might change the whole situation, there still remains a chance that, provided collective farms succeed, there will after two, three, or four years be some improvement in the workers lot."[33] Jones correctly predicted what was about to happen in the coming years: a series of bad harvests coupled with bitter class hatred, persecution of individual thought and freedom, abandonment of *korenizatsiia*, and crushing of the intelligentsia resulted in one of the worst tragedies of the twentieth century.

'Pen Pictures'

The next series of three articles was published under the headline "My Russian Diary—I, II, III" in *The Star*, a Liberal newspaper with a circulation of more than 800,000 readers that was also the sister newspaper of the *News Chronicle*. The articles are by-lined with Jones' name, not surprising given the very personal quality of the articles. *The Star* introduces them as "Some of the most brilliant and realistic pen-pictures yet made of the New Russia...*from the diary of a young Englishman* who speaks Russian fluently and has just returned from an unescorted trip"[34] (emphasis added).

Because no diary directly related to this journey has been unearthed, it's difficult to take this introduction literally. However, given the fact that Jones was an inveterate note-taker and given his description in the first *Times* article in which he states that the "conversations quoted in the following articles were written down at the earliest possible moment after the Russian had left the writer's presence,"[35] it seems reasonable to assume Jones wrote down the conversations used in the *Star* articles in some manner. Furthermore, the three *Star* articles are comprised of twenty-eight vignettes, ranging in length from two sentences to more than a dozen paragraphs. While it's possible Jones could have recreated the incidents and conversations from memory, the more reasonable explanation comes from Jones himself in *The Times* piece, and he did record the conversations, though that notebook or diary was eventually lost.

The three *Star* articles do indeed read like diary entries: short slice-of-life moments without continuity accompanied by cryptic commentary. In style, they are almost the exact opposite of the highly analytical *Times* pieces. The very first vignette reuses the lack of "small coin" theme established on the train ride in "Glimpses of Russia." Not having the correct change to pay for his ten kopeck ticket, Jones has to tell the ticket collector, who laments, "Nobody's got change."[36] In a separate vignette from "My Diary—II," Jones also retells how while riding a tram along the streets of Rostov he heard about men having been executed for hoarding change. "Then the tram stopped and a paper boy rushed up with *Labour*, the Rostov daily. He was shouting: 'Nine men shot for hoarding small coin. Nine men shot for hoarding small coin!'"[37]

Many of the vignettes illustrate the everyday frustrations faced by ordinary citizens. When Jones enters a barber shop to get a shave, the barber asks him if he has a razor for sale. Jones tells the man he only has a safety razor, and the barber falls silent. Jones offers this terse comment: "He was more interested in razors than in Communism."[38] With a mildly sarcastic tone, Jones records the inanities of Moscow life, a place where one loses what day of the week it is because there is no such thing as a week-end, where pedestrians walk in the busy streets without regard to their safety, where a living room is adorned with an icon of Christ on the wall and on the desk an image of Lenin, and where a woman cleaning streets turns her hose on a young man who dares to criticize her work.

Several of the vignettes play upon Jones' being a foreigner. A waitress in a co-operative restaurant asks him if he's ever been to New York where she longs to go and join her brother. "I don't like living here. The food's bad. It would be fine if I could get to my brother in America."[39] While riding on a train through the steppes in North Caucasia, a Georgian tells Jones the story of a pilot who sees a drowning man, swoops down, and saves him. The man turns out to be none other than Stalin, who grants the pilot any wish. "The airman scratched his head and thought. Then he said, 'Well, there's only one favour I want, but it's very important. It's this. For goodness sake don't tell a single soul I saved you, or my life won't be worth living!'"[40] Jones would repeat this parable two years later during a BBC broadcast.

Others openly criticize the capitalist system, as a young boy does at the circus when Jones asks him if he'd like to go to England. "Don't you know it's a capitalist country? I'd never want to go there," he said in a shocked tone. "There's so much oppression in the capitalist countries. I'm sure it can't be nice there."[41] Another man believes that all English communists are rounded up and kept in the Tower of London. In another vignette, Jones states that young communists believe the English upper classes are plotting war against the Soviet Union by manipulating the church and the socialists as tools. But Jones also made sure to show ordinary people without a political agenda. When Jones looks at his watch while riding a tram, a woman warns him that there are thieves in this town. "You be careful, young man. I don't know if you're a German or an Englishman, or what you are. Still, take my tip, and keep your eye on that watch of yours."[42]

Jones was able to strike up a conversation with almost anyone. On a park bench beneath a tree looking at the red walls of the Kremlin, an Asiatic-looking man tells him a riddle about Armenians. At the end, Jones caustically remarks, "No wonder the Turks massacred them, I thought, after I had shaken hands with my companion and strolled towards the Tverskaya, or the Regent-street of Moscow."[43] This rather insensitive, flippant remark does not characterize the overall tone of the articles, for Jones could be quite poignant when he wanted to be. The last vignette in the first article tells the story of having lunch and stealing a glimpse of a mirror in the room where the waitresses left their hats and coats. He sees one of the waitresses applying rouge on her lips and powder on her face.

> The paint and the powder were not applied with skill, the operation in England would not be greeted with any joy by one of the Puritanical upbringing, and yet here in Moscow it warmed the cockles of my heart, for it was so human, so feminine, in a country where personal adornment is not encouraged and where the machine is sometimes placed on a higher level than the human being.[44]

The passage is significant if only because it illustrates Jones' concern with the person, and that empathy for the human side also characterized the greater part of his famine reporting.

'Man of Steel'

In early December, Jones prepared a brief for Lloyd George on "Soviet Russia and the Caucasus." In preparation, he interviewed the prime minister and foreign minister of the Republic of Georgia, Mr. Chenkeli, who described the character of Stalin. In his memorandum to Lloyd George, Jones notes, "...all power is concentrated in the hands of

Stalin.... He is disinterested, has no material ambition, is very honest, absolutely ruthless and brutal.... He sits in his room in the Kremlin, and handles men like pawns."[45]

Significantly, on December 10, 1930, Jones published his first article for the *Western Mail*, titled "Russia's Man of Steel," in which he offers a biographical sketch of Stalin. Jones begins by comparing Wales' attempt to fight off British influence with Georgia's fight against Russian influence, and he notes another similarity in that both countries have been led by foreigners. Lloyd George, "from the once conquered mountainous race," led the British during their hour of need while in Russia the dictator "is a foreigner whose ancestors sniped the invading armies."[46] Jones delineates Stalin's character traits, focusing on his shyness, his shrewdness, and his grim and unattractive features. Providing some historical context, Jones explains how Stalin vanquished Trotsky and was in the process of dismantling the Right-Wing Opposition led by Rykov, Tomsky, and Bukharin. "But Stalin has been too clever for them and has made them declare openly that they are wrong. Although the leaders have recanted in most humble terms, the Right-Wing Opposition will remain a thorn in the flesh of Stalin."[47] The Rightists were first forced to admit their mistakes in November 1929 and then again in December 1930 shortly before this article was written. Jones ends with a series of questions about whether or not Stalin would be able to retain power. However, the most significant passages are those in which Jones contrasts each side's talking points.

Stalin says: "We must industrialise at full speed. We must be willing to deprive Russians of food in order to get machines. We must have no mercy for the richer peasants (the Kulaks), but must socialize agriculture as quickly as possible. Full speed towards pure Communism!"

The Right-Wing Opposition replies: "No. You are going too quickly. We must not export wheat and butter and other foods when the Russian worker is almost starving. We must not exterminate the rich peasant or there will not be enough food. We must slow down."[48]

While it is doubtful these quotations were taken verbatim from speeches published in *Pravda*, *Izvestia*, or agricultural journals, they succinctly capture the positions taken by each side over the course of 1929-1930, as Stalin shifted policy from the market-driven economics of NEP to the command economy of the Five-Year Plan. Jones was correct in supposing the Right-Wing Opposition would grow stronger "as the suffering of the Russian people becomes more acute with the setting in of the cruel winter."[49] What Jones did not anticipate was the ruthlessness with which Stalin carried out his policies and eliminated the opposition. Nonetheless, framing the debate around food deprivation and starvation and not merely around forced collectivization at this early date marks a significant milestone in his reporting.

'A War of Construction'

In the five signed articles under the umbrella title "Russia's Future" for the *Western Mail*, published between April 7-11, 1931, Jones analyzes the Five-Year Plan, then in its third year, based on first-hand observations recorded on his trip the previous August, his reading of Soviet newspapers, and interviews with industrial, agricultural, and political experts. These articles bring together all previous research for Lloyd George as well as his travels through the Soviet Union.

In "Communists' Five-Year-Plan," Jones sets up the polarity of Communism versus Capitalism in his narrative lead: "Two men were standing on the roof of a grey, straight-lined skyscraper in Moscow. One was a tall dark Russian Communist... the other a Welshman looking just like any other Welshman in the streets of a Glamorgan port or mining town."[50] Standing in front of the Kremlin, the communist, a man of the future, points to an electric station and explains why the capitalist is a man of the past. "That electric station over there is symbolic of the efforts of the Bolshevik revolution to build a new industrialised Russia where the machine will take the place of God."[51] The Bolshevik's weapon, of course, is the Five-Year Plan, which Jones calls the third act of the revolution.

The first act began in November 1917 with war on all sides—against the Whites, against the Allies, against the Poles. This first act was characterized by "ruthless terror" and the abolition of private enterprise, and by the time the curtain goes down, "the bodies of millions of Russians dead or dying in the terrible famine of 1921."[52] The second act, the New Economic Policy, spanned the years 1921-1927. Lenin compromised with Capitalism and allowed peasants and shopkeepers to profit from their labors, but in the middle of this act [1924], the drama reached its climax with the poignant death of its leader. With the Five-Year Plan, Stalin was able to ignite "a new revolution"[53] of pure communism that no longer accommodated any vestiges of Capitalism. Jones quotes *Pravda's* description of the Five-Year Plan, which is described as the "great plan of World Revolution."[54] By the end of the Five-Year Plan the idea of World Revolution would change to one of state socialism or socialism in one country.

Jones examines how the communists, numbering one and one-half million, could lead a population of more than one-hundred-fifty million in the second article, "Russia's Future: Stupendous Plan of Communists." Propaganda is the Party's means of explaining the Five-Year Plan. Jones began collecting propaganda posters during his travels, and he uses several of the slogans in this article. Three main aims characterize the Five-Year Plan: (1) industrialize Russian and set up factories and mines everywhere; (2) turn millions of privately-owned parcels of farmland into collectivized, state-owned, and operated farms; (3) exterminate all capitalist elements. "That means that by 1933 every hawker, shopkeeper, barber, tailor who worked or sold for his own profit and not for a State shop or co-operative shop would disappear."[55] Jones then outlines how the Plan would be carried out in other branches of industry—coal, iron and steel, and agriculture. Jones provides production goals for each industry, but he clearly realized that agriculture posed the greatest problem in attempting to do away with the millions of individually owned parcels of land, something that would impact one-hundred-thirty million peasants. "Will it be carried out? This problem is puzzling, worrying and tormenting the men and women in all countries."[56]

Jones begins his third article by quoting a factory commissar: "We are in a state of war. Russia is fighting a war of construction, the war to build up the Socialist State and to change the whole face of the earth. We are fighting a battle royal for the Five-Year Plan."[57] This passage bears a striking resemblance to a diary entry Jones recorded shortly after visiting the Soviet ship *Felix Dzerzhinsky* on May 3, 1930.

Russia is now in a state of war, but in a state of a war of construction, not of destruction. We are to evolve a new collectivist psychology. We are battling for the Five-Year Plan.... Of course we cannot tolerate defeatists; that is why we oppose any counter-revolutionary force. The spirit of competition between factories increases the production in a 'spirit of war.' Russians are being asked to sacrifice for the present to gain in the future.[58]

Whether or not Jones was recycling this material is unclear, although the similarities seem too close to be coincidental. Jones then outlines factors that improve the Plan's chances of success. These include the Soviet Union's vast resources—the largest supply of lumber in the world, one-third of the world's oil reserves, and the vast granary in the south of Russia, more precisely the Soviet Socialist Republic of Ukraine. The régime's stability, fortified by the OGPU, the law courts, and the Red Army, concentrate absolute power in the hands of Stalin. "This ruthless, honest man is just the man to drive a nation. He is brutal and has no mercy. He allows nothing to stand in his way when his mind is made up."[59] Again, this greatly resembles the memorandum Jones prepared for Lloyd George in February 1930 based on an interview with Chenkeli.

Still another factor in the Plan's favor is the enthusiasm of youth, which is being "trained to devote itself to the Five-Year Plan by the excellent work done for education in Russia."[60] Additionally, the government's monopoly of foreign trade allows for rapid influx of cash, needed to build the factories, textile-making machinery and improve coal production. As he did in the previous article, Jones ends with a discussion of agriculture. A bountiful harvest is "a great stroke of good fortune for their policy of collectivization.... A great deal, however, will depend upon the number and the quality of the tractors which can be produced under the Five-Year Plan.... Large State pig and cattle farms are to make up for the terrible shortage of meat which was caused by the peasants massacring their cattle a year ago, when being forced to join the Communist collective farms."[61]

These are the very conditions which changed the war of production into a war against the peasants in Ukraine, North Caucasus, and Donbas, who ultimately were blamed for the famine when they were unable to meet unrealistic grain quotas and were subsequently robbed of planting seeds, livestock, and all foodstuffs. Stalin blamed these areas for the defeat of the first wave of collectivization, even though a greater percentage of the peasant population had been collectivized in Ukraine by mid-1932 than in the *kolkhozy* of the republic of Russia (70 percent to 59.3 percent).[62] Stanislav Kosior, First Secretary of the Ukrainian Communist Party, articulated this rationalization in which failure to meet grain quotas was attributed to a strategy of the peasantry to withhold grain in order to starve the towns. As early as the summer of 1930, Kosior told members of the Ukrainian Central Committee:

> The peasant...wants the bread grain to die in order to choke the Soviet government with the bony hand of famine. But the enemy miscalculates. We will show him what famine is. Your task is to stop the kulak sabotage of the harvest.[63]

Kosior's explanation reflects pure Stalinist doctrine about the need to punish the peasants for the famine. It is they who are not working, it is they who are hoarding the harvested grain, and it is they who are keeping the *kolkhozy* from reaching their quotas. More than seven million tons of grain had been provided by Ukraine during the good harvest of 1930, and the same quota was set for 1931, despite the fact, as Conquest notes, that the conditions of collectivization reduced the harvest by two-thirds of that of 1930. The failure to meet grain quotas in 1931 would lead to purges of Ukrainian Communist Party officials in January 1932 and a propaganda campaign in *Pravda* during the first half of the year.

Jones documents the scarcity of food and clothing in his fourth article on the Five-Year Plan, titled "Russian Workers Disillusioned," which certainly shares similarities with the second *Times* article and begins with the words of a Russian miner: "Why can't they give us workers enough to eat?"[64] Jones had no difficulty getting people to tell him stories of privation during the August 1930 trip, and he uses several quotes that appeared in earlier articles. One young, slightly drunk worker decries what is happening. "That's what they are doing to us in Soviet Russia. The Communists are killing us workers and peasants. Everything's bad, bad, bad. We can't get boots and we can't get clothes. We can't get food, except bread. How can we work all day with our bellies empty. There's nothing in Russia. The Five-Year Plan? It's all lies, lies, lies!"[65]

Jones explains that the Plan's progress was being slowed due to formidable difficulties rooted in a lack of skilled labor, specifically because of untrained and unskilled engineers, mechanics and workers. Other problems stemmed from an inferior railway system that left millions of tons of coal standing idle in the Donetz Basin because there were not enough cars to transport it. Unable to get enough to eat, workers were leaving factories and mines, precipitating a decree from the Soviet Government forbidding workers from leaving their jobs. Jones points to a general state of malaise caused by unrealistic expectations and the threat of death. "During the last winter hundreds of men have been shot for failures in the branches of industry in which they had leading posts. When your actions are dictated according to a set plan and when failure may bring about death, your feeling of initiative is sure to suffer."[66]

Jones provides a final evaluation of the Five-Year Plan in the fifth article, published on April 11, 1931, under the headline "Mixture of Successes and Failures: Progress at the Expense of Happiness." As delineated in earlier articles, the Plan's achievements could be seen in emerging branches of industry, particularly electrical power developments, growth of aviation, exports of oil and grain, and the spread of education, all bolstered by a propaganda machine that effectively steered people toward health and temperance. On the other side of the ledger, Jones was blunt in his criticisms. "The rapid speed at which Stalin is trying to industrialise Russia has led to great hunger and suffering. Food is scarce. The health of the nation may be affected by the present privations. The discontent of the masses has been tremendous, and there has been talk of revolution against the Communists."[67] As he had done in his earlier profile of Stalin, Jones identifies the anti-Stalin group as the Right-Wing Opposition, which had already been forced to cower in December 1930 and admit their ideological mistakes, tied to slowing down the Plan and paying more attention to the happiness and comfort of the working class.

Jones concludes by retelling a story he was told in the Donetz Basin involving Stalin having a dream in which Lenin appears and criticizes Stalin's handling of the first Five-Year Plan and his plan to have a second one: "By that time every man, woman, and child in Russia will have died and joined me, and you'll be the only man left to carry out your second Five-Year Plan."[68] Jones then suggests that if there were more hunger and suffering Stalin's hold on the country would be compromised. Jones, like many other Westerners, underestimated Stalin's absolute control over the Communist Party and the lengths he would go to fulfill the Plan.

Notes

1. Gareth Jones, "Glimpses of Soviet Russia," *The Liberal Woman's News*, 18 September 1930, 483.
2. Ibid.
3. Ibid.
4. Ibid.
5. Ibid.
6. Ibid.
7. Ibid.
8. Gareth Jones, "The Snobbery of Soviet Russia," *News Chronicle*, 3 October 1930, n.p.
9. Conquest, *Harvest of Sorrow*, 186.
10. Jones, "The Snobbery of Soviet Russia."
11. Ibid.
12. Ibid.
13. Colley, *More than a Grain*, 86-89.
14. From a Correspondent [Gareth Jones], "Rulers and Ruled," *The Times*, 13 October 1930, 13.
15. Ibid.
16. Ibid.
17. Conquest, *Harvest of Sorrow*, 146.
18. Ibid., 148.
19. Correspondent [Jones], "Rulers and Ruled," 13.
20. Ibid.
21. Ibid.

22. Gareth Jones, Letter dated August 26, 1930. Gareth Vaughan Jones papers, National Library of Wales. File B6/2.
23. From a Correspondent [Gareth Jones], "Fanaticism and Disillusion," *The Times*, 14 October 1930, 15.
24. Conquest, *Harvest of Sorrow*, 159. For a complete discussion of peasant resistance to forced collectivization, see Lynn Viola, *Peasant Rebels Under Stalin: Collectivization and the Culture of Peasant Resistance* (New York: Oxford University Press, 1996).
25. J. V. Stalin, "Dizzy with Success: Concerning Questions of the Collective-Farm Movement," *Works*, Vol. 12 (Moscow: Foreign Languages Publishing House, 1955), 198.
26. Ibid., 203.
27. Correspondent [Jones], "Fanaticism and Disillusion," 15.
28. Strong, *The Soviets Conquer Wheat*, 71.
29. From a Correspondent [Gareth Jones], "Strength of the Communists," *The Times*, 16 October 1930, 15.
30. Ibid.
31. Ibid.
32. Ibid.
33. Ibid.
34. Gareth Jones, "My Russian Diary—I," *The Star*, 22 October 1930, n.p.
35. Correspondent [Jones], "Rulers and Ruled," 13.
36. Gareth Jones, "My Russian Diary—I," n.p.
37. Gareth Jones, "My Russian Diary—II," *The Star*, 27 October 1930, n.p.
38. Jones, "My Russian Diary—I," n.p.
39. Jones, "My Russian Diary—II," n.p.
40. Gareth Jones, "My Russian Diary—III," *The Star*, 29 October 1930, 6.
41. Jones, "My Russian Diary—II," n.p.
42. Jones, "My Russian Diary---III," 6.
43. Jones, "My Russian Diary—I," n.p.
44. Jones, "My Russian Diary—I," n.p.
45. House of Lords Archives, David Lloyd George files. Gareth Jones, "Soviet Russian and the Caucasus," 9 December 1930.
46. Gareth Jones, "Russia's Man of Steel," *Western Mail*, 10 December 1930, 11.
47. Ibid.
48. Ibid.
49. Ibid.
50. Gareth Jones, "Communists' Five-Year-Plan," *Western Mail*, 7 April 1931, 6.
51. Ibid.
52. Ibid.
53. Ibid.
54. Ibid.
55. Gareth Jones, "Russia's Future: Stupendous Plan of Communists," *Western Mail*, 8 April 1931, 5.
56. Ibid.
57. Gareth Jones, "Forces Behind Stalin's Dictatorship," *Western Mail*, 9 April 1931, 14.

58. Gareth Jones, Diary of Service with Lloyd George, 1929-1930. Gareth Vaughan Jones Papers, National Library of Wales. File B1/3.
59. Jones, "Forces," 14.
60. Ibid.
61. Ibid.
62. Conquest, *Harvest of Sorrow*, 220.
63. Quoted in Conquest, *Harvest of Sorrow*, 221. See also Petro Grigorenko, *Memoirs* (New York: Norton, 1982).
64. Gareth Jones, "Russian Workers Disillusioned," *Western Mail*, 10 April 1931, 5.
65. Ibid.
66. Ibid.
67. Gareth Jones, "Mixture of Successes and Failures," *Western Mail*, 11 April 1931, 12.
68. Ibid.

4

'We Are Starving'

'New Enthusiasms'

On the day before his series on the Five-Year Plan began in the *Western Mail*, Jones sailed for America aboard the *Ile de France* with his new employer Ivy Ledbetter Lee, to whom he had been introduced by Sir Bernard Pares shortly after returning from that first journey to the Soviet Union in September 1930. Lee, who was then serving as Vice-President of the American League of Nations Union, wanted to write a book about the USSR titled *What of Russia Now?* He offered Jones £800 to do essentially the same work as Jones had done for Lloyd George, only in New York City and Washington, D.C., beginning in late April 1931. Lee was writing the book to promote better relations between the Soviet Union and the United States, since one of his clients, Standard Oil, was buying a lot of Soviet petroleum and selling it in Asia. Some of Jones' work involved researching the Russian Revolution and the policies of Lenin as well as following the Soviet press and developments in the oil and sugar trades.[1]

That Lee was fascinated with the Soviet Union is evidenced by the fact that he had already written two other books about the USSR, the first, titled *Present Day Russia*, was published in 1923; the second, titled *USSR: A World Enigma*, appeared in 1927. As Lee explains in the second book's introductory author's "Note," the book made no presumptions as to literary quality; rather, it was written primarily for clients and friends.

> In light of these reservations, it is distributed primarily to clients and friends purely for what it is worth in the hope that the subject matter will be judged as a whole and not in part, and that the picture presented will be accepted as a *general impression only*.[2]

Louis Fischer of *The Nation* was one of the correspondents to whom

Lee sent the book. Fischer responded in a letter to Lee in which he compliments Lee for having captured the essence of the new Russia.

> You seemed to have caught and expressed the new tendencies, new spirit, new enthusiasms now sweeping Russia. I, myself, returning after an absence of six months, scarcely recognize the place. Much has happened, and if the outside world wants to understand, it must listen, read, study without bias and without thoughts fathered by wishes.[3]

Lee corresponded again with Fischer as he prepared another book on the USSR, one written ostensibly to commemorate the fifteen anniversary of the Revolution. The work on that book was largely researched and prepared by Gareth Jones.

'In Skyscraper Land'

The offices of Ivy Lee and Associates were situated across from the New York Stock Exchange. Jones was given an office with a view of the Hudson River, the Empire State Building and New Jersey. In a letter home, he drew a detailed diagram of Manhattan, complete with the numbering of streets, starred designations of where he lived and worked, a sketch of Central Park, the water front, and directions for uptown and downtown (Illustration 6). In another letter, he describes the scene. "I found myself in the middle of the capitalist world...in the heart of skyscraper land."[4] Before long, however, he was sent off to Washington, D.C., to do research at the Soviet Information Bureau. While there, he met Paul Scheffer, the Washington correspondent of the *Berliner Tageblatt*, whom Jones called "the great authority on Russia."[5] In 1929 Scheffer became the first Western journalist to be refused a re-entry visa to the USSR because of his criticisms of the Five-Year Plan. During the grain crisis of 1928, Scheffer reported that bread riots were occurring in Ukraine, as well as along the Don and Volga river regions, and he accurately predicted that those regions were heading for catastrophic famines.[6] Scheffer had already decried the use of state terror, oftentimes employed against the very people who had effected the regime change. He writes:

> History has never invented anything more ironical or cruel than the spectacle of these victorious revolutionaries who, under both systems, the one they destroyed and the one they led to victory, receive the same reward for their efforts—the silence of Siberia.[7]

Scheffer became one of Jones' most trusted and supportive colleagues; he was the last person Jones met with before leaving for the USSR in 1933 and the first person to confer with him upon his return to Berlin where Jones held a press conference to announce his discovery of famine. On his trip to Washington, Jones also had occasion to meet Secretary of State Henry L. Stimson and President Herbert Hoover. He wrote that even though newspapers were trying to be optimistic, the Great Depression was likely to persist.

> It is difficult for anyone not in business or production to realize how the world has crashed in the last year. From the American point of view, there is little change and hardly any hope on the war debts, League of Nations attitude or consultation.... The Congress is very weak in the resolutions, and there was a general atmosphere of failure. The unemployed all over the world are having an awful time, and all the countries are having the same problem.[8]

Upon his return to New York City, Jones moved into the home of the Savelieffs, a Russian-speaking family, so that he might continue "to speak Russian and go to the Russian club to read newspapers."[9] As things turned out, the Savelieffs were not particularly interesting, so Jones befriended another Russian family on the same street, East 121st Street, the Jukoffs. Jones describes Mrs. Jukoff as a Russian noble, sixty-five years old, whose son was a former officer.

> They look proletarian, because the son, who was an officer by profession, has been working in a factory for 10 years. He lost his job and is now doing some translating. I help him in the translating, and in exchange they talk to me. I feel my Russian getting better and better.[10]

Two days later he wrote again, describing the activities that he and Jukoff were enjoying, as well as an assessment of his language development.

> Tonight I am taking Mr. Jukoff out to dinner and to a Soviet film.... They want me to go and see them whenever I can, to read Russian and to talk Russian. They gave me supper last Thursday and have invited me to supper this Thursday night. There is something childish and simple about them. They speak French well, but English hardly. I help the son with English translations.... Mr. Jukoff knows so little English that if I did not help him to give a good translation from Russian, he might

get the sack. I went last night to see them and I learnt a lot of
Russian.[11]

A week later, Jones writes that the son lost his job and was miserable,
the translation job over and the family's only source of income coming
from the Russian lessons for which Jones was paying them.
Part of the reason for Lee's interest with the Soviet Union stemmed
from what Jones in a letter to his family called "the Great Oil War"
between Standard Oil and Royal Dutch, which sold Shell oil. Lee
wanted to publish a book charging the competition with malpractice.
The reason for the book about the Soviet Union that Jones was hired
to work on "is that Mr. Lee is favourable to the Soviet Union, probably
because his clients, Standard Oil are keen on good relations. Standard
Oil buys a lot of Soviet Petrol and sells it in Asia."[12] Jones relates that
he was to begin his work on the book in earnest on May 11, because
Lee wanted his book in the hands of the publisher by August 1. In early
July, Jones writes that he and Lee were staying at Montauk Manor at
the furthermost end of Long Island, where Lee planned "to write his
book on Russia in one week so he says."[13] Jones was confident that
as a result of all the work he was doing he would be able to do some
lecturing in the winter. "Russia is all the rage, and I think the Foreign
Policy Association will help me to get bookings. Anything from £10
to £25 is paid for a lecture. There is complete freedom for anyone on
Mr. Lee's staff to write articles or lecture."[14]

For his part, Jones spent a considerable amount of time at the
New York Public Library researching documents pertaining to the
revolution, especially Lenin's time in Germany. He outlined the other
topics he was working on, including Russia's repudiation of debts,
private property in Russia, the terror of Soviet justice, religion, social
code, and anti-Bolshevik propaganda.[15] Weeks later he writes again,
updating his family about the research he was doing, "studying the
Bolshevik papers at the time of the revolution, and also the secret
documents of the Tsarist period showing how the Tsarist agents bribed
the French newspapers with the exception of *L'Humanité*. They even
paid subsidies to *Le Temps*."[16] Jones never tired of the research he
conducted for projects that, in some cases, never came to fruition, as
with the Lee book.

'Through my Interpreter'

During the middle of June, Jones was introduced to a family member
of another Lee client, H. J. "Jack" Heinz II (Illustration 7), heir to the

Heinz fortune who had recently graduated from Yale and wanted to go to the Soviet Union. Lee suggested that because Jones knew the language, he would be much better than any official Soviet Intourist guide. By early July, Jones provided Lee and the Heinz family with a detailed itinerary for the trip to the Soviet Union, complete with railway schedules, departure times, routes, and length of stay at each destination.

I am going with Jack Heinz, in order that he shall really learn what is happening in Russia and not be taken round by guides, Mr. Lee says. Also to get the "latest dope" for Mr. Lee.... Young Heinz is really first-class—keen, intelligent and sense of humor.[17]

Heinz and Jones set sail from London on August 8 aboard the steamer *Rudzutak* bound for Leningrad by way of Hamburg, Germany. In addition to a stay in Leningrad, Jones scheduled stops in "Moscow, Nijni-Novgorod, down the Volga on a steamer to Stalingrad, then to Kharkoff, Dnieperstroy, Kiev and into Poland at Krakow."[18] The pair spent the first nineteen days in Leningrad and Moscow before heading to Nijni-Novgorod where they began a tour of the countryside, visiting *kolkhozy* and *sovkhozy*.

The themes that dominate Jones' diaries, the three articles he wrote for *The Times*, and *Experiences in Russia 1931—A Diary*, Heinz's book based on Jones' diaries, include many of the same topics he had explored in the first series of articles; namely, the use of propaganda by the Communist Party, the persecution of religion, rapid industrialization, and the deteriorating conditions in the countryside as a result of forced collectivization and dekulakization. Significantly, these works include the words "starve" and "starving" by the peasants they spoke with; the word appears more than a half dozen times in the diaries and *Experiences*. The works also document meetings with a number of Westerners living and working in the USSR, including correspondents Duranty, Fischer, and Lyons, as well as Maurice Hindus, Cecile B. DeMille, and members of the Albert Kahn team of engineers and architects stationed in Moscow. *Experiences in Russia 1931—A Diary* was published anonymously in 1932 by Heinz through the Alton Press in Pittsburgh. That Heinz was the author of *Experiences* and that he travelled to the Soviet Union with Jones are facts not widely known; scant information exists about the book, its composition and publication, or its author.

What is clear from a close reading of all three works—Jones' diaries, the three articles Jones wrote for *The Times*, and *Experiences*—is the correspondence among the three works in the use of anecdotes, accounts of peasants, factory workers, and party officials, and Jones' and Heinz's observations and experiences. Even though Heinz is never named in the book, he relates one meeting with the president of the *Torgsin* stores "concerning the purchase of the '57.' It was a lot of fun, and I arranged to send him samples, after giving him a fight talk for the goods through my interpreter."[19] In that same anecdote, Heinz also relates that he told the commissariat that the prices being charged for Heinz's canned goods in Leningrad were too high. He then continues, "I wanted Mr. Jdanoff, of *Torgsin*, to try some hot beans, and made an appointment to see him in an hour. Just as I arrived, with my hot tins, the rascal drove off in his car. Audible comment on Russian politeness and business ethics!"[20] It seems clear from this passage that Heinz was not deliberately attempting to conceal the company brand, even though he never offers up his own identity by name.

Throughout *Experiences*, Heinz mentions Jones by name, even though he does not explain that they were introduced through Ivy Lee and Associates or that Jones was serving as his tour guide. Upon arriving in Leningrad, Heinz narrates that they got through Customs before anyone else, "courtesy of the port for Lloyd George's former secretary! (Jones.)"[21] In places, Heinz assumes a reportorial tone, as in the very beginning: "Jones and I embarked from London on the Soviet steamer *Rudzutak* at 7:30 p.m."[22] Any time Jones translated a propaganda poster or discussions with people, Heinz attributes the translation to him. And after one particularly heated debate with other passengers on the sixth day of their journey, Heinz notes that "the revolutionaries were so numerous and so unreasonable that they might have swamped me, had it not been for the timely arrival of Joneski. Then we flayed 'em!"[23] This playful Russification of the Jones name by Heinz evidently left an impression, for Jones used it in a letter to describe himself three years later.

Heinz's use of sarcasm is evident in several parts of the book, especially when Heinz wants to draw attention to some flaw in the Soviet system, an ideological contradiction, or the primitive conditions they endured on the journey. For example, after being told by the people's food commissariat that every meat shop would eventually have some sort of refrigeration, Heinz notes, "There's a pipe dream for you!"[24] After waiting three hours for a boat to take them to an auto factory only to watch it sail by loaded with soldiers, Heinz relates that they walked to the factory, commenting, "Ah, the vagaries of travel and Russian uncertainty!"[25] In describing a church service, Heinz contrasts the poverty of the people with the rich robes and gold crown of the officiating priest. "Lighted candles, much gilt work, and innumerable icons with lamps in front, completed the picture—aside from the usual Russian smell!"[26]

Heinz's sarcastic tone was typical of American capitalists, evidenced in a similar travelogue by Carveth Wells, titled *Kapoot*, which chronicles his 1932 journey through the USSR in search of Mount Ararat and Noah's Ark. For example, in describing his stay at the New Moscow Hotel, Wells bemoans a balky bathroom tap.

The tap had worked once upon a time, perhaps before the Revolution, but all the plumbers in the country had probably been executed or exiled together with the rest of Russia's intellectuals, and as the present generation have no use for plumbing or any other such bourgeois luxuries the wash basin and bath had fallen into disuse.[27]

While Heinz maintained his anonymity, no attempts were made to keep Jones' identity secret. His full name is given after the "Preface," in which Jones explains how they travelled:

With a knowledge of Russia and the Russian language, it was possible to get off the beaten path, to talk with grimy workers and rough peasants, as well as such leaders as Lenin's widow [Nadezhda Krupskaya] and Karl Radek [editor of *Izvestia*]. We visited vast engineering projects and factories, slept on the bug-infested floors of peasants' huts, shared black bread and cabbage soup with the villagers—in short, got into direct touch with the Russian people in their struggle for existence and were thus able to test their reactions to the Soviet Government's dramatic moves.[28]

At the time of their journey in 1931, Westerners were relatively free to travel through much of the USSR, confirmed by a number of references to people like Maurice Hindus and Sidney and Beatrice Webb, as well as George Bernard Shaw, mentioned by several peasants who spoke with the pair. It was not until February 1933 when famine conditions were severe that travel was restricted for Western journalists. Ralph W. Barnes, a correspondent for the *New York Herald Tribune*, wrote about those travel restrictions. "The present [1933] restrictions represent a definite change in policy from the time in 1931 when Premier Vyascheslav M. Molotov invited the resident foreign correspondents to investigate and satisfy themselves as to whether forced labor existed in the Soviet lumber camps."[29]

In addition to the accounts of Western journalists and tourists, some of the most vivid descriptions of conditions in the Soviet countryside were provided by agricultural experts like Otto Schiller and Andrew Cairns, the latter a Canadian wheat expert. He first visited the Soviet Union in 1930 for the Canadian Wheat Pools and then in the spring of 1932 was assigned by the Empire Marketing Board in London to assess the significance of Soviet agriculture for the world wheat market. His revelations provided the British Foreign Office with some of the earliest evidence of famine in the countryside.

'The Attack of Capitalism'

Heinz's account is largely based on his observations, material from Jones' diary entries, and conversations, newspapers and propaganda posters that Jones translated for him. An example is related on the very first day aboard the *Rudzutak* when they visited the crew's quarters and came upon a bulletin board that was plastered with propaganda and "amazingly true statements regarding the present world depression."[30] Jones' translation of this newspaper's message resembles the same battle between capitalism and socialism that Jones articulated in his first series of articles for *The Times*. "The attack of Capitalism on the workers' standards of living has led to increased mortality, suicides, and crime. The world bourgeoisie is struggling, with the active help of the Social Democrats, to guarantee a way out of a crisis at the expense of the working masses."[31] Sailors, sixty percent of whom were members of the Communist Party, parroted the latest party slogans. For example, one tells Jones:

> There will be complete equality. We are working toward that; we must now be sure to act according to the doctrine. 'He who will not work, shall not eat.' So if a man doesn't work, he is not to have money nor bread nor anything else. We started off in the beginning with equal pay, but it gave advantages to the lazy man, so we soon abolished that.[32]

Not surprisingly, the sailor quotes a doctrine from the 1918 Constitution of the Union of Soviet Socialist Republics, (Sec. 2, Chap. IX, paragraph 18), which was adapted from the biblical aphorism and later repurposed by Stalin to justify punishment of those who were forced onto the collective farms but would not work.

In addition to the crew, Heinz and Jones engaged a number of passengers, one an avowed Scotch communist; a White Russian who had lived in Chicago for thirty years and been ruined by the Great Depression; Mrs. Bromley, a working woman from England; and Dr.

Salter, a Labor Party Member of Parliament. Jones catalogues these conversations in his diary for August 13-15, one of the few places in the diary where the three dates are consolidated under one heading. In *Experiences*, Heinz uses bits and pieces of these conversations for his narrative of the fifth, sixth and seventh days of the journey, not necessarily following the same topical order as they appear in Jones' diary. For example, one of the first conversations that Heinz discusses related to religion, which he attributes collectively to the Scotch communist and Mrs. Bromley. Jones also lists these two together under the topic of Religion, although it comes as the last topic in this section. Heinz does not quote them directly, instead presenting their views together. "They object to what they call the insincerity and outward sham of the Catholic Church.... They ridicule what they call the ceremonial hokum, and decry the custom of paying money to the priest when one marries."[33]

The Scotch communist, identified as "Comrade Reid," [Heinz's spelling; spelled "Reed" in Jones' diary] is described by Jones as having "yellow-sandy hair, out of work for 9 years."[34] While he doesn't offer a physical description, Heinz explains that Reid had been a member of the Communist Party for ten years and out of work for nine, which certainly helps to explain his hatred of capitalism. Reid was Heinz's first extended contact with a devoted communist "who knew quite a bit about his Marxian philosophy."[35] Over a two-day period the men engage in a wide ranging conversation that covers topics like the impending decline of capitalism, world revolution, the Five-Year Plan, religion, money, and communism in Great Britain. Even though Jones provides clear headings and attribution in his diary, Heinz was not always accurate in his attribution. For example, he mistakenly attributes to Reid the idea that Al Capone and Jack Diamond are "tools of the bourgeois employed to break strikes and intimidate workers."[36] However, the quote should have been attributed to the White Russian, which makes more sense given his residence in Chicago. In his diary Jones records Reid speaking about world revolution, the Third International, the obligations of the Soviet government, and great men. This last topic offers an example of how Heinz used Jones' diary entries. In his diary, Jones underlined Great Men and above it wrote and underlined Scotch.

> Lenin is the only great man who has lived. A great man is a man who will sacrifice everything in the interest of [the] proletariat. Edison was not a great man because he was exploited to benefit the bourgeois.[37]

In *Experiences*, Heinz narrates part of this and then fleshes out the idea with dialogue.

> We talked of great men. Comrade Reid, the Scotsman, believes that Lenin and Marx are the only true great men of the past or present, because they have constructively aided the proletariat.... "What about a man like Edison?" I inquired. "Did he not benefit humanity and the civilized world?"
>
> "No," he declared. "Edison was exploited by the bourgeois, too. But unconsciously he abetted the rationalization of the Capitalist world by his inventions, and in so doing his work caused greater unemployment, and consequently helped to destroy Capitalism."[38]

The passages illustrate just how Heinz fleshed out Jones' entries, doubtlessly working from memory since no notebook or manuscript has been unearthed. After the trip, the two men met in London in October, shortly before Jones returned to America to continue his employment with Lee. In a letter home, Jones writes, "Jack H. came to see me at the Reform [Club] on Tuesday evening and Wednesday was a very busy day getting my [*Times*] articles typed and beginning my last article. Jack H. came in again to finish his *Diary*, which he was basing on my notes."[39]

Jones' diary entries present challenges in terms of flow, legibility, transliteration of entries in Russian/Ukrainian, German, French, and Welsh, and use of shorthand, so it's understandable that Heinz may have struggled figuring out attribution. For example, under the heading White Russian, Jones records several opinions related to the definition of a capitalist, how justice works in America, and how American youth have lost respect for their parents, all of which Heinz uses, almost verbatim. However, then Jones underlines five different topics: Freedom, Cheka, Money, World Revolution and Third International, and he clearly attributes the Cheka, World Revolution and Third International quotes to the Scotsman. What is unclear is whether the other two topics should be attributed to the White Russian. Even though they are on the same page, Jones clearly marks the end of the White Russian's quotations by drawing two lines to separate his from the next set of topics. Not having attribution, these quotations may have come from other sources. After giving the White Russian's opinions, Heinz relates, "I read and wrote until tea time, after which I started a casual talk with the Scotch Communist. Three hours later we quit, having gathered fifteen or more persons into the argument."[40] It is reasonable to assume that because Jones did not attribute those quotes to any of the three named people, they might be from among the fifteen others who joined the conversation.

Finally, after recording another rather lengthy conversation with the Scotch communist in which he attributes the <u>Freedom</u> quote to him, as well as quotes pertaining to the three periods of capitalism, the contradictions in the capitalistic system, and the problems with bourgeois doctors. In Jones' diary, the first two of these have no attribution, as they follow his introduction of Reid, Mrs. Bromley, and the White Russian. Later that night another debate ensued, which, Heinz notes, involved "a considerable number of saloon passengers, both Communist and non-Communist participating. Each of the warriors was housed in a rhinoceros hide of righteousness, and armed with the mighty sword of oratory and the dagger of invective. Cut and slash as they might for nearly two hours, no book was drawn. Then someone yawned, and someone else said it was bedtime, anyway."[41] That Heinz concluded this episode with mock-heroic sarcasm is not surprising, for he doubtlessly recognized that for his family and friends, such anti-capitalist ideology would be tiresome. Nonetheless, Heinz deserves credit for not glossing over this period of the journey when they were confined aboard ship with little else to do but engage other passengers. Arriving in Leningrad the following day, he and Jones were about to confront the harsh realities of the communist system.

'The Real Russia'

The three articles Jones wrote for *The Times* upon his return from the Soviet Union with Heinz were published anonymously on three consecutive days from October 14-16, 1931. The editors note that "the same writer" had the previous year contributed a series of articles and now "contributes further impressions of the country...."[42] The series title was "The Real Russia," and the first part of the series was titled "The Peasant on the Farm: Increase and its Cost." Just as he had drawn a contrast in the 1930 series between the "Two Russias," with the ten percent minority ruling the ninety percent, Jones contrasts the Russia of the cities and towns "inhabited by a small minority of the population" with the real Russia, which can only be found "in the distant villages never, or rarely, seen by the traveller."[43] At the heart of real Russia is the peasant, "the central figure of the Soviet Union," who not only forms the majority of the population but upon whom the rest of the vast country depends, particularly upon their production of grain. "The peasant problem will always be the most important in Russian affairs."[44]

Significantly, Jones does not follow the chronology of their journey.

Rather, he begins this series dealing with the most important issues of the day—forced collectivization, dekulakization, and the radical changes effected during the previous two years, including the disappearance of large-scale individual farms, the splitting up of the land among twenty-six million individual households, and the re-emergence of a kulak class. Deemed as dangers to the authority of the Communist Party, these obstacles were overcome "with energy, ruthlessness and confidence"[45] in the policy of forced collectivization. Jones then lists four questions that he addresses in the remainder of the article. As he did in the first series of articles, as well as in the preface to the Heinz book, Jones explains how he gathered the information:

> The writer, who had no difficulty in travelling wherever he wished and wandered on foot to whatever farms he pleased, was able to gain the confidence of a large number of peasants in different parts of Russia. The unanimity of their views was striking.[46]

Jones does not explain that his knowledge of the Russian language enabled him to travel so freely, most often unescorted by Soviet guides, or that his association with Lloyd George facilitated meeting people of influence like Karl Radek, Madame Nadezdha Krupskaya [Lenin's widow], and Maurice Hindus, as well as several Western journalists—Fischer, Duranty, and Lyons.

Jones then focuses on the "Stalin" *kolkhoz*, a collective farm in a district that was completely collectivized, explaining that "the kolkhoz had been in the turmoil of class warfare, but now ... all was calm again."[47] He then uses a long quote from the president of the village soviet, who explains how unity had been achieved in this village.

> We had 40 kulak families and we sent them all away. We sent the last one a month ago. It was not enough to send the men only, because we must pluck up all the kulak elements by the roots. So we sent the women and children too. They went to Solovki, [a corrective labor camp located on the Solovetsky Islands in the White Sea] or to Siberia to cut wood or to work on the railways. In six years, if they have shown themselves on our side, they will be allowed to return. We leave the very old kulaks here, because they are no danger to the Soviet power. Now the fight against the kulaks has ended in our victory for the last kulak went a month ago....[48]

This last sentence is different from the end of the same quote as it appears in Jones' diary and in the section of Heinz's book dealing with day twenty-eight, which reads: "Thus we have already liquidated the Kulak!"[49] Both the diary and the Heinz book continue with the village president's quote about a campaign in June and July against illiteracy, but *The Times* article continues by associating this last kulak with religious agitation.

> He was the ringleader of a religious sect in the village. He collected a number of peasants in his house and told them in meetings that the Communists wished to starve all the peasants. He prophesied that war would come and that the Pope from Rome would visit the village and would hang all the Communists. That was counter-revolutionary agitation, so now that ringleader is in Siberia doing hard labour. He is working as hard as those farm labourers he used to hire.[50]

In Jones' diary, this anecdote appears on the same page but as part of a separate discussion with the village president, and in *Experiences*, it appears as part of the next day's entry when the village president drove them around the *kolkhoz*. Jones uses the Russian term *batrak* in the diary instead of farm labourers. Lewin argues that in the time period before collectivization, the *batraks* continued to occupy, as they had before the Revolution, the lowest stratum of society, even though in 1926 a majority of them owned small farms and a third of these had tillable land and livestock. Additionally, the employment of labor was not limited to kulaks, for it was common practice in the villages. The state of the *batraks* "weighed heavily on the revolutionary conscience of many activists."[51]

Heinz adds his own touch to the quote by changing the pronoun to a stronger term. "The villain was a Kulak. He said that the Communists wanted all the people to die. Imagine!"[52] Heinz added a sarcastic clincher, as he did in many episodes involving communists. Significantly, Jones introduces into the article the president's accusation that the ringleader was telling the peasants that "the Communists wished to starve all the peasants." The reference to starving the peasants is not in this part of his diary or this section of the Heinz book, even though it does appear in several other places uttered by peasants themselves. Perhaps Jones opted to graft the idea of starvation onto this sequence for effect, having the village president condemn as counter-revolutionary agitation the very means the communists employed to punish the peasants for withholding grain during the 1932 harvest. It is also ironic that as a type of propagandistic "scare story" used by the communists to mollify the population in the countryside, it anticipates the accusation Duranty leveled against Jones after he reported on the famine when he returned from Ukraine in March 1933.

Jones ends this section about the fate of the kulaks by relating an incident that occurred as they travelled down the Volga River en route to Samara on the twenty-fifth day of their journey. From the deck of a steamer, Jones and Heinz watched as a hundred peasants sat motionless on the bank. A doctor's wife tells them:

> Do you see those? They are kulaks, being exiled, just because they have worked hard throughout their lives. The peasants have been sent away in thousands to starve. It is terrible how they have treated them. They have not been given bread-cards or anything. A large number were sent to Tashkent and were left bewildered on the town square. They did not know what to do and very many starved to death.[53]

Jones leaves out a question that appears in the diary, "Didn't you see them in Kazan?"[54] Kazan is located approximately halfway between Nijni-Novgorod and Samara on the Volga River. Tashkent, located in Uzbekistan, would have been almost completely foreign, so the wife's assessment of their not knowing what to do and starving to death is arguably quite apt.

Who is a Kulak?

The next section, titled "The German Colonists," makes use of four anecdotal stories from peasants, only one of which is from a German collective farm that Jones visited alone on the thirty-seventh day [September 5] of their journey. This *kolkhoz* was a village of six hundred inhabitants, most of them German Mennonites. Six families with women and children had been recently exiled. One woman describes how others had previously been exiled from the district.

> We received letters telling us that from the German colony of several villages in the district ninety kulak children had died on the journey to Siberia or on arrival there. We are afraid of being sent away as kulaks, because they might say you were a kulak for political or personal reasons. We had a letter from one of the kulaks saying that they were cutting wood far away in Siberia, that life was terribly hard and that they did not have enough to eat.[55]

Jones relates in his article that the fear of being branded a kulak and exiled had a powerful effect in drawing peasants onto the collective farms. As William Strang notes in a memorandum to Sir John Simon at the British Foreign Office in August 1932, what constituted a kulak changed as conditions devolved in Ukraine and the North Caucasus.

> Kulak and speculator are elastic terms. A kulak is a peasant who has enriched himself by the employment of other men's labour. In other times, a kulak has been a peasant possessing certain machines or more than a certain number of cows or other livestock, the number varying from district to district according to the needs of the newborn collectives for animals to stock them.[56]

Strang explains that kulak was being broadly applied to anyone who disagreed with collectivization, stole or hid grain, or "preaches that all collective farm workers should receive equal wages."[57]

Jones uses the three other peasants' stories to relate how the kulaks were being liquidated in the villages, and sixty percent of the peasant households were forced onto collective farms where a peasant was allowed one cow in his *dvor* [courtyard], and a woman's rations were limited to ten pounds of black bread and cabbage soup for the month. For those who refused to enter the *kolkhoz*, they received nothing at all. When the peasants fought back, retribution was swift and brutal. The peasant woman Jones quoted in his section on the German colonists relates one such incident that Jones chose not to include in his article but which appears in *Experiences*. "I heard that in a village thirty versts away they came to seize the grain and the peasants killed three militiamen. They wanted to have enough grain for themselves instead of starving. The Communists then shot sixteen peasants."[58]

In addition to delineating the plight of the kulaks and peasants, Jones also discusses the administration of the *kolkhoz* by a brigadier, who was generally a young communist sent out by the Party to oversee the modernization of agricultural production. The brigadiers decided how many workers threshed, how many plowed, and how many tended livestock. The brigadiers also decided how much work each peasant has carried out, following Stalin's speech of June 23 that the Left Opposition's idea of equal pay [*uravnilovka*] should be abandoned for piece work [*sdelshchina*]. Stalin notes:

> In order to put an end to this evil we must abolish wage equalisation and discard the old wage scales. In order to put an end to this evil we must draw up wage scales that will take into account the difference between skilled and unskilled labour, between heavy

and light work…. Hence, the task is to put an end to the fluidity of manpower, to do away with wage equalisation, to organise wages properly and to improve the living conditions of the workers.[59]

The article's section titled "Piecework" conveys the information Jones and Heinz were told while at the Stalin *kolkhoz* by the village president. The article's information corresponds to what is in the diary as well in *Experiences* when the village president explains:

> Last year we had "*uravnilovka*" [equal pay] and a lot of people were lazy and said that whether they worked or not they got the same pay. But we introduced "*sdelshchina*" [piece work] this spring, and now they work far harder. We use a system of brigades with a brigadier in charge.[60]

Jones explains how the system works by using simple mathematics. If the worker "carries out the task, his day's work counts as one working day. If he exceeds the task by 20%, then his day is 1.20 working day; if he only ploughs half the average set, his work for the day is inscribed in his book as 0.50 working day."[61] Workers were paid monthly advances on the basis of the number of "work days" up to sixty percent of what the average pay should be with the remainder of the collective farm's profits divided at year's end. After this description Jones offers commentary that outlines both the system's advantages and disadvantages. "The piecework system, while imprisoning the worker in the shackles of bureaucracy, leads to better work than the system of equal pay. It demands, however, good accountants, who are not numerous in Russia."[62] Jones illustrates the polarity of viewpoints among the peasants for the *kolkhoz* movement by offering an exchange between an attractive old man of about seventy-five and a middle-aged woman. When the old man complains that he used to have three horses and three cows but they are now all gone, the woman yells at him. "It's little pity you deserve! You had your horses. You had your cows and you had little pity for us poor peasants then. I had no cow and no horse. I am better off under the *kolkhoz*."[63] In both the article and *Experiences*, Jones notes that only the poorest peasants [*bednyaks*] have anything good to say about the new regime. Jones makes it clear that forced collectivization and the ruthless suppression of dissension have simplified the task of grain collection. With "a stable supply of bread for the towns, for the Red Army or the GPU, it is able to devote its energies to its plan of industrialization."[64]

Eating Figures and Growing Apples

Stalin's belief in "socialism in one country," articulated as state policy in the January 1926 article "On the Issues of Leninism," was predicated on the idea that despite deeply rooted obstacles the proletariat working class and the peasantry could together build a socialist state. Until Stalin abandoned the program of practical measures, based on Bukharin's theory of co-operation, there was no indication that he believed collectivization offered a way of overcoming the non-socialist inclinations of the peasantry.

It is said that our peasantry, by its position, is not socialist, and, therefore, incapable of socialist development. It is true, of course, that the peasantry, by its position, is not socialist. But this is no argument against the development of the peasant farms along the path of socialism, once it has been proved that the countryside follows the town, and in the towns it is socialist industry that holds sway.... The peasantry is non-socialist by its position. But it must, and certainly will, take the path of socialist development, for there is not, and cannot be, any other way of saving the peasantry from poverty and ruin except the bond with the proletariat, except the bond with socialist industry, except the inclusion of peasant economy in the common channel of socialist development by the mass organisation of the peasantry in co-operatives.[65]

While this development sounded fine on paper, Stalin still had no practical means of achieving it. And it was not until the very end of the Fifteenth Party Congress in December 1927 that the Central Committee embarked on a two-pronged plan to implement a full-scale programme of socialist construction and to build socialism in the countryside "on the basis of collectivization and the socialization of the peasant economy."[66] Another year passed before the grain crisis of 1928 precipitated the implementation of the Five-Year Plan.

That the difficulties in forging "socialism in one country" had persisted into the third year of the Five-Year Plan can readily be seen in the second article in the series, "From the Farm to the Factory." Jones focused on the rapid industrialization that took place after forced collectivization began to stabilize grain collection and the use of machinery liberated surplus peasants [*otkhodniki*] to be recruited for the industrial areas. As the basis for the Soviet reorganization of labor, Jones cited a speech Stalin delivered on June 23, 1931, to a group of business executives titled "New Conditions—New Tasks in Economic Construction," in which he outlined a six-point plan for the reorganization of industry. The first part of this speech deals with manpower. Stalin makes two points that follow from the new conditions in regard to the supply of manpower for the increased number of factories. The first is that an automatic influx of manpower must be replaced with a policy of organized recruitment through contracts with collective farms. The second calls for the increased mechanization of heavy labor even though that did not preclude the use of manual labor, which continued to play an important part in production. Mechanization, however, is the new and decisive force, "without which neither our tempo nor the new scale of production can be maintained." Stalin warns that those executives who "do not believe" in the new processes and who long for "the good old times" are delusional. Difficulties with manpower cannot disappear of themselves. "Hence the task is to recruit manpower in an organised way, by means of contracts with the collective farms, and to mechanise labour."[67]

In the first part of his article, Jones delineates the progress in many branches of industry, including the manufacturing of tractors, the oil industry, housing, and transportation, "attained at the expense of profound suffering," especially in districts like the Donetz Basin, "where living conditions are pitiable, where there are insufficient houses, and where epidemics are rife..."[68] Most striking of all, Jones notes, is the absence of unemployment. Jones draws a distinction between Russian beggars, who "are all of a dying generation and are a striking contrast to the workless youths who beg in the streets of Berlin and other capitals."[69] This is arguably Jones' most explicit criticism of Western governments' failure to find solutions to the unemployment problem plaguing nations. In February 1933, Jones wrote an article, "How Germany Tackles Unemployment," which lauded the Nazi's use of labor camps to forestall unemployment.

The second section, titled "Hungry Workers," explains the difficulties confronting the Soviet plan of rapid industrialization. Jones writes that the most notable difficulties are the "strain of living conditions and the disillusionment of the workers," punctuated by "food shortages, a dearth of quality goods, and the lack of liberty."[70] Cooperative shops were not providing enough basic goods, forcing workers to buy on the private market at exorbitant prices. When asked about completing the Five-Year Plan in two and one-half years, a factory worker dismisses the accounting. "You cannot eat figures. The Five Years Plan is on paper. You see that tree over there; it is no apple tree, is it? But the Communists say, 'Tomorrow that tree has to grow apples.'"[71] This passage is also used in *Experiences*, and the worker debunks the idea that everything is voluntary. "In our factory we cannot say a single thing. They say that everything is voluntary. Voluntary, indeed! They get up a meeting, and pass a resolution by asking who is against it. Nobody wants to get into trouble by putting up his hand. If he did, they would say, 'Oh, you're against the government, are you?' You may disappear. Oh, yes, a lot have disappeared!"[72] The wording in Jones' article is slightly different and leaves off the worker's final sentence found in the diary: "They have been shooting people, too, and they have places in Siberia for the opposition."[73]

Although Jones did not include this grim reminder of what happened to those who openly opposed the government, he was not deliberately glossing over such ruthlessness, for in the next section he relates the fate of "engineers of the old school," who interfered with the schemes of party enthusiasts. Jones notes, "The fear with which they were inspired throughout last winter, when many were arrested for sabotage and many were shot had a serious effect upon their work."[74] Other practices that alienated workers included the way in which "workers were 'voluntarily' obliged to pay one month's wages to the various loans,"[75] such as the "Third Decisive Year Loan," as well as devoting "voluntarily" their free day to work as *subbotniki* [persons who work in factories, other than the ones in which they are regularly employed, on their free days]. Moreover, the most debilitating problem was "the nervous strain caused by under-nourishment and over-crowding that makes the life of the average Russian a misery."[76]

Significantly, in his address of June 23, Stalin warns that industrialization must be accompanied with improved conditions for the workers, who had markedly changed from years past.

The worker today, our Soviet worker, wants to have all his material and cultural needs satisfied: in respect of food, housing conditions, cultural and all sorts of other requirements. He has a right to this, and it is our duty to secure these conditions for him. True, our worker does not suffer from unemployment; he is free from the yoke of capitalism; he is no longer a slave, but the master of his job. But this is not enough. He demands that all his material and cultural requirements be met, and it is our duty to fulfill this demand of his.[77]

Although Stalin acknowledged the importance of food and living conditions, those conditions only deteriorated as the decisive Third Year of the plan was pushed through with alarming mismanagement, exacerbated by the exportation of grain and a poor distribution network, which resulted in food supplies needlessly lost or "arriving in a decayed state."[78]

In the final section, "Dearth of Skill," Jones analyzes the lack of labor efficiency, another condition Stalin addressed in his June 23 speech. Labor efficiency was an important topic Jones and Heinz encountered in their journey, beginning with their time in Moscow and continuing with their visit to the Autostroy factory outside of the city of Nijni. However, in his article Jones uses none of the sources who provided a wealth of information about this "the test year in industry."[79] In *Experiences*, they met with "Mr. S.," a reference to G. K. Scrymgeour, an engineer with Albert Kahn Inc., and the only American on the National Technical Soviet. Heading up a group of twenty-five American engineers, Scrymgeour also became the chief of *Gosproekstroi* [State Project Construction Trust], the major Soviet design and construction organization.[80] At dinner, Scrymgeour related that poor planning and lack of coordination were two of the Soviets' greatest faults. Heinz narrates one of the many illustrations Scrymgeour provided:

> Mr. S. had plans submitted to him for building a huge carburetor plant — bigger than the one constructed for Ford. But they want to locate it six miles from the railroad! All materials must therefore be trucked six miles. Mr. S. warned them, but the plant must go there![81]

They also met with Spencer Williams of the American Chamber of Commerce, who told them about the problems associated with labor inefficiencies, lack of quality control, and no managerial initiative.

> Diesel engines are being turned out in quantity, but quality is lacking. Two or three boats on the Black Sea have proceeded at too fast a tempo, and, also, there is a general tendency for managers to be easy in making inspections.
> Labour has too high a turnover and is nomadic. Food and housing rumors fly about to the effect that better conditions exist elsewhere, so workers move off.[82]

Jones articulates these same points, noting that the labor turnover has "become alarming and no factory has a stable number of hands.... The reliable works manager and the foreman with authority and initiative are also lacking, for it is difficult to produce such men under a system where freedom plays no part."[83] One-party dictatorship forced party members into leadership roles for which they were ill-prepared, and the desire to outperform rival factories "in Socialist competition has led to high figures being obtained at the expense of quality."[84]

Jones concludes this second article by referring to a decree from the Supreme Economic Council published in *Izvestia* on September 8, 1931, that blamed the grave situation of the iron and steel industry on the very conditions Stalin had outlined in his June 23 speech — namely, the deplorable shortage of labor, the intolerable equalization of wages, and the absence of piecework. Jones astutely surmises that the problem was mainly rooted in transportation. "Transport has become a danger spot in the whole Plan. Large quantities of ore, grain, food and other supplies are lying idle because of the disorganization on the railways."[85] Not surprisingly, disorganization on the railways also exacerbated the famine as loads of grain rotted beside railway stations. Ironically, Stalin pointed to the changes made in the railways as a shining example of what had to happen in industry, explaining that personal responsibility had prompted significant improvement.

> Naturally, when there is no personal responsibility there can be no question of any important increase in the productivity of labour, of any improvement in the quality of production, of the exercise of care in handling machinery and tools. You know what lack of personal responsibility led to on the railways. It is leading to the same result in industry. We have abolished the system under which there was lack of personal responsibility on the railways and have thus improved their work. We must do the same in industry in order to raise its work to a higher level.[86]

'Youth and the Future'

"A Blessed Word," the final article in the series, focuses on youth and the future, particularly on the fight against illiteracy. In the first paragraph Jones applies the same technique he had used in other articles, namely posing questions framed around polarities.

> Will he [young peasant] cling to the "Land and Liberty" ideal of his parents and grandparents or will he firm himself into a socialistic system of agriculture? Will the peasant be happy as a cog in a great agricultural wheel, or will he always yearn for his little patch, his own cow, and freedom to buy and sell as he wishes?[87]

This "battle royal" for the hearts and minds of the new generation, Jones asserts, is being influenced through communist education, worship of the machine, anti-religious agitation, militarization, and propaganda for world education. Significantly, in the entire article Jones offers only two direct quotes from Soviet citizens, both about the persecution of religion—one from the 10-year-old daughter of a Leningrad mother and the other from a young schoolteacher. While he uses several propaganda slogans and themes that can be traced to Jones' diaries and sections within *Experiences*, this article paints a compelling portrait of how "minds are being molded along Communist lines.... And it is upon them that powerful influences are working which in time will result in the emergence of a new type of citizen."[88]

What distinguishes the new type of citizen is education, thanks to the introduction in 1928 of the polytechnic school. Parts of this section are based on their interview with Lenin's widow, who is addressed in Jones' diary and *Experiences* as "Madame [Nadezhda] Krupskaya." It is not altogether surprising that the interview with Krupskaya focused on education and not the agricultural situation. In January 1929, Krupskaya published an article in *Pravda*, titled "Lenin and Kolkhoz Construction," in which she criticized the imposition of large-scale farming as feudal, arguing that it was antithetical with Lenin's beliefs. She argues, "The reconstruction of the very foundations of agriculture is a long-term affair. Such sweeping changes in agriculture cannot be imposed 'from above.'"[89] Interestingly, Jones did not broach the subject of collectivization with Krupskaya in his article or the fuller one he wrote for the *Western Mail* that was published on November 7, 1932, titled "Lenin's Widow Talks to a Welshman." As Jones notes in that piece, the relationship between Krupskaya and Stalin was contentious.

> She has, however, been associated with the [Right-Wing] opposition to Stalin, and her real relations with the present dictator are not so cordial as they are stated to be in the official press.
>
> The anecdote is whispered in Moscow that Stalin and she had a quarrel. Suddenly Stalin lost his temper, turned to her and shouted: "Look here, old woman, if you do not behave I'll appoint another widow to Lenin!"
>
> It would be better, therefore, I thought, as I mounted the stone steps to her room not to talk about politics, but about education.[90]

Jones' tactfulness and sense of humor are clearly evident in this passage. In the 1931 article, he focused exclusively on education. The most important aspect of the polytechnic education is "production," which serves as the title of this section. Jones notes:

It is remarkable to note what importance is attached to the word "production," a word which is surrounded with a halo of respect. At an early age children are introduced to factory life and learn to handle machines. An enthusiasm for technical things is engendered, and the knowledge which children have of machinery is surprising.[91]

This is very similar to the way that Heinz summarizes Krupskaya's views.

Each school has an arrangement with a factory or collective farm. The pupil frequently visits the factory and learns about production by practical experience in handling machines.[92]

And in the 1932 article, Jones uses almost the identical information.

She told me that in order that the children might be able to learn about machines and factories a new system of education, called "polytechnical education," had been introduced, by which each school was attached to a factory. The pupils were to visit the factory frequently and thus become acquainted with the processes of production.[93]

Jones relates that it was the children in the Communist Pioneers and the *Komsomoltsi* [young communists] who encouraged peasants to study as well as brought them culture. Children also are seen "marching with banners" with propaganda messages about the importance of education in carrying out the Five-Year Plan.

On this trip, Jones brought back from the Soviet Union a collection of propaganda posters, at least one of which advocates for the end of illiteracy (Illustration 8): "We will fulfill the decisions of the Party about the elimination of illiteracy."[94] Jones decries the subordination of music, art, and literature to a political aim, providing a rare critical opinion. "It is inconceivable that there should not be some day a reaction against this limited conception of all branches of learning as weapons of class warfare."[95] He then illustrates the effects of this education in the 10-year-old girl who came home from school one day and challenged her mother: "Show me God! You cannot. There is no God."[96]

Jones uses this child's atheism to transition to the Soviet war on religion, which is proclaimed in propaganda posters as a weapon for oppression, interventionists, and allies of the Pope. Drinking is connected with religion, yet Jones suggests that this propaganda "often produces an effect quite different from that which it intends."[97] This assertion reflects what had been the Central Committee's warning about using heavy-handed antireligious propaganda; as early as 1922 after Yaroslavsky's newspaper *Bezbozhnik* (*The Godless*) appeared in Moscow, the party warned against using mocking messages "since they were offensive to the feelings of believers and tended to strengthen their fanaticism."[98] In other words, there are still many adherents to religious sects and many communists who hide their beliefs behind their atheism. Jones illustrates this by quoting a young schoolteacher, whom they met on a train heading back to Moscow. This sequence in the article is somewhat different than it is in *Experiences*.

I am a believer, but I can repeat Communist speeches as eloquently as any Commissar in Moscow. If I do not become a young Communist I shall not receive a good education, so I pretend to rejoice in their long-winded foreign words like "industrialisation," but what my tongue says my heart does not believe.[99]

In *Experiences*, this interaction is given considerably more development. In addition to addressing the issue of religion and education, the young woman also speaks about opposition to collectivization.

When I get back to Moscow, I am going to become a *Komsomolka*. I am a believer, but I won't tell them. There are many others like that, too. The reason for this deception is that it gives me a chance to go to a university and study more music. It is very hard for one to learn the piano these days, and I have been lucky. It is considered bourgeois, you know.... In school I have to make reports and speeches. I learn my Communist phrases and sentiments, but I don't have to believe them, do I? Anybody can repeat things—and lots do![100]

It is interesting to see how Jones condenses material and repurposes it for effect. Doubtlessly, he had to be concerned about the article's length. For example, in the section about the Leningrad mother whose daughter tells her there is no God, she also tells them how much easier it is to get divorced now as well as get abortions. "It is easy to get married and divorced now and morals have declined.... Abortions and abortions all the time—75,000 last year in Moscow!"[101] In his article, Jones ends this section by stating unequivocally that among young people religion is now losing ground and "together with the lessening of the religious basis, stable family is in the towns also losing its importance."[102]

The plight of children constitutes one of the most compelling themes in Jones' reporting and in *Experiences*. One particularly noteworthy exchange occurs when they meet with "a little boy with fair hair and an intelligent face,"[103] who asks Jones if he has any foreign money to sell. The boy wants foreign money because he can get almost anything in the foreigner's shops, but very little in the cooperatives. When Jones asks him if he believes in God, the boy answers that he does. "My parents do, too.... They took me to a meeting once. I fell asleep! I like sport. In my class some believe in God, but they are a minority." The boy also says that he doesn't care what happens in the factories, and he never reads the newspapers because they are dull. "I like the radio and cinema and sports magazines."[104] They encounter other young people who express similar views. The following night they again run into the young boy, who tells them that most of his friends' houses have icons on the walls, as well as pictures of Lenin, but almost none of Stalin because he is not liked at all. As the boy guides them along a street, a police patrol comes by and the boy tells them, "There is trouble for someone. The Solovki is full nowadays—it is hard for religious people."[105]

'A Keen Desire'

In the final main part of his third article, Jones addresses the concerns of militarization. Much of the information in this part serves as a summary of his interviews with key journalists, including Fischer of *The Nation*, Duranty of the *New York Times*, and Karl Radek of *Izvestia*, as well as a member of *Osoaviakhim* [Society for Aviation and Chemical Defense], who is not named in the diary, but is described by Jones as "very sincere, fanatic. One view. No humor." This *Osoaviakhini* tells Jones, "All workers are trying to make the Soviet Union powerful and unconquerable. All our beliefs come from Lenin."[106] The speaker says that he is one of eleven million members with branches in factories and collective farms, and non-workers are not allowed, although workers can join from the age of sixteen and from seven to sixteen, there are "Young Friends of *Osoaviakhim*." Everyone must be prepared to defend the country.

In a theatre in Nijni-Novgorod, Jones relates that patriotic fervor was evident in propaganda posters: "Be prepared at any moment to defend your Socialistic fatherland" and "Struggle always and continuously for the Soviet Union for the successful international proletarian revolution," and "No revolution can last until it can defend itself."[107] During intermission between acts "of a brilliant performance in an opera house a gas mask demonstration may take place." The *Osoaviakhini* also relates that the population must "learn how to handle gas masks. The children learn how to make anti-poison gas objects."[108] Physical strength and service are greatly encouraged, as are shooting sports. Not surprisingly, at one collective farm, Jones notes that the church was transformed into a house of culture, "a section of which was to be devoted to military purposes."[109] In the Park of Culture and Rest, propaganda was visible on banners, and radio speakers broadcast patriotic messages: "We must have more and more Shock Brigade workers." "We must know the heroes of the Soviet Union."[110] One particular poster impressed both Heinz and Jones, who made a crude drawing of it in his diary (Illustration 9). Heinz describes it at length:

> Another poster showed a group of silk-hatted Capitalists seated around a table on which there was a sheet of paper bearing the word "Crisis." On the table was a sign reading, "The Hoover Plan." Towering above this scene was a great red figure of a worker brandishing a rifle.[111] (Illustration 10)

Despite all this military preparedness, Jones notes that there is "a keen desire for peace, based on the necessity of good relations with capitalist powers, essential for the industrialization of the country."[112] This idea, especially in regards to foreign intervention in Germany, can be found in Jones' diaries and *Experiences*. The *Osoaviakhini* tells him, "It is not a military organization. We do not want to form a second army. We want a policy of peace. We do not want to attack. We have too many tasks at home. We now think that only the workers in their own countries can make revolutions."[113] This attitude, which evolved from "socialism in one country," was a Stalin policy condemned by Trotsky as "National Communism," an idea that betrayed the ideals of Marx and Lenin. An interview with Duranty was the source for this information, though he is not mentioned in *The Times* article.

Additionally, in interviews with Fischer and Radek, the same ideas are discussed. Fischer tells Jones that Russia is "a bull country.... This country breaks through stone walls." However, he also tells him that "nobody takes the Komintern seriously. Personnel, revolutionary bureaucrats. They do want world revolution, but their methods are different.... Moscow is not ready to sacrifice Russia for world revolution. Its hand is not going to be in every revolutionary fire."[114] Significantly, in *Experiences*, Heinz ends this section by quoting Fischer as saying, "This country is starving itself great."[115] The line is also used in Dr. Colley's biography, and the footnote cites the Heinz work rather than the diary as its source. In "Modernization from the

Other Shore: American Observers and the Costs of Soviet Economic Development," David C. Engerman also uses the quote and attributes it to Heinz. However, in Jones' diary, the line does not appear on any of the pages that document the Fischer interview. That Jones would not have recorded such a quotable statement seems peculiar given his penchant for detailed note-taking. At one point during the interview, Fischer tells them, "The People's Commissariat told me, 'My God, I hope Germany doesn't go smash.' <u>Don't quote me here</u>."[116] If nothing else, this shows the level of detail within Jones' diary. Although unlikely, the "starving itself great" quote may be a statement Fischer wrote in another article, but it cannot be found in the Jones diaries for the 1931 trip to the Soviet Union. Could Heinz possibly have remembered it after consulting the diaries or after speaking with Jones? Was Heinz ad-libbing? Heinz, of course, was not a trained journalist and would not have had a set of rules governing the use of quotes. In much of *Experiences*, his quotations follow closely Jones' diary entries. There are, however, differences in terms of how Heinz used source material. Both men handled quotes according to personal rules or predilections rather than professional guidelines. Without any other evidence, it's difficult to discount the quote and equally difficult to believe that Jones would have failed to record it.

In his article, Jones asserts that the Third International is subordinate to "the cold common sense of the Foreign Office," meaning the Soviets were not going to risk valuable assets for a "weak revolution in Germany."[117] This last phrase comes from Karl Radek, who also tells Jones:

> Every nation must be its own savior. A feeble revolution in Germany would be a great set-back for us. We would be obliged to help them. I do not think that a German revolution is a concrete possibility.... We have no reason from an international point of view to force developments. Besides, the German worker knows that they would have to fight from the first day against intervention. As long as two worlds exist, there is always the danger of intervention.[118]

Radek reiterates that the masses of people want peace, and that it is nonsense to believe that the USSR will be independent and self-sufficient. "The more a country develops, the greater its foreign trade relations will grow. Thus we have every reason for peaceful relations, and for strengthening them."[119]

Jones concludes this article by offering a summary that affirms the importance of youth in increasing the power of the Communist Party, thanks in large part by crushing all dissension. However, Jones notes that even Soviet indoctrination faces two key barriers: "the originality of the Russian mind and the human passion for liberty which is intensified by tyranny and which will increase with the spreading of education."[120] Jones astutely synthesizes the ideas he has presented in this article. While noting how important education has become in molding the hearts and minds of young people, he also suggests that education engendered a passion for human liberty. Over the next two years, however, class warfare only intensified, and forced collectivization and dekulakization necessitated increasingly more stringent and more crushing policies resulting in rampant suffering. Having witnessed considerable upheaval in the Soviet Union of 1931, Heinz and Jones began their journey back across Europe and to the United States.

'A Tremendous Thrill of Freedom'

In *Experiences*, Heinz relates his mixed feelings upon arriving in Berlin:

A tremendous thrill of freedom once again, and the pleasure of a really good dinner. Russian experiences begin to have an unimagined glamour and romance. Our curses of Russian discomforts are now but inaudible murmurs, and our most unpleasant experiences have become the best of fireside tales. But perhaps we are all wrong; perhaps others once doubted the glory that was Greece, the grandeur that was Rome![121]

The two men spent several days in London before Jones sailed back to America aboard the *S.S. Deutschland* in October 1931 to resume employment with Ivy Lee. In a letter to his family, Jones wrote about meeting Heinz on two separate occasions, so that the American could work on his book. The letter certainly confirms that *Experiences in Russia 1931—A Diary* was indeed the work of Heinz, however much it is based on the Jones diaries. Jones also relates that on the day before he was to sail, he stopped in at the offices of *The Times* and saw Barrington-Ward, who told him that it was doubtful his articles would be published due to "stress of election and interest in home crisis."[122] Despite the prognosis, Jones was not concerned since he believed he could place the articles with a newspaper in the United States "and receive much more for them."[123]

Jones was a voracious reader, and he relates that while on board ship he was planning to read H. R. Knickerbocker's *Five-Year Plan* and study a number of magazines and articles thoroughly. Clearly, he was still very much consumed with what was happening in the USSR, and over the next year he continued his research into conditions there, ultimately writing two articles that accurately predicted the famine. By the time he reached America, he was able to add a brief postscript to his letter, telling his family that he'd received a cable from *The Times* notifying him that the series of three articles had been accepted for publication. They would be the last articles Jones ever wrote for that prestigious publication but certainly not the last newspaper articles he was to write, and they would gain the attention of Soviet authorities.

In New York, Jones lunched at the Recess Club with Howard Heinz, Jack's father, who thanked him for accompanying his son to Russia. Heinz told Jones that Jack had written to thank his father for selecting someone fluent in the language and attuned to the political situation. The elder Heinz told Jones he would convey to Ivy Lee how pleased he was that the tour had been a success. Lee shared Heinz's letter with Jones.

I had hoped to see you in New York to personally thank you for the privilege of having Gareth Jones join my son, Jack, in Russia. It was a well worthwhile trip and the results could never have been accomplished had it not been for Jones. My boy paid him a very high compliment, and after my interview with him at the Recess Club on Tuesday, I wish to heartily endorse what my son said about him. I am quite sure the two young men have sized up the Russian situation better than any authorities of whom I know.[124]

Jones was invited to speak to a number of civic organizations about his experiences in Russia. He received $1,000 for his lecture to more than a thousand people at the First Presbyterian Church of Buffalo and was interviewed by the *Buffalo Evening News*. In November he spoke to a group of Russians in a Russian students' club, but they left him with a terribly uneasy feeling.

It went off very well, but I had the feeling when I talked to them—they were White Russians—that they were also hopeless at governing, fanatical and unreliable, and I prefer the Communists to the White Russians. I hate the atmosphere of spying and dictatorship that pervades Russian places. It is exciting when one gets first into such an atmosphere, but when one gets used to it becomes very underhand and despicable.[125]

Jones' admission that he preferred the communists to the White Russians speaks to his liberal background. Even though he was highly critical of the Soviet régime and the Five-Year Plan, he could not abide a return to Tsarist policies.

Jack Heinz II published *Experiences in Russia 1931—A Diary* in 1932 through the Alton Press in Pittsburgh. Given its very limited distribution, the book hardly caused a stir; it was not reviewed by any major book reviewers and is not listed in *Book Review Digest* for 1932. Nonetheless, the book is noteworthy for several reasons. As stated by Heinz in the "Foreword," the book's object was "to obtain a cross-section of public opinion about the things that are transpiring in their country's remarkable experiment in practical Socialism."[126] Any reasonable evaluation would have to conclude that Heinz certainly met that objective, having presented the unadulterated opinions of individuals from almost every segment of Soviet society as well as the most recognizable correspondents writing for American and British journals—Fischer, Duranty, and Lyons. Heinz also succeeded in illustrating both the successes and failures of the Five-Year Plan, especially in terms of the impact of collectivization on the peasantry. Arguably, the book presents one of the most comprehensive accounts of collectivization that had been published up to that time in English. Most importantly, the book establishes that some peasants were already dealing with starvation conditions in the countryside. While neither Heinz nor Jones suggests that starvation was prevalent in the areas that they visited, historians have established that in 1931 starvation killed more than one million people in Kazakhstan.[127]

Despite its accomplishments, the book did not merit even a single mention at the Heinz Family website (while the Phantom Corsair, a futuristic vehicle designed by Jack's brother Rust, was mentioned, and which was later featured in the movie *The Young at Heart*). Why those responsible for maintaining the Heinz family legacy have chosen to minimize the publication of this work is not altogether clear. Nigel Linsan Colley believes that Jack Heinz wrote the book to impress both his grandfather, H. J. Heinz, and his father Howard Heinz.[128] The Heinz Company was known as "a pioneer in labor relations" and spearheaded the drive for passage of the Pure Food and Drug Act of 1906. As his father had done after World War I, Jack Heinz II "was tapped to assist England with its food shortages and also toured the Netherlands to assist that nation with food aid."[129] Heinz continued that work in Europe at the conclusion of World War II. It is interesting to speculate just what impact his tour of the Soviet Union in 1931 had on these efforts to assuage food shortages.

Notes

1. See Colley, *More than a Grain*, 105-107.
2. Ivy Ledbetter Lee, *USSR: A World Enigma* (New York: Privately Printed, 1927), iv.
3. Louis Fischer, Letter dated February 16, 1930. Ivy Ledbetter Lee Papers; 1881-2003, Public Policy Papers, Department of Rare Books and Special Collections, Princeton University Library.
4. Gareth Jones, Letter dated April 21, 1931. Gareth Vaughan Jones Papers, National Library of Wales. File 6/3.
5. Ibid.
6. See Henry Regnery, "Paul Scheffer: At the Eye of the Storm," in *Perfect Sowing: Reflections of a Bookman*, ed. Jeffery O. Nelson, (Wilmington, Delaware: ISI Books, 1999), 232-248.
7. Ibid., 235-236.
8. Gareth Jones, Letter dated April 29, 1931. Gareth Vaughan Jones Papers, National Library of Wales. File 6/3.
9. Gareth Jones, Letter dated May 10, 1931. Gareth Vaughan Jones Papers, National Library of Wales. File 6/3.
10. Gareth Jones, Letter dated June 19, 1931. Gareth Vaughan Jones Papers, National Library of Wales. File 6/3.
11. Gareth Jones, Letter dated June 21, 1931. Gareth Vaughan Jones Papers, National Library of Wales. File 6/3.
12. Gareth Jones, Letter dated April 29, 1931. Gareth Vaughan Jones Papers, National Library of Wales. File 6/3.
13. Gareth Jones, Letter dated July 7, 1931. Gareth Vaughan Jones Papers, National Library of Wales. File 6/3.
14. Gareth Jones, Letter dated May 12, 1931. Gareth Vaughan Jones Papers, National Library of Wales. File 6/3.
15. Ibid.
16. Gareth Jones, Letter dated July 7, 1931. Gareth Vaughan Jones Papers, National Library of Wales. File 6/3.
17. Gareth Jones, Letter dated July 18, 1931. Gareth Vaughan Jones Papers, National Library of Wales. File 6/3. For the itinerary, see Gareth Jones, Itinerary of Tour in Russia, August 1931. Gareth Vaughan Jones Papers, National Library of Wales. Bundle 24.
18. Gareth Jones, Letter dated July 3, 1931. Gareth Vaughan Jones Papers, National Library of Wales. File 6/3.
19. [Jack Heinz II], *Experiences in Russia 1931—A Diary* (Pittsburgh: Alton Press, 1932), 130-131. See also Gareth Jones, Journal of Russian Travels, 1931, August 21-September 4. Gareth Vaughan Jones Papers, National Library of Wales. File B1/12.
20. Ibid.
21. [Heinz], *Experiences*, 43.
22. [Heinz], *Experiences*, 15.
23. [Heinz], *Experiences*, 38.
24. [Heinz], *Experiences*, 129.
25. [Heinz], *Experiences*, 156.
26. [Heinz], *Experiences*, 107.

27. Carveth Wells, *Kapoot* (New York: Robert M. McBride & Company, 1933), 31.

28. Gareth Jones, "Preface," in *Experiences in Russia 1931—A Diary* (Pittsburgh: Alton Press, 1932), 7-9.

29. Ralph W. Barnes, "Million Feared Dead of Hunger in South Russia," *New York Herald Tribune*, 21 August 1933, 7.

30. [Heinz], *Experiences*, 16.

31. [Heinz], *Experiences*, 16. See also Gareth Jones, Journal of Russian Travels, 1931, August 21-September 4. Gareth Vaughan Jones Papers, National Library of Wales. File B1/11. Diary 1, Part 1, 3. **N.B.** Page numbers refer to the pagination provided by Nigel Linsan Colley for the pdf files provided at http://www.colley.co.uk/garethjones/diaries/1931-1/gareth_jones_1931_diary_1a.pdf
Briefly, Mr. Colley assigns one page for each set of facing pages, not each individual diary page.

32. [Heinz], *Experiences*, 22. See also See also Gareth Jones, Journal of Russian Travels, 1931, August 7-15. Gareth Vaughan Jones Papers, National Library of Wales. File B1/11. Diary 1, Part 1, 2.

33. [Heinz], *Experiences*, 31. See also Gareth Jones, Journal of Russian Travels, 1931, August 7-15. Gareth Vaughan Jones Papers, National Library of Wales. File B1/11. Diary 1, Part 1, 9.

34. Gareth Jones, Journal of Russian Travels, 1931, August 7-15. Gareth Vaughan Jones Papers, National Library of Wales. File B1/11. Diary 1, Part 1, 7.

35. [Heinz], *Experiences*, 30.

36. Ibid. See also Gareth Jones, Journal of Russian Travels, 1931, August 7-15. Gareth Vaughan Jones Papers, National Library of Wales. File B1/11. Diary 1, Part 1, 8.

37. Gareth Jones, Journal of Russian Travels, 1931, August 21-September 4. Gareth Vaughan Jones Papers, National Library of Wales. File B1/11. Diary 1, Part 1, 9.

38. [Heinz], Experiences, 31-32.

39. Gareth Jones, Letter dated October 4, 1931. Gareth Vaughan Jones Papers, National Library of Wales. File B6/3.

40. [Heinz], *Experiences*, 34-35.

41. [Heinz], *Experiences*, 39-40.

42. From a Correspondent [Gareth Jones], "The Peasant on the Farm: Increase and Its Cost," *The Times*, 14 October 1931, 13.

43. Ibid.

44. Ibid.

45. Ibid.

46. Ibid.

47. Ibid.

48. Ibid.

49. [Heinz], *Experiences*, 176. See also Gareth Jones, Journal of Russian Travels, 1931, August 21-September 4. Gareth Vaughan Jones Papers, National Library of Wales. File B1/12. Diary 2, Part 2, 21.

50. Correspondent [Jones], "The Peasant," 13. Gareth Jones, Journal of Russian Travels, 1931, August 21-September 4. Gareth Vaughan Jones Papers, National Library of Wales. File B1/12. Diary 2, Part 2, 21.

51. Lewin, *Russian Peasants*, 52.
52. [Heinz], *Experiences*, 184.
53. Correspondent [Jones], "The Peasant," 13. See also [Heinz], *Experiences*, 159-160.
54. Gareth Jones, Journal of Russian Travels, 1931, August 21-September 4. Gareth Vaughan Jones Papers, National Library of Wales. File B1/12. Diary 2, Part 2, 18.
55. Correspondent [Jones], "The Peasant," 13.
56. Marco Carynnyk, Lubomyr Y. Luciuk and Bohdan S. Kordan, eds., *The Foreign Office and the Famine: British Documents on Ukraine and the Great Famine of 1932-1933* (Kingston, Ontario: The Limestone Press, 1988), 196.
57. Ibid.
58. [Heinz], *Experiences*, 222-223.
59. J. V. Stalin, "New Conditions—New Tasks in Economic Construction: Speech Delivered at a Conference of Business Executives," *Works*, Vol. 13 (Moscow: Foreign Languages Publishing House, 1954), 59.
60. Correspondent [Jones], "The Peasant," 13. See also [Heinz], *Experiences*, 183. See also Gareth Jones, Journal of Russian Travels, 1931, August 21-September 4. Gareth Vaughan Jones Papers, National Library of Wales. File B1/12. Diary 2, Part 2, 21.
61. Correspondent [Jones], "The Peasant," 13.
62. Ibid.
63. Ibid. See also [Heinz], *Experiences*, 188-189. See also Gareth Vaughan Jones Papers, National Library of Wales. Folder 35. Diary 3, Part 1, 4.
64. Correspondent [Jones], "The Peasant," 13.
65. J. V. Stalin, "Concerning Questions of Leninism," *Works*, Vol. VIII (Moscow: Foreign Languages Publishing House, 1954), 85-86.
66. Quoted in Lewin, *Russian Peasants*, 209.
67. Stalin, "New Conditions," 56-57.
68. Correspondent [Jones], "From the Farm to the Factory," *The Times*, 15 October 1931, 13.
69. Ibid.
70. Ibid.
71. Ibid.
72. [Heinz], *Experiences*, 115. See also Gareth Jones, Journal of Russian Travels, 1931, August 21-September 4. Gareth Vaughan Jones Papers, National Library of Wales. File B1/12. Diary 2, Part 1, 13.
73. Ibid.
74. Correspondent [Jones], "From the Farm to the Factory," 13.
75. Ibid.
76. Ibid.
77. Stalin, "New Conditions," 61.
78. Correspondent [Jones], "From the Farm to the Factory," 13.
79. [Heinz], *Experiences*, 112.
80. Anthony C. Sutton, *Western Technology and Soviet Economic Development* (Stanford: Hoover Institution Press, 1971).
81. [Heinz], *Experiences*, 106.
82. [Heinz], *Experiences*, 111. See also Gareth Jones, Journal of Russian Travels,

1931, August 21-September 4. Gareth Vaughan Jones Papers, National Library of Wales. File B1/12. Diary 2, Part 1, 9.

83. Correspondent [Jones], "From the Farm to the Factory," 13.
84. Ibid.
85. Ibid.
86. Stalin, "New Conditions," 63.
87. Correspondent [Jones], "Youth and the Future: A Blessed Word," *The Times*, 16 October 1931, 13.
88. Ibid.
89. Quoted in Lewin, *Russian Peasants*, 319.
90. Gareth Jones, "Lenin's Widow Talks to a Welshman," *Western Mail*, 7 November 1932, 6.
91. Correspondent, "Youth and the Future," 13.
92. [Heinz], *Experiences*, 97. See also Gareth Jones, Journal of Russian Travels, 1931, August 21-Septermber 4. Gareth Vaughan Jones Papers, National Library of Wales. File B1/12. Diary 2, Part 1, 2-3.
93. Jones, "Lenin's Widow," 6.
94. Political Propaganda Posters from the Collection of Gareth Jones. Accessed on 23 July 2012 from http://www.garethjones.org/soviet_articles/soviet_posters/elimination_text.htm
95. Correspondent [Jones], "Youth," 13.
96. Ibid. See also [Heinz], *Experiences*, 55. See also Gareth Jones, Journal of Russian Travels, 1931, August 7-15. Gareth Vaughan Jones Papers, National Library of Wales. File B1/11. Diary 1, Part 1, 19.
97. Correspondent [Jones], "Youth," 13. In *Peasant Rebels Under Stalin*, Lynne Viola notes that collectivization was viewed by the peasantry in apocalyptic terms, providing them with a lexicon of current events and a frame for rebellion. "The alien culture of the state became the antithesis of peasant culture, the Communist Antichrist to the peasant Christ, through its association and, in the popular consciousness, merger with atheism, amorality and force.... The apocalyptic tradition was used to delegitimize the collective farms and the state that backed them, thus becoming an idiom of peasant protest" 55.
98. Quoted in Joan Delaney, "The Origins of Soviet Antireligious Organizations," in *Aspects of Religion in the Soviet Union 1917-1967*, ed. Richard H. Marshall, Jr. (Chicago: The University of Chicago Press, 1971), 113.
99. Correspondent [Jones], "Youth," 13.
100. [Heinz], *Experiences*, 201-202. See also Gareth Jones, Russian Diary 1931. Gareth Vaughan Jones Papers. National Library of Wales. Folder 35. Diary 3, Part 1, 6-7.
101. [Heinz], *Experiences*, 55-56. See also Gareth Jones, Journal of Russian Travels, 1931, August 7-15. Gareth Vaughan Jones Papers, National Library of Wales. File B1/11. Diary 1, Part 1, 19.
102. Correspondent [Jones], "Youth," 13.
103. [Heinz], *Experiences*, 53-54. See also Gareth Jones, Journal of Russian Travels, 1931, August 7-15. Gareth Vaughan Jones Papers, National Library of Wales. File B1/11. Diary 1, Part 1, 18.
104. Ibid.
105. [Heinz], *Experiences*, 66. See also Gareth Jones, Journal of Russian Travels,

1931, August 7-15. Gareth Vaughan Jones Papers, National Library of Wales. File B1/11. Diary 1, Part 2, 5.

106. Gareth Jones, Journal of Russian Travels, 1931, August 15-September 4. Gareth Vaughan Jones Papers, National Library of Wales. File B1/12. Diary 2, Part 2, 4.

107. Gareth Jones, Journal of Russian Travels, 1931, August 15-September 4. Gareth Vaughan Jones Papers, National Library of Wales. File B1/12. Diary 2, Part 2, 4-6.

108. Ibid.

109. Correspondent [Jones], "Youth," 13. See also [Heinz], *Experiences*, 184-185.

110. [Heinz], *Experiences*, 72-74. See also Gareth Jones, Journal of Russian Travels, 1931, August 7-15. Gareth Vaughan Jones Papers, National Library of Wales. File B1/11. Diary 1, Part 2, 8.

111. [Heinz], Experiences, 73-74. See also Gareth Jones, Journal of Russian Travels, 1931, August 15-September 4. Gareth Vaughan Jones Papers, National Library of Wales. File B1/12. Diary 1, Part 2, 9.

112. Gareth Jones, Journal of Russian Travels, 1931, August 15-September 4. Gareth Vaughan Jones Papers, National Library of Wales. File B1/12. Diary 2, Part 2, 5.

113. Ibid.

114. [Heinz], *Experiences*, 83-84. See also Gareth Jones, Journal of Russian Travels, 1931, August 7-15. Gareth Vaughan Jones Papers, National Library of Wales. File B1/11. Diary 1, Part 2, 19-20.

115. [Heinz], *Experiences*, 85.

116. Gareth Jones, Journal of Russian Travels, 1931, August 7-15. Gareth Vaughan Jones Papers, National Library of Wales. File B1/11. Diary 1, Part 2, 19.

117. Correspondent [Jones], "Youth," 13.

118. [Heinz], *Experiences*, 124. See also Gareth Jones, Journal of Russian Travels, 1931, August 15-September 4. Gareth Vaughan Jones Papers, National Library of Wales. File B1/12. Diary 2, Part 1, 23.

119. [Heinz], *Experiences*, 123. See also Gareth Jones, Journal of Russian Travels, 1931, August 15-September 4. Gareth Vaughan Jones Papers, National Library of Wales. File B1/12. Diary 2, Part 1, 22.

120. Correspondent [Jones], "Youth," 13.

121. [Heinz], *Experiences*, 235.

122. Gareth Jones, Letter dated October 4, 1931. Gareth Vaughan Jones Papers, National Library of Wales. File B6/3.

123. Ibid.

124. Howard Heinz, Letter dated October 1931. Ivy Ledbetter Lee Papers. Seeley G. Mudd Manuscript Library, Princeton University. Box 2, Folder 27.

125. Gareth Jones, Letter dated November 1931. Gareth Vaughan Jones Papers, National Library of Wales. File B6/3.

126. [Heinz], *Experiences*, 5.

127. See Conquest, *Harvest of Sorrow*, 178-189; Davies and Wheatcroft, *The Years of Hunger*, 321-331.

128. Personal interview with Nigel Linsan Colley, 9 June 2012, London, England.

129. "The Heinz Family," John Heinz: A Western Pennsylvania Legacy. Accessed on 23 December 2011 from http://www.johnheinzlegacy.org/heinz/heinzfamily.html

5

'The Hunger Year'

'Light Music in a Depression'

Over the course of the next year, Jones, unlike millions of unfortunate people, managed to keep working and even changed jobs. In fact, given the deteriorating conditions worldwide, he considered himself fortunate to remain gainfully employed. Even though he would not return to the USSR for sixteen months, Jones closely followed developments there as well as in Germany. In November 1931 he predicted a Nazi dictatorship in Germany and a government led by Adolf Hitler. And by the following October, he wrote two more articles about the imminent famine in the USSR under the prescient title, "Will There Be Soup?" Knowing what conditions in the countryside would be like after consecutive poor harvests, Jones warned that the winter of 1932-33 would be one of famine and death for millions of peasants. That he focused on the human suffering is testimony to the journalism he practiced.

When Jones returned to New York in October 1931, conditions there had also deteriorated, noting in a letter home that "in one month, 600,000 have lost their jobs in the US.... Many teachers have not been paid for months. People who had vast fortunes two years ago are now almost starving."[1] Invited to have tea with a Mr. Koznov of Rothschild's, Jones was somewhat taken aback by Koznov's focus of making money. "I much prefer the Communist outlook of work for the Society than that of Mr. Koznov. An orchestra played light music as we discussed the Depression."[2] Not surprisingly, Jones conveys the irony of the posh environment, one which left him feeling uncomfortable given the deprivation in much of the city. In November he sent his family money for them to buy a house in Barry, in the Vale of Glamorgan, South Wales, and the following month he arranged with the Heinz office in London to send them a supply of baked beans. He accurately predicted that Ivy Lee would never write a book on the Soviet Union.

"It would be much better for him if he had asked me to follow the current situation in Europe."[3]

As he settled into his tasks at Ivy Lee and Associates, Jones found time to deliver a speech, titled "Whither Germany?" to the Town Hall Club, which was covered by the *New York Times*. In his speech, Jones attributed the revolt happening in Germany to three betrayals: by German politicians, by the treaty of Versailles, and by capitalism. Jones predicted that unless conditions changed and Germany was allowed to rejoin the ranks of foreign states, a dictatorship "seems inevitable"[4] and would lead to either civil war or bolshevism. The *New York Times* coverage prompted a call from the *New York American* requesting permission to publish the speech in their Sunday paper, which, Jones notes, was "quite an achievement to get liberal anti-Tariff views and anti-reparation views into a Hearst paper."[5] This marked the beginning of a long and ultimately disastrous relationship with the Hearst newspaper chain.

One thing that emerged from this presentation was that Jones felt much more affection for the Germans than the Russians, and in his speech, he laments the annihilation of the German middle class due to inflation, tariffs imposed on German exports, and reparations from the war. "A great class has been annihilated, the German middle-class. Their savings swept away by the inflation, educated Germans have been reduced to proletarian conditions. That is the situation, which we must bear in mind in considering the new Germany."[6] His views on the world economic situation were sought after by many in the Wall Street community and among Lee clients. He polished off an article for the *Western Mail* in December, titled "The World in 1931: A Retrospective of the Banking Crisis," in which he analyzes the reasons for the precipitous fall of world economies, thanks in large part to heavy tariffs imposed on international trade and a banking crisis that evolved out of German inflation.

> The story of 1931 is the story of how, creeping unawares upon an unsuspecting world, this new crisis, the world-banking crisis, came to add its burden to the already heavy load which trade and politics had placed on mankind.... Germany had borrowed too much money which would be recalled at short notice, and the short-term credits were now flowing full speed out of the country. Wagons sped from the *Reichsbank* to the station packed full of gold leaving the country, and the life-blood of German finances was running dry.[7]

Jones asserts that banks in England and the United States "began to withdraw their holdings in London and the stock of the yellow metal in the Bank of England grew smaller and smaller."[8] The crisis brought down the British government, and on September 21, England went off the gold standard. However, it is in the article's opening paragraph that Jones most effectively dramatizes the world situation by employing techniques honed in his articles on the USSR's Five-Year Plan, using a personal experience from New Year's Eve 1930 to get at these global problems:

> ...a Welshman was walking down the most famous and most elegant street of Berlin when he heard shouting and scuffling. Turning round, he saw a pale-faced, white-collared clerk shrieking hysterically, "We've been betrayed! We've been betrayed by the capitalists and betrayed by the Versailles Powers. The capitalists and the French are out for our blood! We've not got enough bread and next year it will be worse.... It's going to be a hunger year, a hunger year."[9]

Jones explains how the global economic crisis gained momentum throughout 1931 as tariffs choked off world trade, prices for commodities plummeted, and world banking almost collapsed.

War Debts and Reparations

In January, Jones' position at Ivy Lee and Associates radically changed from foreign affairs to "the business side of the office—the side which brings in money."[10] Despite the apparent change, Jones continued to work on foreign affairs, writing memoranda for two speeches Lee delivered in February—"The Revision of War Debts" and "International Cooperation." Jones had already lectured on "The Revision of the Treaty of Versailles" and "The Polish Corridor Problem" in Ridgefield, Connecticut. He also sent Lloyd George two letters about the American Depression that were included in George's new book *The Truth about Reparations and War Debts*.

Days after Lee delivered his speeches, he informed Jones on February 25 that he wanted to enlarge the speech on war debts into a book that he asked Jones to prepare. In typical fashion, Jones conducted research for the book at the Foreign Policy Association and the British Library of Information. Within days he had outlined twelve chapters for the book. In a letter home he expresses pleasure to be working on something worthwhile.

The book is to argue in favour of cancellation of War Debts and Reparations. So I may be doing a bit of work for better conditions and world peace. Mr. Lee wants the book ready by April 15. He'll have to rush because he hasn't begun writing it yet.[11]

As Jones prepared material for another Lee book, he was informed in early February that "the staff had to be cut down, and I was to be one of the victims."[12] He was to finish out his year with Ivy Lee and Associates before rejoining David Lloyd George upon his return to Europe.

Before leaving the United States, Jones wrote a two-part series for the *Western Mail*, titled "A Welshman Looks at America," published on March 30-31, 1932. In the first part, "Land of Tragedy and Disillusion," Jones frames the story with a newsworthy event and then personalizes it by focusing on his encounter with homeless men. He uses the suicide of Robert J. Levine, who jumped to his death after losing his entire savings during the bank crash, to illustrate how disillusionment has become "the dominant note in America today..." only three years after Hoover had declared that the country was in sight of "the day when poverty will be banished from this nation."[13] Jones contrasts the "riot of Broadway extravagance" with a "queue of hundreds of bedraggled men, waiting sheepishly as passers-by stared at them."[14] He then personalizes the narrative by telling how he experienced "a rare example of how men thrown upon their own resources can struggle along in the face of adversity."[15]

While bringing mail to the steamship *Berengaria*, Jones "came upon a patch of wasteland covered with bricks, where several large buildings had been torn down. Primitive hovels had sprung up, built by hand from old boxes and pieces of timber."[16] Here Jones encounters four unemployed men listening to a black man from South Carolina play a banjo and sing spirituals. The men survived by picking up fruit that was thrown out or standing in bread lines like the million other unemployed people "in the heart of the richest city in the world!"[17] He ends the article by explaining that Chicago, which he had only recently visited, was also experiencing the same "shattered prosperity" with its civil servants having received six weeks' pay in the last seven months.

In the second article, "Amazing Poverty amid Glut of Gold," Jones takes a broader look at the banking crisis over the past year. He begins the article by relating a story that he had heard from the previous April aboard the *Ile de France*, which he was taking to come to America to begin his work for Ivy Lee and Associates. While much was going on throughout the ship, the real drama was playing out in the Stock Exchange room. "A telegraph message would arrive and some of the men would bite their lips as the figures on the board fell lower and lower. Upon those figures depended their fortunes and the lives of their dependents."[18] Jones explains how fortunes had been gambled in "a riot of speculation"[19] with banks providing credit recklessly and people extending their credit beyond their ability to pay. Thanks to the false reassurances of politicians that prosperity was right around the corner, many Americans did not realize that "tariffs were strangling world trade; that the thousand million pounds worth of gold in America was obtained at the impoverishment of the other nations; that war debts and reparations were leading to Welsh miners losing their jobs and striking a blow at the whole system of world economics."[20] Jones shows his Liberal point of view by making it clear how tariffs imposed by the victors were having a deleterious impact on his Welsh readers.

Jones then delineates the plight of various industries like the collapse of steel, farming, and small businesses, noting that the fall in living standards and the fear of banks collapsing "have made Americans lose faith in their leaders."[21] That includes business leaders as well as politicians, especially foreign politicians, who engender an "extreme isolationist feeling" and blame Europe for the depression. Curiously, Jones concludes by explaining that despite this anti-European feeling, "sentient towards Great Britain is excellent, hospitality to British guests is lavish, and there have been many tributes to Britain's financial courage and moral character."[22] This abrupt change in tone arguably dilutes the article's effectiveness, but perhaps Jones felt compelled to offer an uplifting message. Six months later after completing two articles about the deteriorating conditions in the USSR, Jones wrote a letter of complaint to the editors that they were using his articles as "Tory Propaganda."

The change in tone is also noteworthy in that before leaving America Jones spent considerable time and effort interviewing American politicians, including Al Smith, John W. Davis, and Norman Thomas. Before interviewing him, Jones described Smith as "one of the outstanding personalities of America."[23] However, after the interview, his description changed dramatically, calling Smith "the rudest, cheapest man I have seen, spitting all the time, has a horrible voice and is almost as bad as Jimmie [James J.] Walker."[24] Not surprisingly, Jones wrote a scathing portrait of Walker for the *Western Mail* that was published on September 9, 1932, titled "Mayor Walker's Secret: The Power Behind the Personality." He decries the graft and corruption that marked Walker's tenure, evidenced by his collection of 150 pairs of silk pajamas, his entourage of platinum blondes from the Ziegfeld Follies, and his control of Tammany Hall and public sector jobs. One who opposed Walker's brand of politics was Norman Thomas, "the type of unselfish honourable public man whom we produce so often in

Wales."[25] Jones was highly impressed with Thomas, a socialist with Welsh roots who ran for the U.S. presidency in 1932.

In his profile of Thomas for the *Mail*, Jones highlights his Welsh ancestry, noting that "his love of arguments, his sharp retorts, and his puritanical background have surely been bestowed upon him by generations of Nonconformity, because both his grandfather and his father were Welsh preachers, and he himself was a Presbyterian minister and still preaches."[26] Thomas also held views similar to Jones in terms of the repayment of war debts as well as the dangerous imposition of high tariffs, both of which, they believed, would lead to extreme nationalism. Jones realizes, however, that Thomas "has not the slightest chance of being elected President on November 8th."[27]

Jones was an astute judge of character, and as he prepared to make the journey back to Great Britain on April 28 aboard the *Columbus*, he correctly surmised that Lee would not write the book on War Debts and Reparations. "Mr. Lee has been exceedingly charming to me although a lot of members of the staff say he can be very rude and blustering. He has always been very kind to me."[28] His year's work in America having ended, he was ready for a second opportunity to work for David Lloyd George, bolstered "with a more profound knowledge and understanding of the American character, world finance, and politics than when he left to join Ivy Lee."[29] Once back in Great Britain, he would turn his attention to an imminent catastrophe—famine in the USSR.

'No Proper Organization'

By the time Jones began his second stint working for David Lloyd George in late May 1932, troubling reports about the poor agricultural conditions in the Soviet Union began reaching the West. In the spring, Andrew Cairns began his three-stage tour of the USSR countryside for the Empire Marketing Board in London "to assess the significance of Soviet agriculture for the world wheat market."[30] Throughout his journey, Cairns supplied the British Foreign Office with memoranda regarding the conditions he was finding. Even before Cairns began forwarding the Foreign Office with his observations, reports in May 1932 confirmed that Ukrainian peasants were already in a state approaching famine after stocks of grain had been depleted by successive grain collections for the needs of the cities and towns, the war reserve, and export. In early June, Cairns wrote that a young American journalist had told him that dispatches documented the large number of peasants leaving the *kolkhozy* during the seeding campaign and heading to the towns to search for work and food.[31] In the same memorandum, Cairns writes:

I shall soon forget what little Russian I know, but never will I forget the Russian equivalent of "please give me some bread," or the expression on the faces of the tens to scores of people who made the request at practically every station at which I got out during the late afternoon and night of May 12th and all day of May 13th.[32]

Cairns also relates that the woman who made up his bed in the hotel in Simferopol told him she was receiving 200 grams of black bread per day and nothing else. Another worker from the Black Earth district said that the trains were full of people arrested for not working and were being sent to other districts, as well as the loss of significant numbers of livestock at nearby collective farms.

Even though the government had attempted to ameliorate the problems in May 1932 with a series of neo-NEP decrees with the intention of making more consumer goods available to the villages and decentralizing the channels of food supply, Cairns saw this as a bribe to the peasants, "fearing that without a freer flow of increased supplies of food from the country to the town, the hardships of the coming winter might be event sharper..."[33] Unfortunately, most of these consumer goods never reached the villages, but went instead to the gold, fur, timber, and other industries, which were all classified nominally under "Village."[34] In Vinnitsa, the center of the sugar beet industry in central Ukraine, Cairns found the sugar beets badly infested with caterpillars and choked with weeds. Even though the *sovkhozy* and *kolkhozy* had sown their full quota of sugar beets, the individual peasants had not sowed any. Despite a last minute decree from the state saying the price paid was still too low, it was too late to induce the peasants to sow beets.[35] By the time he reached the Volga region in August, Cairns was seeing land idle or crops infested with weeds. While in this region, Cairns spoke with one Soviet agricultural expert, Professor N. M. Tulaikov, who had made a tour of the region in June and July, and said that "in the upper half of the left side of the Volga ... the crops looked fine, but he motored over the whole country in mid-July and found that the drought and hot winds of late June and early July had practically ruined the crop."[36]

Even before the Politburo convened a conference of regional party secretaries and heads of soviet executive committees in late June to stress the importance of the grain collection plans, changes had been enacted. On January 1, 1932, the administrations of more than two hundred collective farms were disbanded, administrators of 345 collective farms were tried on charges of hampering the work of grain procurements in one quarter of the raions in the Ukraine SSR, and

355 people were dismissed from their posts. To the Conference of the Communist Party of Ukraine, Stalin sent his two most trusted associates, Molotov and Kaganovich, to make it clear that there would be no softening of the grain procurement plan. In the conference's concluding speech, Kosior criticized secretaries of raion party committees for failing to accept their responsibility. "We must put a decisive end to such frames of mind. After what has been said at the conference, after the speeches by comrades Molotov and Kaganovich and your unanimous approval of these speeches, we should unfold work in a Bolshevik manner and ensure that the difficulties being experienced by certain raions of Ukraine are swiftly overcome."[37] In short, delegates were forced to approve a resolution calling for unconditional implementation of the grain procurement plan. To punctuate that the state would rely on coercion and repression to obtain the grain, Stalin sent conference attendees a letter in which he criticized the grain collection campaign of 1931-32 for being mechanical; rather, the upcoming campaign had to account for the special features of every district and every *kolkhoz*, and local plans should be prepared with additional collections to guarantee the plan was fulfilled at all costs. Despite these admonitions and warnings, *Pravda* headlines in early August were anything but positive, as reported by the British Foreign Office: "No proper organization of grain collection in Ukraine. Only two areas in proper organization of grain collection in the Ukraine. Only two areas in North Caucasus have fulfilled the grain plan. No attempt to suppress speculators. State grain fund being illegally sold on the market. Waste of vegetables through transport failures."[38] This assessment doubtlessly was reflected in a letter that Stalin sent Kaganovich on August 11, 1932, in which he thoroughly castigates the unsatisfactory efforts of the Ukrainian GPU to combat counter-revolutionary efforts to undermine the grain procurement plan. The letter reveals not only Stalin's distaste for the Ukrainian peasantry, but also his concern about the entire Communist Party organization of Ukraine.

> The most important issue right now is the Ukraine. Things in the Ukraine have hit rock bottom. Things are bad with regard to the party.... This is not a party but a parliament, a caricature of a parliament. Instead of leading the districts, Kosior keeps maneuvering between the directives of the C[entral]C[ommittee] of the VKP and the demands of the district party committees—and now he has maneuvered himself into a total mess.
>
> Unless we begin to straighten out the situation in the Ukraine, we may lose the Ukraine. Keep in mind that Pilsudski is not

daydreaming, and his agents in the Ukraine are many times stronger than Redens or Kosior thinks.... As soon as things get worse, these elements will waste no time opening a front inside (and outside) the party, against the party. The worst aspect is that the Ukraine leadership does not see these dangers.
Things cannot go on this way.[39]

Almost immediately, Stalin replaced Kosior with Kaganovich, as well as making changes to the Ukrainian GPU in order to effect the changes that would transform Ukraine "into a real fortress of the USSR, into a genuinely exemplary republic."[40] There is little question that the use of the euphemisms "real fortress" and "exemplary republic" merely served to rationalize Stalin's desire to procure as much grain from Ukraine as possible to feed the cities and to purge all social spheres by ending Ukrainization and branding nationalist aspirations as "Ukrainian nationalist deviation." This strategy culminated in a secret Politburo decree on grain collection in Ukraine and the North Caucasus on December 14, 1932. As Martin posits, "This decree was the most important central intervention on nationalities policy since the 1923 decrees that first codified the Soviet nationalities policy. It marked the first time that the Soviet leadership officially declared that the 1923 policy of *korenizatsiia*, as implemented in Ukraine and the North Caucasus, had not disarmed nationalist resistance as was intended, but rather had intensified it."[41] From November 1932 to January 1933, a special commission was dispatched to extract an additional 90 million poods of grain from the Ukrainian countryside. The campaign was spearheaded by grain confiscation brigades that received a percentage of the looted grain and food products with which they fed themselves to survive.[42] These policies left entire Ukrainian villages without any bread or food and resulted in the blacklisting of oblasts that failed to meet grain requisition quotas, with fines imposed even on the grain harvested by collective farmers on their home garden plots. Throughout the summer and fall, Jones received accounts that led him to ask a basic question that became the basis for his two articles in the *Western Mail*, "Will There Be Soup?"

Ruin and Famine

Jones completed two articles in mid-October about the failure of the autumn harvest. The failure precipitated considerable alarm among Western observers as well as members of the Politburo, who instituted drastic measures in a futile attempt to collect whatever grain had not already been turned over, imposed unrealistic quotas for the final two months of the autumn season, and made it a crime to hoard, destroy, or steal grain, livestock, or fodder. As the Soviet Government had done by instituting Article 107[43] of the penal code during the grain crisis of 1928, it issued the decree of August 7, 1932, in an effort to end hoarding and stealing of grain by making all kolkhoz property the "sacred property" of the state. In a July 26 letter Stalin explained the rationale for the decree.

> Capitalism could not have beaten feudalism, it would not have developed and been strengthened, if it had not declared that the principle of private property was a foundation of capitalist society, if it had not made private property into sacred property, the violation of the interests of which was strictly punished and for the defense of which it created its own state. Socialism could not defeat and bury capitalist elements and individualistic self-seeking tendencies, habits and traditions (which are the basis of theft)... if it did not declare that social property (cooperative, kolkhoz and state) is sacred and inviolable.[44]

Offenders were to be considered "enemies of the state," who could summarily be executed or exiled for five to ten years. This decree was published in *Pravda* on August 8 on an inside page, provoking a rebuke from Lazar Kaganovich, who mandated that it be given front page treatment the following day along with an editorial, "Socialist Property is Sacred and Inviolable."[45] An August 21 headline "To the Firing Squad—for Stealing Kolkhoz Grain!" illustrates the drastic lengths that the Politburo was willing to go to punish hungry peasants for attempting to survive repression and starvation by taking grain they had grown.

That Jones titled his two articles for the *Western Mail* "Will There Be Soup?" is noteworthy for its stark simplicity and because the expression that he most often chronicled from the peasants he interviewed was "We have no bread." The emphasis on "soup" rather than "bread" points to the general condition of famine characterized by not only an absence of grain to make bread, but also by severe shortages of all food staples, especially beets and potatoes. This point can also be seen in the fact that widespread illness and disease accompanied the famine. As Davies and Wheatcroft note, "As soon as people in the famine areas began to eat substitutes for normal food, cases of food poisoning were reported by the GPU."[46] Food poisoning resulted from eating poisonous weeds, treated grain seed, and infected animals, but the most common cause of food poisoning was eating moldy grain. Additionally, Jones certainly witnessed conditions in which severe undernourishment led to the spread of infectious and other diseases, particularly typhus, typhoid fever, smallpox, and scurvy. Given the lack of food, people attempted to leave the areas most affected by the famine, congregating at railway stations and on trains where an increased presence of lice facilitated the spread of typhus. From January to June 1933, the rate of incidence in Ukraine increased to nearly ten times the January level and was higher than in the rest of the USSR.[47] An ameliorating factor was the improved medical care afforded the countryside in the increased number of doctors, hospital beds, and other facilities that had not been present in earlier famines.

These two articles reframe first-hand information that Jones collected on his journey the previous year with Jack Heinz II, and he refers to information that he read in *Izvestia*. Jones incorporated information from sources like Bruce Hopper, a Harvard professor who had published *Pan-Sovietism: The Issue Before America and the World* in 1931 and had recently returned from a journey to the Soviet Union; Kingsley Martin, editor of the *New Statesman*; Walter Eliot, the minister of agriculture; and Jules Menken, a professor at the London School of Economics. In a letter to Ivy Lee on September 15, Jones relates what he learned from Hopper.

> The Soviet Govt is facing the worst crisis since 1921. The harvest is a failure and there will probably be starvation for millions this winter. There is at the present moment a famine in the Ukraine. The collective farms have been a complete failure; and there is now a migration away from the farms. There is simply nothing left in many of the collectives and numbers of peasants from as far South as the Bessarabian frontier have wandered up to Moscow to search for bread. Even the Army is short of food and there is grave discontent in it.
>
> Disillusion is spreading rapidly through the ranks of the party. There is now no open opposition, but the silence is dangerous.
>
> Russia, says Hopper, is about to enter a period similar to the NEP. The speeches of Molotov, Yakovlev, and Krylenko all indicate preparations for big changes.
>
> Hopper's cook's rations for four months had been bread and water.
>
> The prospect of exporting grain this winter is very slim and butter is wiped out as an export. Hopper is suspicious as to the amount of the Soviet gold supply and is afraid that the SU will not meet its obligations.

It would be worth while seeing Hopper when he comes to New York.[48]

In a letter to his family, Jones explains Menken's dismay at the appalling conditions.

He [Menken] was appalled with the prospects: what he had seen was the complete failure of Marxism. He dreaded this winter, when he thought millions would die of hunger. He had never seen such bungling and such breakdowns. What struck him was the unfairness and inequality. He had seen hungry people one moment and the next moment he had lunched with Soviet Commissars in the Kremlin with the best caviar, fish, game and the most luxurious wines. I have got heaps of facts from the Press which confirm there is a severe crisis. The harvest is a failure: there is shelter lacking for 1,000,000 head of cattle; potato plans have broken down; in July only 40% of the grain collecting plan was carried out. The peasants are refusing to give up the grain.[49]

According to a memorandum from the Foreign Office, Menken had been summoned by the Soviet Ambassador to Great Britain for his articles published in the *Economist*, "on the ground that they were not up to the *Economist's* usual 'objective' standard and painted too black a picture."[50] Before writing his articles, Jones was typically thorough in his assessment of the situation, having gathered as much information as he could from people who had witnessed conditions on the ground since the previous September when he and Heinz had been there. As Jones makes clear in these two articles, the real victims were the peasants, who, having been forced onto the *kolkhozy*, were now being blamed for shortages that they were incapable of forestalling.

Jones begins the first article by posing the titular question, noting that people in communist Russia and capitalistic America were asking the same question. The use of this dichotomy allows Jones the opportunity to link the competing ideological systems around the continuing worldwide depression, yet distinguish the plight of the two peoples. While capitalist America's soup lines were a by-product of high unemployment, collapse of the banking system, and disillusionment with politicians, in communist Russia "the voices of the questioners are fraught with greater fear, because the harvest is failed and the food is not there."[51] Jones' assertion that the harvest is a failure and the USSR was facing a famine was based on an October 5 article in *Izvestia* about conditions in the Donetz Basin where a woman was described waiting for vegetables in a shop. Even though a shop attendant attempts to calm her, she "looks at an empty basket, thinks of the winter, thinks of the cabbage, potatoes and tomatoes and asks one question: 'Will there be soup?'"[52] By telling the reader what the woman was thinking, Jones certainly was moving beyond the strict boundary of journalism. This technique of entering the consciousness of the woman shopper was borrowed from fiction, and it allows Jones the flexibility to have her then pose the overarching thematic question, "Will There Be Soup?" It is hard to imagine that the woman's question was part of the *Izvestia* article or that her thoughts would have been given. These lead paragraphs provide some evidence that Jones was willing to move these articles beyond straight reporting, and evidently the editors at the *Western Mail* approved.

Jones begins the next section, "In the Countryside," with a series of questions: "Why is there little soup? Why is meat short? Why is bread beginning to be rationed again?"[53] Jones was doubtlessly aware of the Politburo's decision in March 1932 to reduce the bread rations for the whole of ration Lists 2 and 3, "effectively removing 20 million of the 38 million citizens receiving rations from guaranteed central state supply."[54] This measure was followed in May by further cuts in grain allocations to the population and the Red Army. These measures point to the severity of the grain shortage, and despite the fact that the state had forecast a better harvest in 1931-32 than the good harvest of 1930-31, evidence confirms the opposite, including reduced grain exports of more than one million tons. Resources at hand were "utterly insufficient" to meet the increased demand, special allocations for workers in a number of expanding industries, and an increase in the number of "manual and office workers, railwaymen and building workers requiring bread rations from the so-called 'General Supply.'"[55]

As he had done in his other series, Jones explains how he experienced the Real Russia, traveling by train in hard not soft class without a specific destination, alighting "at some small station" and walking to a village or collectivized farm where he could talk to the peasants in the Russian language. This is what allowed him to learn "from the mouths of the peasants themselves why there is not enough soup."[56] He contrasts this with "quite a different picture from that which the Communist had painted to me in Moscow."[57] Jones was not afraid of allowing *apparatchiki* to articulate the Communist Party line, using the words of a "keen, well-built young Bolshevik" in the Commissariat of Agriculture to explain how the Five-Year Plan was going to socialize agriculture. The quotation he uses appears in neither *Experiences in Russia 1931—A Diary* nor his own diaries from that trip, though there are many similar statements about the progress being made in the Five-Year Plan. Nonetheless, the quote outlines major components of the plan as it was conceived and articulated by the Central Committee's department of agriculture in August 1929, namely to "sweep away the private farmer" [kulak], turn villages into collective farms "where land and the cows and the horses and the pigs will be owned in common and the land ploughed in common by tractors." These new methods are already "increasing harvests" and producing "a happy and healthy countryside."[58]

In "Peasants Questions," Jones offers "not a healthy and happy countryside," but one that he documented on September 4-5, 1931, during his trip to the "Stalin" *kolkhoz* located near the Volga River about 1,000 miles from Moscow. In this village, he encounters "a group of shaggy, rough peasants," who ask him if there will be "a Bolshevik Revolution in England" and if "one can get meat in America."[59] When he settles into a simple peasant's hut and talks to the peasant's wife, he asks if there is enough food.

> Of course, there isn't. How could there be? They've taken the land from us to make these Communist collective farms. We want our own land and look what they've done to our cows. My husband and I had a fine cow. They took it away and put all the cows of the village together and now the cow is thin and scraggy and we don't get enough milk.[60]

This differs from the version in Jones' diary from September 4, 1931, which was also recounted in *Experiences* by Heinz.

> Oh, it is terrible! We used to have three cows, two horses, sheep, and ten chickens: now look around. The *dvor* [farmyard] is empty, and we only have two chickens. Now we only get half a litre of milk a day. We used to have as much as we liked; one cow used to give fifteen litres a day. That is why my children look so pale and ill. How can it get better when we have no land and no cows?[61]

The next section chronicles an exchange that took place the following morning. Jones again blends several exchanges with different peasants into one longer quotation for the 1932 article.

> It's a dog's life now, ever since they've forced us into collective farms. 1926 and 1927 were fine years when we still had our own land. But it will be better to be under the earth than to live

now. Land, cow and bread they've take away from us. Nearly all our grain—and it was little enough—has been carted away and sent to the towns and we're afraid to speak. What will we do during the winter?[62]

In the 1932 article, the man is described as "a handsome blackheaded peasant with flashing eyes and prominent white teeth."[63] In his diary entry dated Sept. 5, 1931, Jones describes the man as a "keen supporter," who the previous night had spoken favorably about what the *kolkhoz* was doing. The man "whispered to the Vice-Pres., then he came and there was a complete change in his attitude" about life on the collective farm.

It's terrible. We can't speak, or we'll be sent away. They took away our cows and now we only get a crust of bread. It's worse, much much worse than before the Rev.[olution]. But 1926-7, those were the fine years.[64]

Jones also notes in the diary, "Absolute change in attitude and gestures." He adds another quote from the man. "We've got to keep quiet or they'll send us to Siberia. We're afraid."[65] After this exchange, Jones and Heinz went to offices of the Village Soviet, outside of which were several *muzhiks*, one of whom approached them and "whispered."

It is terrible in the kolkhoz. They took my cow and my horse. We are starving. Look what they give us. Nothing. Nothing. Nothing. How can we live with nothing in our *dvor*. And we can't say anything or they'll send us away as they did the others. All are weeping in the villages.[66]

The changes made from the previous year are slight; in effect, Jones creates a composite character—another technique of fiction—by fusing together several different exchanges in order to render peasants' reactions more succinctly.

Collectivization of Livestock

What Jones presents in the article accurately reflects what was happening with livestock. That several peasants refer to livestock can be attributed to the decree of July 30, 1931, which mandated the socialization of livestock. The campaign to collectivize livestock began in the autumn of 1930, in part as a response to kulak wrecking by killing their livestock during the initial phases of collectivization. At the Sixteenth Party Congress in July 1930, Stalin predicted that it should be possible to solve meat shortages within a year, leading to the establishment of *kolkhoz fermy* [units] in the autumn of 1930.[67] By July 1931, more than eight thousand cattle *fermy* and six thousand pig *fermy* had been established. The Politburo's decree of July 30 included three important directives. The first established livestock *sovkhozy* and market units in *kolkhozy*, supported by increased production of silage and concentrated fodder and the training of livestock experts, including women. The second decision approved the construction of meat combines, similar to those on American farms, to develop meat-canning shops that would produce tins of canned meat. Jones' 1931 diary and *Experiences* document a meeting with S. O. Zuckerman, chief of the supply department of *Narcomsnab* [the people's food commissariat], who tells him:

> When the canning industry is complete, it will be as modern as the American industry. Cold storage and refrigerator plants will be built. We are now building three dry ice plants and sixteen new cold storage houses were put in operation this year. Eventually we will have some sort of refrigeration in every meat shop.[68]

The final part of the decree set quotas for the collection of livestock to be transferred to the socialized animal herd. The decree was made despite awareness that the numbers and condition of livestock were worsening. As Jones documents, peasants complained that the state was taking their last cow, horse or pig, leaving them destitute. Additionally, when livestock were taken, the conditions under which they were kept in the *kolkhoz* were terrible. On the same visit to the "Stalin" *kolkhoz*, Jones describes a brief incident that illustrates this point.

> We stood outside; there was a horse tied to a gate. Old man almost with tears. "That was my horse. I fed him well. Look at him now, scraggly." Then a boy came and jumped on the horse and drove away using his whip. Old man followed the horse out of sight with his eyes. Said nothing. Sad look in his eyes.[69]

The deterioration in both the condition and number of livestock had an especially negative impact in 1932, resulting in not enough draught power during the spring plowing and sowing, not enough silage to feed the livestock, and not enough livestock for the peasants to eat.

One of the most obvious differences in the "Soup" articles is the emphasis on winter, especially in looking ahead to a bleak winter (1932-33) without sufficient food. Even though the harvest of 1931 was very bad, none of the diary entries from this period look ahead to winter (1931-32), which can be explained by the fact that Jones and Heinz were there in late August and early September, perhaps too early in the season for many to be worried about winter; their focus was on the grim conditions the peasants were confronted with on a daily basis. That their concerns were focused on the present is evidenced by the seven statements about starving that can be found in *Experiences* and Jones' 1931 diaries. This certainly raises the question as to why Jones didn't use any references to starving in "Will There Be Soup?" The point lingers in the question he has the man ask about what they will do during the winter. In using the conditions and experiences he documented in 1931 to make what was happening in October 1932 come to life for his readers, Jones would have had to feel fairly certain that the 1932 harvest was as bad as, if not worse than, the harvest of 1931. It is important to remember Jones was working not with substantive data, but with anecdotal evidence from people like Hopper, Martin, and Menken. That he asserts "the harvest is a failure" testifies to his belief in what he knew to be happening. Not surprisingly, then, he titled the second article, "Russia Famished under the Five-Year Plan."

Jones begins this article by pointing to one reason why the harvest, including both grain and vegetables, failed, namely, "that a couple of million of the most energetic kulaks (the richest peasants) have been exiled."[70] As already noted, the term kulak referred to not only the most well off peasants but also came to include anyone who opposed collectivization. According to Tauger, the number of exiled kulaks (and their families) has been substantiated as being 381,026 families, or a total of 1.8 million people.[71] Other scholars estimate the number to be more than four million peasants exiled between 1930 and 1933.[72] Jones then presents an anecdote from his 1931 trip to the "Stalin" *kolkhoz* with Heinz, dated September 4 in his diary. Jones alters the time sequence, moving the account, which they had heard on their first day, to the following morning, "after a night on the wooden floor of the stuffy room which I shared with the whole of the peasant's family."[73]

In the article, Jones accompanies the president of the village Soviet in his carriage as they "were bumping over the fields of the collective farm." The village president then tells how they defeated the kulaks. "We've defeated the *kulaks*, those peasants who had a lot of land and employed labour. We exiled 14 families from here and now they're cutting wood in the forests of the north or working in Siberia. We must root them out because they are of the enemy class. We sent the last *kulak* a month ago."[74] In the diary, this exchange occurs on the previous night, and forty families were sent away. The entry specifies that the families were sent to Solovki or Siberia to cut wood or work on the railways and that they can return in six years "when they have justified themselves, they are allowed to return.... We have almost liquidated the kulaks."[75]

The article's next section, titled "Counter Revolution," continues the conversation with the president by appending a small part of a much longer exchange that took place the following day, material that he used in the 1931 articles for *The Times*. It focuses on the leader of a religious sect. "He used to collect the peasants in his hut and tell them that the Communists wanted the peasants to starve but that there would be a war and when there was war the Pope of Rome would come to their village and hang all the Communists. That was counter-revolution. So we sent him away. These kulaks are terrible. It was they that urged the peasants to massacre their cattle."[76] In the diary entry, the sect leader uses the word "die," not "starve." Jones adds the final four sentences to move the discussion to peasant resistance, a topic which was not attributed to the village president in either the diary entries or *Experiences*. While Jones was doubtlessly aware of sabotage by the peasants, including the killing of cattle and horses, having the village president explain this was an expeditious way to incorporate this topic into the article; the village president asserts that killing livestock was "another reason why food was scarce."[77] Jones then adds that Stalin in his June 1930 speech estimated that one-third of the cattle and one-fifth of the horses in Russia had been massacred by peasants not wanting "to give up the animals for nothing to collective farms."[78] This assertion warrants consideration on several points.

First, Jones effectively uses the village president to label the kulaks as "the enemy class"; it should be remembered that Stalin was able to defeat the Bukharinists in 1929 by branding their reluctance to quarrel with the kulak as a step backward.

> The Bukharin-ites' misfortune is that they do not understand the mechanics of the class struggle, do not understand that the kulak is an inveterate enemy of the working people, an inveterate enemy of our whole system. They do not understand that a policy of making things easier for the kulak and untying his hands would worsen the entire political state of the country, improve the chances of the capitalist elements in the country, lose us the poor peasants, demoralise the middle peasants, and bring about a rupture with the working class of our country [*smychka*].[79]

Blaming the food shortages on the kulaks' killing of cattle and horses as well as their refusal to turn over reserves of grain was used as the main propaganda theme throughout the duration of the Five-Year Plan.

State collection of livestock began in 1929 and increased again in 1931, when drought conditions had a deleterious effect on the grain harvest, precipitating a reaction by the peasants, some of whom preferred to slaughter rather than surrender their livestock to the *kolkhoz*. As one *Narkomzem* commissar notes, "There was nothing voluntary about the socialization of animals."[80]

Second, the June 27, 1930, speech Jones refers to was Stalin's "Political Report of the Central Committee to the Sixteenth Congress," published in *Pravda* on June 29. A part of that speech addressed the agricultural situation, divided into sections related to grain production, livestock farming, and production of industrial crops. Stalin set 1916 figures as the standard with which to compare present levels, noting that the numbers indicate "obvious signs of the beginning of a decline in livestock farming." Even more alarming were the numbers for "marketable livestock," which had been steadily declining since 1926. Stalin's "way out" of the livestock farming crisis was the same solution used to turn around grain production, namely, "by developing *large-scale* agriculture, by establishing large farms with modern technical equipment.... It can and must take only the line of organizing large farms of a *socialist* type, equipped with modern machines."[81] By the time of Jones' articles, the number of horses had dropped from more than 30 million to 20 million, and the number of cattle had declined by more than 45 percent as well as a reduction of 33 percent in the weight of grown cattle slaughtered for state collections.[82] It is not clear exactly where Jones got his figures on the number of animals slaughtered by peasants, for Stalin did not mention anything about peasant resistance in his speech, and livestock statistics were not published in the Soviet press in 1932-1933. On his tour in the Volga region, Andrew Cairns reported to the British Foreign Office that the number of livestock was down significantly. "He [Professor Tulaikov] thought the figures of the decreases were too high, but said they now had on the average only one horse to 17-18 hectares of cultivated land whereas 3 years ago they had had one horse to not more than 4 hectares of land. In other words, he admitted that they had lost two thirds of their horses. The fact that all the crops were full of weeds and that much of the grain was sown far too late he attributed largely to the loss of livestock."[83]

While traveling from Samara to Moscow on the railway system, Jones relates that he saw "a mass of debris-shattered coaches and torn up rails...another clue as to why food was so short, and that is bad transport."[84] The Five-Year Plan had spurred efforts to improve the railway system by laying miles of railroads and building new locomotives, but the system was often ineffective and rarely on time. On August 4, *Pravda* ran a headline complaining about the inefficiency of the railway system: "Waste of vegetables through transport failures." Jones also quotes from an October 7 story he read in *Izvestia* that reported on a "mountain of cabbages" heaped into the center of Kaluga awaiting transport. "Then it started raining and only when the cabbages began to go rotten was anything done about it. It was taken as fodder for the cattle and to feed the pigs. In a word there was a regular 'cabbage panic' in Kaluga."[85] Such mismanagement, Jones notes, hindered fulfillment of the Five-Year Plan.

A Looming Disaster

In the final section, "Gloomy Forecast," Jones reports that only 40 percent of the July grain plan and 60 percent of the August grain plan had been carried out in North Caucasus and Lower Volga, two of the chief grain growing areas. September was the only month in which the collections were successful, and October was perhaps the worst since only 33 percent was collected in Ukraine, 34 percent in North Caucasus, and 54 percent in Lower Volga. Even though the numbers improved slightly in November, collections for the two months combined barely reached 60 percent in those three areas. Jones cites *Izvestia's* figures on potatoes and industrial plants such as sugar beets also not meeting the plan's goals, leaving the chief towns with supplies of vegetables that were "disastrously small."[86] Jones concludes by pointing out that the forecasts for the last winter of the Five-Year Plan gave little indication that the question driving the article would not be answered affirmatively.

Jones' articles may have contributed to the acknowledgement of the harvest's failure from two of the USSR's most supportive reporters, Walter Duranty and Louis Fischer. Duranty published a six-part series the following month, and on December 7 Fischer published an article in *The Nation*, titled "Soviet Progress and Poverty," in which he openly criticized the grain collection policy. Fischer suggests that despite a bad harvest caused by too much "rain when it needed dry weather and dry weather when it needed rain,"[87] there was no starvation in Ukraine. Fischer acknowledges that weather was only part of the problem, pointing to the loss of livestock and inadequate supplies of fodder as worsening the situation. However, what he finds most disturbing is the policy of grain procurements.

I am convinced that the whole system of grain procurements [*kldebo-zbgotooka*] must soon disappear. Moscow cannot perpetuate an arrangement which permits official stores to charge a ruble for a small roll when the peasant gets only one ruble eighty kopecks for a whole pood.[88]

Fischer began this questioning of the grain procurement policy in "Private Profits," published on August 24. In that article, he suggests that the grain procurement policy, the government's "largest single economic activity,"[89] was woefully mismanaged. That mismanagement created an anomalous situation in which peasants had to buy bread at a higher price than what they had been paid for it.

Peasants, moreover, were deprived of so much grain through the state's procurements that they lacked seed for the current season, and when the government subsequently lent them seed they ate at least part of it. The practice of taking every last ton of cereals out of the village in order to meet the state's needs is destructive of the government's best interests, and will have to stop if agriculture is to progress.[90]

Fischer's admonition of the grain procurement policy overshadowed his concern for human suffering, and throughout 1933 he, like Duranty, denied that there was famine. It would take years before Fischer could bring himself to abandon his support for the totalitarian tactics of the Bolsheviks.

For his part, Duranty wrote a six-part series that the *New York Times* published in late November, accompanied by two editorials about the food shortages. In the November 26 editorial, the *Times* notes that the serious food situation in the USSR was widely known, thanks in large part to information Duranty had gathered from "government statements on harvesting troubles, by reports brought out of Russia by visitors, and with increasing frequency by dispatches dealing openly with food shortages."[91] Significantly, these are similar to the sources Jones used in his two articles, except that Jones also included first-hand accounts. Not surprisingly, the editorial board lauded Duranty for speaking out "with unprecedented detail and vigor."[92]

A close reading of this series of articles reveals Duranty's ambivalence about the causes of worsening food shortages. On the one hand, in a front page story to begin the series Duranty unabashedly called the campaign to collectivize agriculture a success that is "the most startling of all."[93] On the other hand, even though two-thirds rather than one-third of peasant holdings had been collectivized, "the nation is short of food and the effects of that shortage are becoming ever graver and more evident."[94] Duranty cites the very same statistics about the loss of livestock supply that Jones and Fischer used. He also notes the harvest was 20 to 30 percent below the 1931 level, as well as a lack of winter fodder, both of which were accompanied by "human discouragement and lowered standards."[95]

The same ambivalence can be seen in the second part of the series, which the *New York Times* headlined "Food Shortage Laid to Soviet Peasants." In attempting to explain the food shortage, Duranty offers critiques from those inside and outside of the USSR. Internally, he points to an overly ambitious program, unbridled enthusiasm in carrying out the plan, and a lack of capital and investment. None of these, Duranty asserts, can adequately explain the food situation. The cause goes deeper, he asserts.

> The food shortage must be regarded as a result of peasant resistance to rural socialization, or, perhaps more accurately, as a result of the measures taken to overcome that resistance. The measures have proved effective and the resistance has been overcome—the operation was successful, but it left the patient low.[96]

Duranty then explains that it is useless to suggest that the Bolshevik's headlong drive to collectivization was the cause or that a "slow siege" would have been better. He then offers two hypotheticals. First, he suggests that perhaps the Bolsheviks' "storm attack" was the only way to conquer peasant conservatism because only by closing their markets and suppressing the private traders could agriculture become socialized. Second, and more telling, was his indictment of the means employed by the Politburo to achieve the desired ends.

> Perhaps, too, the central authorities underestimated the effects of abuse or misuse of their instructions by local leaders, failed to foresee the extent of the muddle and confusion and placed too high hopes in the management of the new collectives or on the readiness of the peasant masses to realize the benefits of cooperation and the new system.[97]

Duranty almost discounts this critique, arguing in the very next paragraph that as the authorities went "full steam ahead," food production dwindled "as the peasants killed their live stock and abandoned the production of surplus foodstuffs." While acknowledging that extraneous factors such as the collapse of world prices and the threat of war with Japan exacerbated the crisis, upsetting an already delicate balance that "became involved in a vicious circle, each difficulty breeding others," Duranty notes that it would be a mistake to exaggerate the gravity of the situation. Barring an international disturbance, "remedies will be found, and the Soviet program, though menaced and perhaps retarded, will not be seriously affected."[98]

In the remainder of the series, Duranty reaffirms his conviction that the problem lies not in the Soviet agrarian policy "except for defects and difficulties due to a laissez-faire attitude or compromise with opponents because of a lack of support or allies."[99] He again argues that time and enthusiasm are the bulwark of the Soviets and that they have faced far graver crises in their history. That Duranty would return to the same refrain he had been singing for the Soviets for ten years speaks to the "vigor" with which his dispatches championed the Soviet cause. That the *New York Times* praised Duranty's reporting for its "unprecedented detail," which was nothing more than a recitation of official Soviet statistics, testifies to the blindness with which his editors read and disseminated his work without compunction. The Soviets were not nearly so accommodating, for they noted Duranty's ambivalence and chose this opportunity to tighten the screws on the doyen of Western correspondents.

In a confidential letter to the Foreign Office in December 1932, William Strang describes a meeting he had with Duranty, in which the reporter impressed Strang as "waking up to the truth" about the food shortages. After mentioning that Duranty had sent an article out "by safe hand to Paris and had it telegraphed to New York," Strang notes that as a result Duranty "was visited by emissaries from governing circles here (not the Censorship Department of the People's commissariat for Foreign Affairs, but from higher spheres) who reproached him with unfaithfulness."[100] Warned about possible dire consequences for such "unfaithfulness," Duranty feared that he might suffer a similar fate as Paul Scheffer, who had been expelled from the Soviet Union in 1929 and not allowed to return. Duranty even delayed a trip to Paris for a few days, as the authorities were "in such a state of nerves that there is no knowing what they might do."[101]

Duranty made his trip to Paris, was allowed to return to Moscow, and became far more boisterous in denying that famine conditions were worsening in many areas of the USSR. What Strang described as an awakening was little more than a momentary vacillation, and Duranty remained securely ensconced in Moscow until September 1933 when he toured the countryside during which he ridiculed any notion of a famine. By that time, several other reporters, including Barnes, Stoneman, Muggeridge, and Jones had provided blunt, first-hand accounts of the truly horrific famine that was devastating the Soviet countryside.

Notes

1. Gareth Jones, Letters from New York 1931. Gareth Vaughan Jones Papers, National Library of Wales, File B6/3.
2. Quoted in Colley, *More than a Grain*, 151.
3. Gareth Jones, Diary for December 5, 1931. Gareth Vaughan Jones Papers, National Library of Wales, File B3/7.
4. "Declares Germany Can Pay No More," *New York Times*, 25 November 1931, 5.
5. Gareth Jones, Letters from New York 1931. Gareth Vaughan Jones Papers, National Library of Wales, File B6/3.
6. Our Correspondent, "Fascist Dictatorship for Germany Now Possibility," *New York American*, 29 November 1931.
7. Gareth Jones, "The World in 1931: A Retrospect of the Banking Crisis," *Western Mail*, 31 December 1931, 6.
8. Ibid.
9. Ibid.
10. Gareth Jones, Letter dated January 20, 1932. Gareth Vaughan Jones Papers, National Library of Wales, File B6/3.
11. Gareth Jones, Letter from New York 1932. Gareth Vaughan Jones Papers, National Library of Wales, File B6/3.
12. Gareth Jones, Letter dated February 5, 1932. Gareth Vaughan Jones Papers, National Library of Wales, File B6/3.
13. Gareth Jones, "Land of Tragedy and Disillusion," *Western Mail*, 30 March 1932, 6.
14. Ibid.
15. Ibid.
16. Ibid.
17. Ibid.
18. Gareth Jones, "Amazing Poverty Amid Glut of Gold," *Western Mail*, 31 March 1932, 6.
19. Ibid.
20. Ibid.
21. Ibid.
22. Ibid.
23. Gareth Jones, Letter dated April 17, 1932. Gareth Vaughan Jones Papers, National Library of Wales, File B6/3.
24. Gareth Jones, Letter dated April 18, 1932. Gareth Vaughan Jones Papers, National Library of Wales, File B6/3.
25. Gareth Jones, "Mayor Walker's Secret," *Western Mail*, 10 September 1932, 6.
26. Gareth Jones, "Welshman's Bid for Presidency," *Western Mail*, 10 October 1932, 6.
27. Ibid.
28. Gareth Jones, Letter dated April 21, 1932. Gareth Vaughan Jones Papers, National Library of Wales, File B6/3.
29. Colley, *More than a Grain*, 169.
30. Carynnyk, ed., *The Foreign Office and the Famine*, 77-78.

31. Ibid., 30.
32. Ibid., 170.
33. Ibid., 135.
34. Davies and Wheatcroft, *The Years of Hunger*, 143-144.
35. Carynnyk, ed., *The Foreign Office and the Famine*, 135.
36. Ibid., 190-191.
37. Quoted in Yurii Shapoval, "Understanding the Causes and Consequences of the Famine-Genocide of 1932-1933 in Ukraine: The Significance of Newly Discovered Archival Documents," in *Famine in Ukraine, 1932-1933: Genocide by Other Means*, ed. Taras Hunczak and Roman Serbyn, 84-97, (New York: Shevchenko Scientific Society, 2007), 92. III Conference of the CP(b)U. 6-9 July 1932. Stenographic report. Kharkiv, Partvydav, 1932, 145, 147. See also See Davies and Wheatcroft, *The Years of Hunger*, 144-146.
38. Carynnyk, ed., *The Foreign Office and the Famine*, 171-172.
39. J. V. Stalin, *The Stalin-Kaganovich Correspondence 1931-1936* compiled by R. W. Davies, Oleg V. Khlevniuk, E. A. Rees, Liudmila P. Kosheleva, and Larisa A. Rogovaya. Trans. By Steven Shabad. (New Haven: Yale University Press, 2003), 180-181.
40. Ibid., 181.
41. Terry Martin, *Affirmative Action Empire: Nations and Nationalism in the Soviet Union, 1923-1939* (Ithaca: Cornell University Press, 2001), 302.
42. Shapoval, "Understanding the Causes," 94.
43. See Lewin, *Russian Peasants*, 218-220.
44. Quoted in Davies and Wheatcroft, *The Years of Hunger*, 164.
45. Davies and Wheatcroft, *The Years of Hunger*, 167.
46. Ibid., 429.
47. Ibid., 430.
48. Gareth Jones, Letter dated September 15, 1932. Ivy Ledbetter Lee Papers, Seeley G. Mudd Manuscript Library, Princeton University. Box 2, Folder 27.
49. Gareth Jones, Letter dated October 5, 1932. Gareth Vaughan Jones Papers, National Library of Wales.
50. Carynnyk, ed., *The Foreign Office and the Famine*, 71.
51. Gareth Jones, "Will There Be Soup? Russia Dreads the Coming Winter," *Western Mail*, 15 October 1932, 6.
52. Ibid.
53. Ibid.
54. Davies and Wheatcroft, *The Years of Hunger*, 101.
55. Ibid., 103.
56. Jones, "Russia Dreads the Coming Winter," 6.
57. Ibid.
58. Ibid. For a full discussion of the origins of the Five-Year Plan, see M. L. Bogdenko, "About the History of the Initial Phase of Massive Collectivization of the Rural Economy of the USSR," *Problems of History of the Communist Party of the Soviet Union*, No. 5 (1963), 19-35.
59. Jones, "Russia Dreads the Coming Winter," 6. See also [Heinz], *Experiences*, 174.
60. Ibid.
61. [Heinz], *Experiences*, 175. See also Gareth Jones, Journal of Russian Travels,

1931, August 15-September 4. Gareth Vaughan Jones Papers, National Library of Wales. File B1/12. Diary 2, Part 2, 20.

62. Jones, "Russia Dreads the Coming Winter," 6. See also [Heinz], *Experiences*, 177-178. See also Gareth Jones, Journal of Russian Travels, 1931, August 15-September 4. Gareth Vaughan Jones Papers, National Library of Wales. File B1/12. Diary 2, Part 2, 22.

63. Jones, "Russia Dreads the Coming Winter," 6.

64. Gareth Jones, Journal of Russian Travels, 1931, August 15-September 4. Gareth Vaughan Jones Papers, National Library of Wales. File B1/12. Diary 2, Part 2, 22.

65. Ibid.

66. Ibid.

67. Davies and Wheatcroft, *The Years of Hunger*, 301.

68. [Heinz], *Experiences*, 129. See also Gareth Jones, Journal of Russian Travels, 1931, August 15-September 4. Gareth Vaughan Jones Papers, National Library of Wales. File B1/12. Diary 2, Part 2, 2.

69. Gareth Jones, Journal of Russian Travels, 1931, August 15-September 4. Gareth Vaughan Jones Papers, National Library of Wales. File B1/12. Diary 2, Part 2, 22. See also [Heinz], *Experiences*, 179.

70. Gareth Jones, "Russia Famished under the Five-Year Plan," *Western Mail*, 17 October 1932, 6.

71. Tauger, "Natural Disaster and Human Actions in the Soviet Famine 1931-1933," 24.

72. See Davies and Wheatcroft, *The Years of Hunger*, 46-47.

73. Jones, "Russia Famished," 6.

74. Ibid.

75. Gareth Jones, Journal of Russian Travels, 1931, August 15-September 4. Gareth Vaughan Jones Papers, National Library of Wales. File B1/12. Diary 2, Part 2, 21.

76. Jones, "Russia Famished," 6.

77. Ibid.

78. Ibid.

79. J. V. Stalin, "Bukharin's Group and the Right Wing Deviation in Our Party," *Works*, Vol. 11 (Moscow: Foreign Languages Publishing House, 1954), 336.

80. Quoted in Davies and Wheatcroft, *The Years of Hunger*, 323.

81. J. V. Stalin, "Political Report of the Central Committee to the Sixteenth Congress of the C.P.S.U.," *Works*, Vol. 12 (Moscow: Foreign Languages Publishing House, 1954), 287.

82. See Tauger, "Natural Disaster and Human Actions in the Soviet Famine 1931-1933," 23; see Davies and Wheatcroft, *The Years of Hunger*, 327.

83. Carynnyk, ed., *The Foreign Office and the Famine*, 190-191.

84. Jones, "Russia Famished," 6.

85. Ibid.

86. Ibid.

87. Louis Fischer, "Soviet Poverty and Progress," *The Nation*, Vol. 135, No. 3518, 7 December 1932, 553.

88. Ibid., 554.

89. Louis Fischer, "Private Profits in Russia," *The Nation*, Vol. 135, No. 3503, 24 August 1932, 159.

90. Ibid.
91. "Soviet Food Scarcity," *New York Times*, 26 November 1932, 14.
92. Ibid.
93. Walter Duranty, "All Russia Suffers Shortage of Food; Supplies Dwindling," *New York Times*, 25 November 1932, 1.
94. Ibid.
95. Ibid.
96. Walter Duranty, "Food Shortage Laid To Soviet Peasants," *New York Times*, 26 November 1932, 9.
97. Ibid.
98. Ibid.
100. Walter Duranty, "Soviet Industries Hurt Agriculture," *New York Times*, 29 November 1932, 6.
101. Carynnyk, ed., *The Foreign Office and the Famine*, 71.
102. Ibid.

FAMINE RULES RUSSIA

The 5-year Plan Has Killed the Bread Supply

By GARETH JONES

MR. GARETH JONES.

Mr. Jones is one of Mr. Lloyd George's private secretaries. He has just returned from an extensive tour on foot in Soviet Russia. He speaks Russian fluently—and here is the terrible story the peasants told him.

A FEW days ago I stood in a worker's cottage outside Moscow. A father and a son, the father a Russian skilled worker in a Moscow factory, and the son a member of the Young Communist League, stood glaring at one another.

The father, trembling with excitement, lost control of himself and shouted at his Communist son: "It's terrible now. We workers are starving. Look at Chelyabinsk, where I once worked. Disease there is carrying away numbers of us workers and the little food there is is uneatable. That is what you have done to our Mother Russia."

The son cried back: "But look at the giants of industry which we have built. Look at the new tractor works. Look at the Dnieprostroy. That construction has been worth suffering for."

"Construction indeed!" was the father's reply. "What's the use of construction when you have destroyed all that's best in Russia?"

What that worker said at least 96 per cent.

"The cattle have nearly all died. How can we feed the cattle when we have only fodder to eat ourselves?"

"And your horses?" was the question I asked in every village I visited. The horse is now a question of life and death, for without a horse how can one plough? And if one cannot plough, how can one sow for the next harvest? And if one cannot sow for the next harvest, then death is the only prospect in the future.

The reply spelled doom for most of the villages. The peasants said: "Most of our horses have died and we have so little fodder that the remaining ones are scraggy and ill."

If it is grave now and if millions are dying in the villages, as they are, for I did not visit a single village where many had not died, what will it be like in a month's time? The potatoes left are being counted one by one, but in so many homes the potatoes have long run out. The beet, once used as cattle fodder, may run out in many huts before the new food comes in June, July and August, and many have not even beet.

The situation is graver than in 1921, as all peasants stated emphatically. In that year

CHILD BEGGARS IN MOSCOW

there was famine in several great regions, but in most parts the peasants could live. It was a localised famine, which had many millions of victims, especially along the Volga. But to-day the famine is everywhere, in the formerly rich Ukraine, in West Russia, in Central Asia, in North Caucasia—everywhere.

What of the towns? Moscow as yet does not look so stricken, and no one staying in Moscow would have an inkling of wh...

1. *Evening Standard*, 31 March 1933.

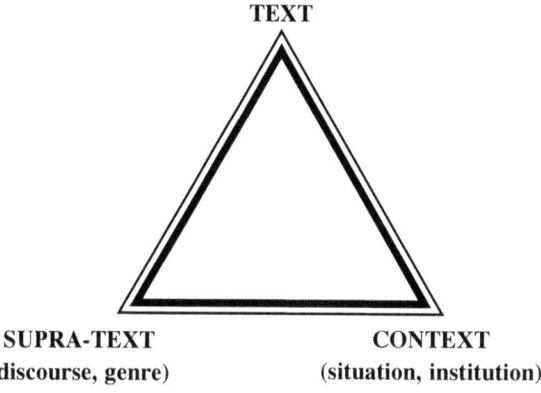

TEXT

SUPRA-TEXT
(discourse, genre)

CONTEXT
(situation, institution)

2. Graphic representation of the relation between text, supra-text, and context.

3. Annie Gwen Jones with the Hughes family.

4. *Bezbozhnik (The Godless)* newspaper, 22 April 1923.

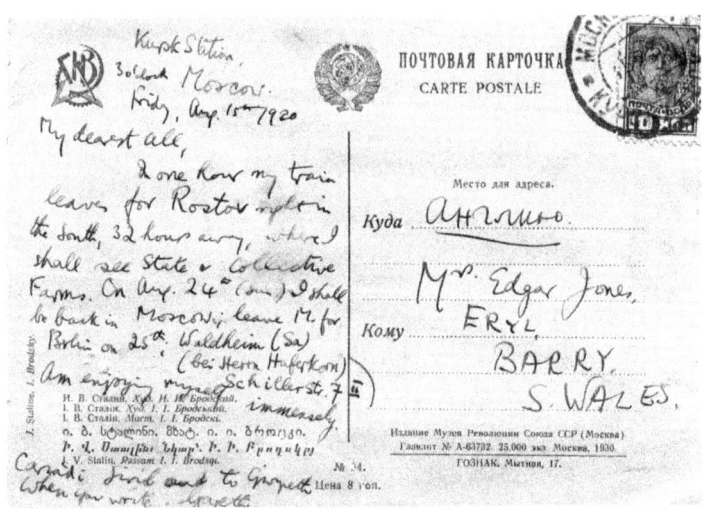

5. Postcard to Mr. Edgar Jones from Gareth Jones, August 1930.

6. Letter from Gareth Jones depicting the location of Ivy Lee and Associates.

7. Jack Heinz II, "On the eve of your departure...".

8. Soviet propaganda poster about eliminating illiteracy.

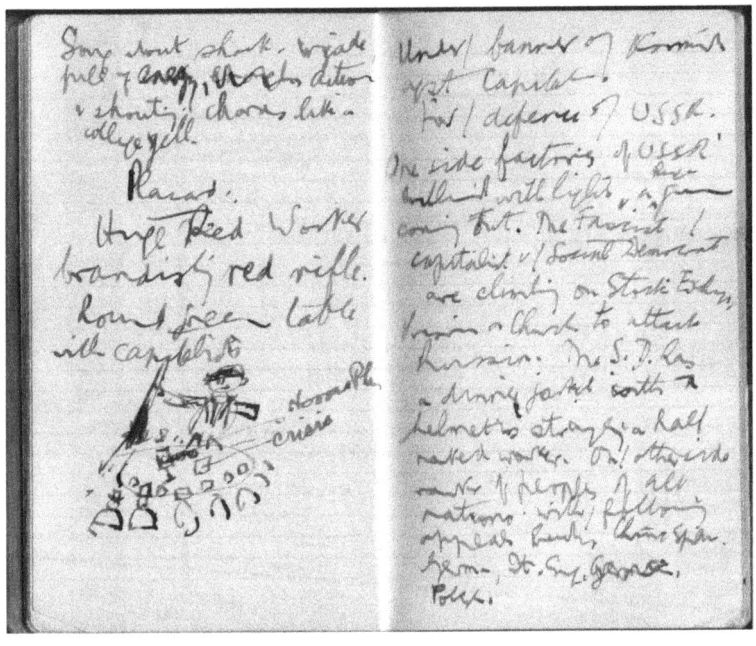

9. Gareth Jones' diary entry drawing of the "Hoover" propaganda poster

10. The "Hoover" propaganda poster, from the archives of Gareth Jones.

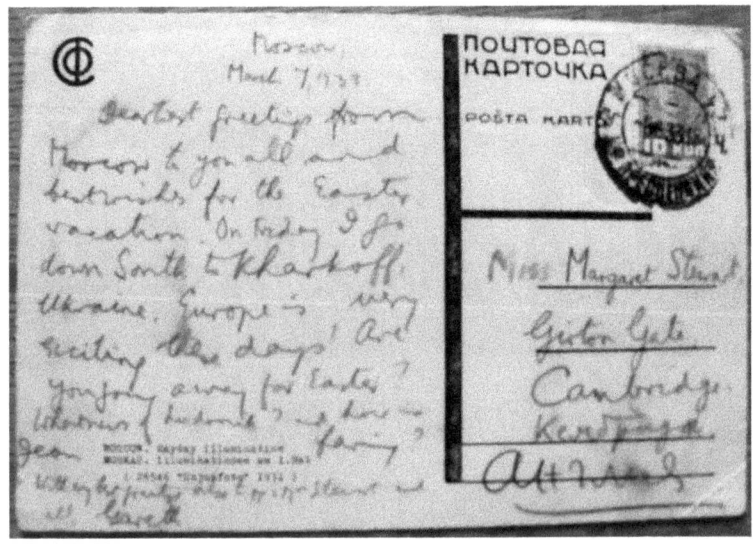

11. Gareth Jones' diary entry with 'See Hamlet'.

12. Postcard to Margaret Stewart, 7 March 1933.

Kharkoff
Tuesday, March 14, 1933.

My dearest All,

Just a short word to say that I am having a splendid time in Kharkoff, staying with the German Consul, who is an uncle of *[illegible]* and who is remarkably kind to me. Tomorrow night we are all going to the opera to see "Eugene Onegin" (Pushkin) and on Thursday, I shall travel with the German Consul-General on the wonderful train, the "Arrow," with

13. Gareth Jones' letter to his family sent from Kharkov, 14 March 1933.

Series on "Tammany's Poor Relations" Continues Today on Pa[ge]

NIGHT EDITION

New York Evening Post

NIGHT EDITI[ON]

Wall Street Closing Prices

Wall Street Closing

THREE 3 CENTS

WEDNESDAY, MARCH 29, 19[33]

THREE

FAMINE GRIPS RUSSIA, MILLIONS DYING, IDLE ON RISE, SAYS BRITON | LEHMAN PLEA ON BEER BILL STIRS STORM | ROOSEVELT DEMANDS U[.S.] CONTROL NEW SECURITI[ES] MESSAGE HITS DISHONES[T]

14. *New York Evening Post*, 30 March 1933.

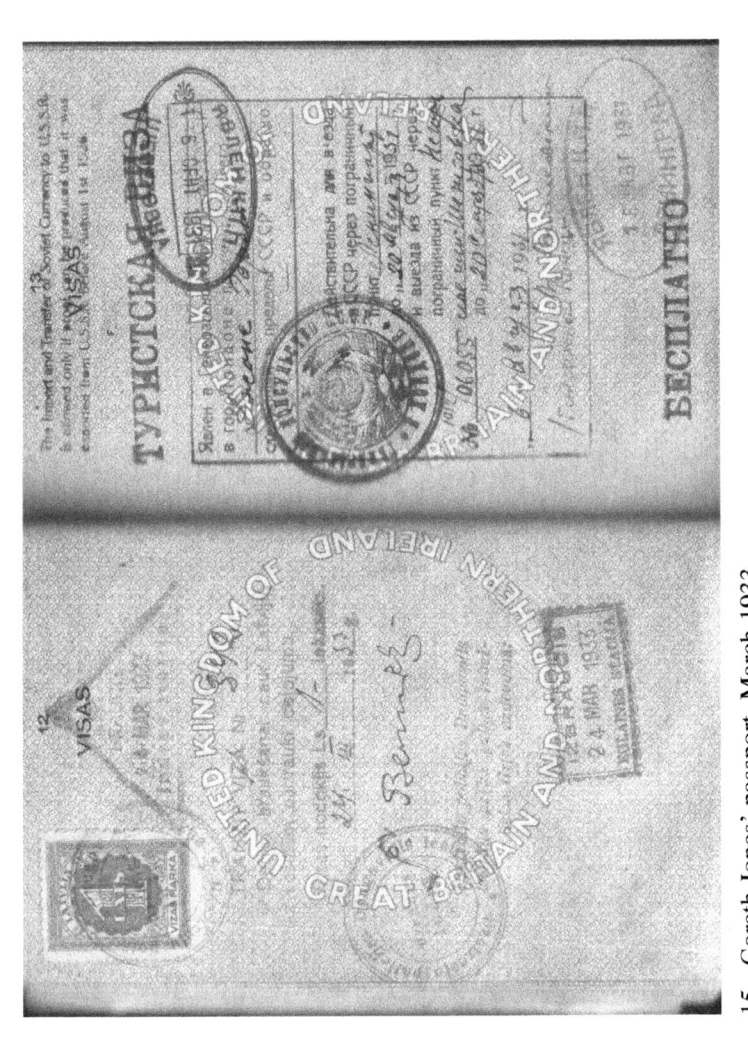

15. Gareth Jones' passport, March 1933.

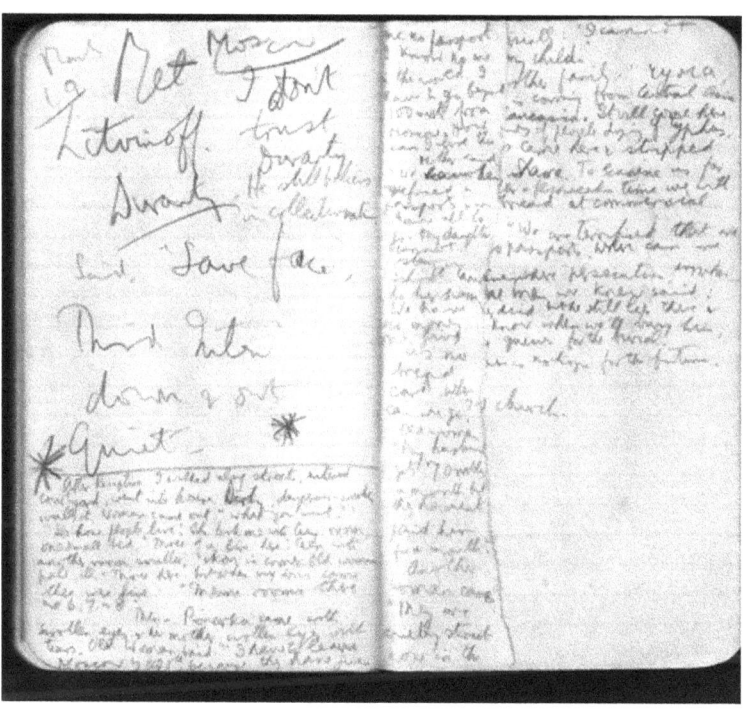

16. Gareth Jones' diary entry, 'I don't trust Duranty'.

17. Picture of an orphanage, from the archives of Gareth Jones.

18. A poster advertising Gareth Jones' 'The Enigma of Bolshevik Russia' travelogue.

19. Gareth Jones in the KFWB radio station, January 1935.

Gareth Jones

In memory of Gareth Richard Vaughan Jones, born 1905, who graduated from the University of Wales, Aberystwyth and the University of Cambridge. One of the first journalists to report on the *Holodomor*, the Great Famine of 1932–1933 in Soviet Ukraine.

Er cof am Gareth Richard Vaughan Jones, ganed 1905, a raddiodd o Brifysgol Cymru, Aberystwyth a Phrifysgol Caergrawnt. Un o'r newyddiadurwyr cyntaf i adrodd ar y Newyn Mawr yn yr Wcrain, 1932–1933.

Пам'яті випускника Валійського університету в м. Аберинствит і Кембриджського університету Герета Ричарда Воена Джоунза (нар. 1905 р.) – одного з перших журналістів, які повідомили про Голодомор у радянській Україні 1932–1933 рр.

Placed in his honour by the Ukrainian Canadian Civil Liberties Foundation, with the assistance of the Ukrainian Autocephalous Orthodox Church in Great Britain, the Ukrainian Orthodox Church of Canada, the Ukrainian American Civil Liberties Association, and the Association of Ukrainians in Great Britain.

2 May 2006

20. The plaque commemorating Gareth Jones at the Old College building, Aberystwyth University.

> initiated by Russia., In conclusion, Duranty point-
> ed out that,"in agreement with the NEW YORK TIMES and
> the Soviet authorities." his official despatches al-
> ways reflect the official opinion of the Soviet régime
> and not his own.
>
> A.W.Kliefoth.
>
> AWK EM

21. Memorandum by A. W. Kliefoth, dated 4 June 1931.

6

'Philological Sophistries'

'A Gentlemen's Agreement'

As 1932 drew to a close, Gareth Jones faced important decisions regarding the direction of his career. He and Lloyd George were nearing completion of the first volume of *War Memoirs of David Lloyd George*, scheduled for publication in the spring of 1933. By January his application for a visa to the USSR had been granted, expedited by the Soviet ambassador to Great Britain, Ivan Maisky. That the Soviets were intent on satisfying Jones and currying favor is evident in correspondence between Maisky and the Foreign Press Department. In a letter dated January 25 to A. F. Neiman, a deputy in the Foreign Press Department overseen by Konstantin Umansky, Maisky implored that Jones be treated with care as he was going to report back to Lloyd George about "the critical situation in the USSR," which, according to "conversations and writings, [were] now flooding Europe..."

> I urge you to take Jones under your special care, give him sufficient attention, and put him in touch with those people and institutions whose assistance he will need. The impressions Jones forms will to a significant degree determine Lloyd George's attitude toward the USSR.[1]

In early February, Neiman wrote back that every attempt would be made to fulfill Maisky's wishes, noting that not only was Jones important because of his connection with Lloyd George, but also because of his journalistic connections, particularly with *The Times*, "which has, on several occasions, taken articles from him of an 'editorial nature...'" That the Soviet press department was aware of Jones' connection with *The Times* is significant because neither the three articles Jones published in 1930, nor those in 1931 carried his by-line. Exactly how the Soviets came to connect Jones with his unsigned work for *The Times* is something that remains a mystery. Neiman also noted that his most recent article, published in the *Manchester Guardian*, "makes us be on guard that his sympathies have changed [from 1930]. It is, of course, our job to persuade him otherwise, but I know Jones a little and am afraid that his impressions will not generally yield to our influence."[2] Significantly, Jones' recent articles in the *Western Mail* about the failed harvest did not attract the attention of anyone at the Soviet embassy in London or the Foreign Press Department in Moscow. As previously noted, other writers had either been banned, like Scheffer, or castigated, like Menken and Duranty, for writing articles critical of the USSR. Whatever good graces Jones enjoyed before his third visit quickly vanished after his revelations of the famine were reported in the Western press upon his return in late March. Those reports drew the ire of Foreign Minister Maxim Litvinov and Konstantin Umansky, head of the Press and Information Department of the Soviet People's Commissariat of Foreign Affairs. Vehement denials also came from Soviet sympathizers like George Bernard Shaw and journalists like Duranty and Fischer.

The story of Jones' reporting of the famine and the denials by pro-Soviet Western journalists is one of the most misunderstood episodes in journalism history. Part of that misunderstanding can be traced to Eugene Lyons of United Press, who more than anyone else was responsible for writing about the episode of "throwing down Jones"[3] by Western journalists stationed in Moscow, purportedly at a party hastily called by Umansky on the night after the first newspaper reports of Jones' tour of the Ukrainian countryside were published in the *New York Evening Post* and *Chicago Daily News*. Lyons' account of this episode was accepted uncritically after it first appeared in *Assignment in Utopia* in 1937. More recently, several scholars, including Crowl, Taylor, and Engerman, have questioned the veracity of Lyons' version of that evening. One obvious problem stems from the lack of details about the event's timing, who was present, and the nature of this "gentlemen's agreement" in exchange for access to the Metro-Vickers trial of six British engineers charged with spying. A second is Lyons' framing of Jones as someone whose reports were based mainly on what Lyons, Duranty, and Muggeridge—all of whom Jones interviewed during his March trip—had told him, a claim that does not stand up to scrutiny.

In *Assignment*, Lyons readily admits to feeling deeply ashamed about his and other journalists' failure to report the famine, and his recounting was supposed to serve as his way of making amends for that failure. However, his version of events is suspect on several counts. For one, he asserts that what Jones reported about the famine "was little more than a summary of what the correspondents and foreign diplomats had told him."[4] The twenty-one articles Jones wrote provide ample evidence to the contrary; in fact, they demonstrate that Jones used far more material from the peasants and workers who were suffering as a result of the famine and repressive Stalinist policies than from official sources. Lyons deliberately undervalued Jones' work to keep the spotlight on what he and the other Moscow correspondents were doing, or not doing as was the case. Secondly, his description of the meeting at which Umansky orchestrated a bargaining session allowing the corps of Western correspondents access to the Metro-Vickers trial in exchange for their "phrases that damned Jones as a liar"[5] is fraught with gaps that strain credulity. Lyons never names any other journalist who was present that evening, nor has anyone ever come forward to corroborate Lyons' version of events. If anyone later had reason to attest to this version of events and deflect criticism from the famine denial and calling Jones a liar, it was Duranty, for he published the only article contesting Jones' reporting of famine conditions in Ukraine.

Lyons begins this chapter in *Assignment* by quoting from Duranty's March 31 article published in the *New York Times* without naming him, yet Lyons refers to the article as "our" denial and "what we did."[6] If this article truly represented a collaboration, it seems only reasonable that at some later point Duranty would have verified that orchestrated effort, in effect, spreading the blame; however, he never did, even after he admitted years later that a famine had indeed occurred. More telling is the fact that the article published in the *New York Times* on March 31 was based almost entirely on a conversation between Jones and Duranty that occurred on March 19, which clearly points to Duranty's being the sole author.

In creating this "Poor Gareth Jones" character who serves as the sacrificial lamb to their ineptitudes, Lyons undermines the importance of Jones' work while deflecting criticism from their failure to cover the famine. Casting Jones as the victim of Duranty's denigration mitigates the importance of his work and deflects attention from his accomplishments back to the Western correspondents in Moscow stymied by the ban on travel. The record shows Jones was anything but a victim; he confronted Duranty's famine denial directly and exposed Duranty and other Western correspondents as "masters of euphemism and understatement,"[7] he criticized liberals like George Bernard Shaw and the liberal press, he wrote a letter to the editor in support of Muggeridge's famine reporting, and he even questioned Lloyd George's "admiration for Stalin."[8] Jones was quite capable of standing up for himself and for what he knew. He was not their stooge or parrot. His reporting was his own. The only tragedy is that for far too long scholars have given more attention to the cowardice of those complicit in manufacturing consent for Stalin's paradise and not enough to the courage of the journalists who exposed what was unfolding there. Almost all of the Western journalists, even Duranty and Fischer, eventually recanted their denials of the famine. Unfortunately, by that point, Jones had largely become the man too easily forgotten.

'A Career in Journalism'

Even while finishing his employment with Lloyd George, Jones had his eyes focused squarely on international affairs in Germany and the USSR. Two anecdotes he told during an early December speech, "A Distant View: From Moscow," for the British Broadcasting Company (BBC) illustrate this point. The first was a tale popular among the anti-Nazi Lutherans in Germany about a Nazi priest who orders any Jew to leave the church before beginning the service. After a brief pause, the figure of Christ comes down from the crucifix on the altar and silently leaves the church. The second was a retelling of a story he had heard on his first journey to the USSR in 1930 that was published in *The Star*; it involved a pilot who sees a man drowning in the water, rescues him, and discovers that the man is Stalin. The pilot immediately considers dropping him overboard "because of what all the other Russians would say for not letting him drown."[9]

A week later Jones interviewed for a position with the BBC, which he ultimately turned down on the advice of friends and colleagues. He writes his parents, "There is the possibility, of course, that they might have had my name in mind as the head of the BBC in Cardiff—a job which I would have disliked intensely."[10] Rather than taking a position with the fledgling broadcasting company, Jones clearly intended on a career in print journalism. Several people advised him to get more experience with a provincial newspaper, and he quickly secured a position with the *Western Mail* beginning on April 1, 1933. Given his Welsh background and the number of articles he had already written as a correspondent, it is not surprising that he accepted. On the other hand, he thought that the newspaper was making use of his "Will There Be Soup?" articles as Tory propaganda. Shortly after their publication, he writes:

It gives me a real kick to be able to set tongues wagging and people buzzing....

I should much rather be associated with Disarmament, Free Trade and the League of Nations than with the *Western Mail's* readers' views. Moreover, it has aroused interest in Communism. I am writing two articles on the Communist International, which is timely on account of the controversy.

Everybody's views are doubted. Have Lloyd George's views always been accepted? Or anybody's for that matter? And it is rightly so![11]

As a journalist with conviction, Jones was not interested in writing views that would placate the greatest number of people. Additionally, he had the full support of writers like Paul Scheffer, London correspondent for the *Berliner Tageblatt*; Kingsley Martin, editor of the *New Statesman*; and Hessell Tiltman, author of *Peasant Europe*.

In late January, he arranged to write a series of article for *The Economist* on Russia, secured a speaking engagement with the Royal Institute of International Affairs for March 30 also on the Soviet Union, a series of articles on Germany for *The Financial News*, and three other articles for *The Times*. He ended up not placing articles with the *Economist* or *The Times* following his trip to the USSR in March. Before leaving for Southhampton en route to Berlin, Jones notes, "Sir Bernard Pares has received confirmation [of famine conditions] from many sources."[12] In his diary he also made a note that news in the city "coincides with Muggeridge's point of view and mine."[13] He delivered a lecture to members of the Flintshire Committee of the League of Nations Union at Rhyl, which was reported in the January 24 edition of the *Manchester Guardian*. The brief article notes that Jones offered a critique of the Five-Year Plan, the success of which was mostly "on paper."[14] Jones reiterated what now was one of his overarching themes—that the plan's forced collectivization of the peasants and dekulakization had led to famine conditions and the ruin of agriculture. Jones also talked about the change in policy from grain collections to a grain tax, introduced in mid-January 1933. Several days later, Jones apprised Lloyd George about many of the same things in a letter he wrote while aboard the *SS Bremen*.

Having met with Ambassador Maisky in London, he reported to Lloyd George the ambassador's summary of problems still confronting the USSR, namely, construction and industrialization. Maisky claimed the first had been carried out by the first Five-Year Plan, and the second would be solved by the second Five-Year Plan. Jones was increasingly less bashful about disputing these kinds of assertions, even with people who were sympathetic to the Soviets. When the ambassador asserts, "In a year or two, everything will be all right," Jones adds parenthetically, "(Exactly the same words as I was told two years ago and also a year ago.)"[15] He closes the letter by adding that he was "not so optimistic as the Ambassador. March will be an interesting month to judge..."[16] He also related two important decisions that had been made in January. The first involved replacing the existing system of grain collections by a grain tax. The new policy was adopted in a joint decree of the Politburo and *Sovnarkom* on January 19, 1933, and given considerable play in the press. Titled "On the Compulsory Delivery of Grain to the State by Kolkhozy and Individual Households," the decree allowed peasants to sell surplus goods on the private market after paying the grain tax.[17] The second, less publicized decision, attached a special political section [politotdel] of the Communist Party to each Machine Tractor Station (MTS), which would make sure peasants were enlightened on policy work in the collective farms and on combating hostile [kulak] elements in the villages.

'Kuban Scoop'

While Jones was reporting on the changing political landscape in Germany, precipitated by Hindenburg's naming Adolph Hitler as Chancellor on January 30, 1933, conditions in the countryside of Ukraine and North Caucasus, particularly the Kuban region, were rapidly deteriorating. Although not reported in the Soviet press, OGPU reports of famine both in small towns and in the countryside were being forwarded to Moscow. In early February, the Ukrainian Politburo passed a secret resolution instructing regional party committees and soviet executive committees to take immediate measures to localize any cases of starvation.[18] Other reports from the OGPU described famine not only in the main grain areas, but also in the Central Black Earth region, the Urals, and the Far East. Complicating matters, the Politburo was forced to abandon its earlier decree not to issue grain from central funds for seed. Between February 11 and March 3 the Politburo issued almost a million tons of grain as seed to North Caucasus, Ukraine, the Lower Volga, Urals, and Kazakhstan. That decree of *Sovnarkom* and the Central Committee was published in *Pravda*, the only occasion during the height of the famine when the distribution of seed grain from central funds to the countryside was openly published in the Soviet press. This relaxation from the policy of drastic grain collections, completed on January 15 and replaced by the new grain tax, did not forestall the growing awareness of famine conditions. If Lyons is to be believed, it was he, more than any other Western journalist, who was responsible for uncovering the gruesome reality that Soviet policy had wrought.

In *Assignment in Utopia*, Chapter XII of Book IV, "Upon Sodom and Gomorrah Brimstone and Fire," Lyons recounts that in January 1933 a European journalist who had to "play ball"[19] with the Soviets turned over local newspapers that carried articles detailing how all the inhabitants of three Cossack towns in the Kuban, North Caucasus, had been packed into cattle cars and shipped to the Arctic forests. Some researchers have speculated that this journalist was Malcolm Muggeridge, who had received newspapers from an anonymous visitor and then published an unsigned article in the *Manchester Guardian* on January 13, 1933, titled "Russia's 'Plan.'" Muggeridge recounts the meeting in his diary entry for December 1, 1932.

> One day a young man came to the door and asked to see the Correspondent for the Manchester Guardian. I asked Klavdia Lvovna to interpret. He said he had secret information to impart. Very sensibly she refused to interpret. He went away. Afterwards he went to see [Alfred T.] Cholerton, whose secretary also refused to interpret. Cholerton asked him to come back in the evening. We both assumed he was a spy. He was, he said, from the North Caucasus where people were starving and being shot for storing grain. He left us a pile of newspapers and a pamphlet.[20]

In his January 13 article, Muggeridge cites headlines from newspaper articles that had appeared in *Molot* [*Hammer*], during November and December 1932, which were "almost wholly devoted to the question of grain collection."[21] Even though Muggeridge does not mention providing Lyons with these newspapers, the dates and content make it likely that they were the same newspapers upon which Lyons based his Kuban story. These newspapers "boasted of it in eight-column headlines, and told how Red Army veterans would be quartered upon the land and in the houses from which the owners had been driven."[22] Armed with this information and the knowledge that "anything published in the Soviet press was ... exempt from censorship,"[23] Lyons wrote an article in which he asserts that 40,000 people had been exiled. He then submitted it to Umansky, who refused to allow that figure into the story since it was based on census information that was two or three years old. Thwarted momentarily, Lyons then discussed the story with Fred Kuh, head of the United Press Berlin Bureau, who agreed to file it for him from Berlin, where Lyons was vacationing. Lyons recounts:

> The world was horrified by the story. More than the generalized talk of peasant troubles, this concrete instance of many thousands of human beings exiled *en masse*, without regard to individual guilt or innocence, dramatized the Soviet agrarian tragedy.... My Kuban story, it thus transpired, started the first serious breach in the conspiracy of silence around the famine. The Soviet authorities, I had reason to learn, never forgave me.[24]

In point of fact, there was no "conspiracy of silence" among Western journalists at this time; Western correspondents stationed in Moscow like Muggeridge, Barnes, and Stoneman were writing stories about the emerging agrarian tragedy in the Soviet countryside, and Jones had broached the possibility of famine in the articles he had written after his 1931 visit with Jack Heinz II and again in 1932 with the two "Will There Be Soup?" articles. Additionally, Lyons' dispatches based on the newspapers his secretary had come across hardly constitute an assault against Soviet reticence around famine conditions in the countryside. As Engerman points out, while Lyons "emphasized the food question and the harshness of government grain demands," he also justified "government repression as a response to peasant laziness."[25] For example, in one undated dispatch, Lyons writes, "Following Molotov's speech legislation expected abandoning present system [of] grain requisitions substituting tax in kind stop represents another effort [to] overcome peasant apathy which past two years created tragic food shortage..."[26]

In explaining the desperate conditions in Ukraine, the North Caucasus, and Lower Volga regions, Lyons adopted the Soviet leadership's language in pointing to peasant apathy as engendering the hardships in the countryside. Lyons concludes the "Kuban scoop" episode by relating that when he went to retrieve his visa to return to the USSR, the Soviet consulate in Berlin held it up and administered a "mild reprimand" before issuing the visa. Then, a "second installment of the reprimand" was issued by Umansky, who explained that matters were no longer in the Press Department's hands. Lyons writes, "I had broken a taboo by giving the outside world a peep into the official closets where skeletons were stored. The miracle is that I survived nine months longer."[27]

Despite having broken this "taboo" and having purportedly breached the conspiratorial silence about the famine, Lyons was nonetheless free to cover the Metro-Vickers trial only months later. While Lyons' "Kuban scoop" could have been used as a fulcrum to extract his complicity in regards to "throwing Jones down," Lyons provides few details about these articles, despite the fact they ostensibly brought to light information about the recently instituted internal passport system, death decrees, politotdel within MTS, and wholesale purges within the Communist Party. Lyons asserts that this singular series of articles "could not be so easily lost upon the outside world,"[28] nor easily explained away by the Soviets. What Lyons called his Kuban sin was "thus made a hundred-fold more culpable,"[29] thanks to the wide distribution of the stories, even more so given the fact that "all Moscow correspondents were obliged to corroborate my facts"[30] to their editors.

Lyons then asserts that two correspondents—Ralph W. Barnes of the *New York Herald Tribune* and William Stoneman of the *Chicago Daily News*—"were emboldened by the interest stirred up by my Kuban scoop to make a surreptitious journey into Ukraine and North Caucasus."[31] The two reporters published a number of articles detailing the deteriorating conditions there. Barnes and Stoneman managed to escape detection and bypassed the censors by mailing their articles from Moscow to Berlin.[32] Muggeridge also visited the Kuban in early February, which ultimately led to a series of three articles published anonymously in the *Manchester Guardian* in late March, shortly before Jones returned from his trip. On February 23, 1933, a ban against travel was confirmed, preventing Western journalists from traveling unescorted within the USSR. If Lyons' Kuban scoop was indeed the spark that alerted the outside world as to the horrors inside the workers' paradise, precipitated the travel ban, and engendered the eyewitness accounts of Barnes and Stoneman, Muggeridge, and later Jones, then the two-stage "mild reprimand" leveled against him becomes fairly incredulous. Access to the Metro-Vickers trial, we are urged to believe, was the sole cause for denigrating Jones' eyewitness account of the famine. More likely, Umansky had the Kuban scoop as the leverage he needed to manipulate Lyons.

Moreover, the "Kuban scoop" was hardly a singular event in that from November 1, 1932, through January 20, 1933, more than 100,000 people were arrested in connection with grain and seed collections, 26,000 were deported from the region, and 70,000 imprisoned. Former Red Army soldiers and their families were among the 50,000 people who were brought in from other areas to resettle the Kuban region.[33] Furthermore, the expulsion of kulak elements and purging of party members began as early as November 1, 1932, when Lazar Kaganovich and Anastas Mikoyan arrived in Rostov-on-Don where "a kulak attitude predominates"[34] among a section of rural communists. The OGPU chief in the region was replaced, retail trade was restricted in twenty districts of the Kuban, and three of its *stanitsy* were placed on a black list, meaning all goods were removed from the shops. Before the end of November, more than three thousand counter-revolutionaries had been arrested in Kuban, and almost one hundred were sentenced to death. On November 12, Boris Sheboldaev condemned peasants who stole grain or failed to contribute to the *kolkhoz*.

We have explicitly made it public that malicious saboteurs, accomplices of the kulaks, those who do not want to sow will be exiled to the northern regions.... We must pose the problem of the deportation of an entire village. In these circumstances

kolkhozy, collective farmers and really honest individual peasants
will have to take responsibility for their neighbours.[35]

More than half of the Kuban's 716 party secretaries and more than
40 percent of the party members were expelled. Many more left the
region. Within days, the Politburo instituted the system of internal
passports, making it more difficult for starving peasants to abandon
their collective farms or villages in search of food or work in the towns
and cities.[36] By the end of 1932, internal passports were required for
travel everywhere in the USSR. Written five years after the fact, Lyons'
description of the episode leaves out significant details and glosses over
the contributions of other journalists. More importantly, it calls into
question his version of events following Jones' reporting of the famine.

'The Taste of Hunger and a Tyrant's Reign'

Before Jones arrived in the USSR, he tried to allay his family's fears
by letting them know he was well prepared. "Please don't worry. I am
inoculated against typhus. I have a very warm fur. I don't want a rug.
The trains are too hot."[37] A week later, he writes that the Schullers
have "stocked me up with medicaments etc. and given me camphor
against insects."[38] Almost immediately after Jones arrived in Moscow
on March 4 at the Hotel Metropole, he began to record his impressions
of conditions in the Soviet capital. The first few pages of his 1933
diary serve as an appointment schedule for his first week in Moscow,
documenting meetings he scheduled with Chamberlin, Muggeridge,
and Lyons, as well as several Soviet officials like Umansky, Radek,
Grinko, and officials at the British and German consulates. Jones'
diaries also provide a detailed account of the numerous exchanges he
recorded with ordinary people in and around Moscow and peasants in
the countryside, as well as prices of goods from sugar to beer to bread,
reports from *Pravda* as well as pamphlets and propaganda posters, and
scenes of everyday life.

As he had done in the 1931 diaries, Jones used key words in the
upper corners of the pages to index what was on them, something which
doubtlessly facilitated the writing of twenty-one articles composed
in the weeks after his return. Far from merely parroting what other
Western journalists told him, as Lyons suggests, Jones used the diaries
to collect eyewitness accounts from everyday people, in the process
painting a stark, uncompromising picture of what would become
the famine's worst period, March through August. However, due to

the fragmentary nature of some entries, the diaries also raise several perplexing questions.

For example, the diary entry for March 8 is significant because in this interview, Jones picked up on the interviewee's assertion about writers having literary freedom. Underlined at the top of the page are the words, *Artistic realism.* "There is more freedom to write about anything.... Give us books for new readers. True books with living truth."[39] Jones then asks, "Would [a writer] describe famine in village? L: Well, there is no famine, [the person responds]. L: Well, a gun would shoot shell far. You must take a longer view. The present hunger is temporary. In writing books you must have the longer view. It would be difficult to describe hunger."[40] Beneath this entry, Jones writes: "prevarication. See *Hamlet.*"[41] (Illustration 11)

Dr. Colley, perhaps believing that Jones' use of the "L" was shorthand for Litvinov, calls the exchange "historically noteworthy, documenting a first-hand famine denial by arguably one of the most powerful politicians in the Soviet Union after Stalin."[42] Even though the interviewee was V. G. Lidin, whose real name was Gomberg and whose phone number and address Jones had recorded on the very first page of the diary, the denial of famine is indeed noteworthy in that Jones was willing to confront this writer openly about the famine and record the interviewee's evasiveness about that specific issue. The conversation is also of interest in that it is devoted to the formation of the Socialist Writers Union, based on a decree by Stalin on April 23, 1932, which liquidated the Association of Proletarian Writers (*Rossiyskaya Assotsiatsiya Proletarskikh Pisateley* or *APPR*). Stalin wanted to organize writers in a socialist way to implement socialist realism. The organizing committee was chaired by Ivan Gronsky, former editor of *Izvestia* and *Novy Mir* [*New World*], with Valery Kirpotin of the Communist Academy in the position of organizing committee secretary.

This March 8 interview, which follows one Jones recorded with Karl Radek, editor of *Izvestia*, very well might have been with someone else from the Writers Union. Lidin's answers quoted above are very similar to Gronsky's explanation of socialist realism that was published in *Literaturnaia Gazeta* in May 1932. "The basic demand that we make on the writer is: write the truth, portray truthfully our reality that is in itself dialectic. Therefore the basic method of Soviet literature is the method of socialist realism."[43] Lidin articulates the very same principles that Gronsky had outlined the previous year. That Jones would leave himself a note to "See Hamlet" adds an additional layer of interest to this particular interview, especially since it immediately follows the writer's assertion that it would be difficult to describe hunger, something that Jones was obviously determined to do and a possible clue to the *Hamlet* reference. Alexey Bartoshevitch explains that the play had been deemed "non-recommendable"[44] for the stage, mainly because Stalin detested the character of Hamlet. "The main reason was: Josef Stalin, who generally favoured the classics, hated 'Hamlet' as a play and Hamlet as a character. There was something in the very human type of this Shakespearean Prince that caused 'the great leader's' scorn and suspicion. His hatred for the intelligentsia was transferred to the hero of the tragedy – with whom Russian intellectuals always tended to identify themselves."[45] Another possible explanation comes from Nigel Colley, who believes that Jones, not knowing about the ban, "made a personal and sarcastic note referring to Shakespeare's own take on tyranny and famine..."[46] The relevant passage in *Hamlet* was from the "To be or not to be" soliloquy in the 1603 First Quarto version of the play:

> Who'd bear the scorns and flattery of the world,
> Scorned by the right rich, the rich cursed of the poor?
> The widow being oppressed, the orphan wrong'd,
> The taste of hunger, or a tyrant's reign,
> And thousand more calamities besides,
> To grunt and sweat under this weary life,
> When that he may his full quietus make
> With a bare bodkin? Who would thus endure
> But for a hope of something after death,
> Which puzzles the brain, and doth confound the sense,
> Which makes us rather bear those evils we have
> Than fly to others we know not of?
> Aye that. O this conscience doth make cowards of us all.

Whether or not this, indeed, was the passage to which Jones was referring rests upon the notion that Jones knew this version of the famous soliloquy, one that scholars often refer to as a corrupted version. The key line, "The taste of hunger, or a tyrant's reign," does not appear in the 1623 First Folio version of *Hamlet*. Was Jones attempting to connect a single line from the First Quarto version to the perpetrator of famine in Soviet Russia in 1933? If nothing else, it points to the difficulty in attempting to account for everything that appears in the diaries.

In contrast to the discussion about Socialist Realism, the interview with Litvinov on March 23 is far different in tone and content, dealing primarily with matters one would expect from the Soviet Foreign Minister, namely, international political affairs, ranging from the Disarmament Conference and the refusal of Japan to sign a non-aggression pact, to the possibility that Hitler would bring about conflict in Poland. More telling perhaps, Litvinov confided in Jones his displeasure with Sir Esmond Ovey and explained what would likely happen with the Metro-Vickers trial. Lastly, Litvinov asks Jones to convey his respects and regards to Lloyd George. "I always enjoyed being with him and always admired him. I always followed with great interest his activities when I was in London as an émigré."[47]

What is most remarkable about the diaries of the 1933 trip is Jones' focus on famine conditions. They clearly reveal what his intention was: To prove that famine was raging in the Soviet countryside. One entry from his first full day in Moscow serves as a fitting prologue for his development of a discourse about famine. Outside of a *Torgsin*, he encounters "a begging woman: 'Want bread for my child.' She was selling flowers: 1 r[ouble] 25 a bunch. Went into *Torgsin*: plenty of everything. Came out. Another beggar, a peasant with boy. 'Please give me something to get bread for my son. We've come up all the way from Ukraine. It's terrible there. No bread. They are starving so we came up North to get bread in the town."[48] This is but one of the thousand calamities that he was to witness that certainly played on his conscience but did not turn him into a coward at all.

'An Imposter'

Jones was in the USSR from March 4 until March 24 when he departed for Danzig, where he arrived the following day to stay at the Haferkorn home. There he read letters from his family and revealed in his responses what he was to reveal to the world in a matter of days. This letter contrasts markedly from those he wrote while still in the USSR, letters he knew would be reviewed by the censors. For example, on March 7, he writes a postcard (Illustration 12) to Margaret Stewart, a Cambridge student: "Dearest greetings from Moscow to all and best wishes for the Easter vacation. On Friday I go down South to Kharkoff, Ukraine. Europe is very exciting these days..."[49] A week later he writes his family from Kharkov (Illustration 13):

> Just a short word to say that I am having a splendid time in Kharkoff staying with the German consul [Ehrte], who is an uncle of Eric Schuller and who is remarkably kind to me. Tomorrow we are going to the opera to see "Eugene Onegin" (Pushkin), and on Thursday I shall travel with the Consul-General on the wonderful train the "Arrow"...[50]

The two pieces of correspondence are significant for a number of reasons. On the one hand, the postcard shows that Jones had every intention of traveling to Kharkov, ostensibly to visit a tractor factory as a guest of the German consulate. He purchased a ticket for the overnight train on March 10, having been provided with the name of the Foreign Press Department's contact in Kharkov, S. I. Brodovsky, with whom he was to check in upon his arrival. What the Press Department did not suspect was that Jones fully intended to get off the slow train before it ever reached Kharkov, with his rucksack filled with provisions bought with foreign currency at the *Torgsin* stores. The letter to his family describing the "splendid time" he was enjoying, after having walked forty miles through famine-ravaged villages, was meant to throw off the censors. As soon as Jones was out of the USSR, he wrote freely and honestly. "The Russian situation is absolutely terrible, famine almost everywhere and millions are dying of starvation. I tramped for several days through villages in the Ukraine and there was no bread there, many children had swollen stomachs, nearly all the horses and cows had died, and the people themselves were dying."[51] Upon his arrival in Berlin on March 29, he shared his findings in a press conference, perhaps arranged by Paul Scheffer of the *Berliner Tageblatt*, with H. R. Knickerbocker (HK) for the *New York Evening Post* (Illustration 14) and Edgar Ansel Mowrer (EM) for the *Chicago Daily News*. News of Jones' tramp through the countryside quickly reached the USSR, prompting considerable anger among the Soviets, especially Maisky, Umansky, Brodovsky, and Litvinov. On the same day as Jones' Berlin press conference, Brodovsky reported to Umansky:

> Jones was here; he looked over the tractor factory and left. The attaché at the German consulate here, von Welck, told me Jones got off at a station before reaching Khar'kov (evidently Belgorod), and walked 70 kilometers to Khar'kov in order to get acquainted with our countryside. He spent one night of his wanderings with a chairman of a village council and one night with a peasant. Jones stayed here with the Vice-Consul, Ehrte, at the German Consulate.... Jones came to see me ... but we did not speak.[52]

In London, Maisky called on Lloyd George's secretary, A. J. Sylvester, and lodged a complaint about Jones; Sylvester wrote back on behalf of Lloyd George, expressing displeasure that Jones had made it seem that he "was visiting Russia for and on behalf of Mr. Lloyd George."[53] Although Sylvester stated that Lloyd George would be communicating with Jones "at once...demanding an explanation of his behavior..." Lloyd George never did communicate with Jones directly again. Not surprisingly, Litvinov was galled by the entire affair, blaming Maisky for having facilitated Jones' request for a visa, the press department for having failed to bring attention to unfavorable articles published in the past, and even himself for having granted Jones a lengthy interview. "We gave this individual all kinds of support, helped him in his work, I even agreed to meet him, and he turns out to be an imposter."[54] On April 2, Litvinov sent out a communication titled "Restrictions on the Freedom of Movement by Foreign Correspondents," which stated that foreign correspondents "must get permission in advance to visit any other places [than Moscow] in the Union."[55]

The stories the two American journalists wrote, as well as those syndicated in British newspapers like the *Sun*, the *Morning Post*, the *Daily Express*, and the *Yorkshire Post*, provided Jones' honest account of the famine. Both of the American journalists' stories about Jones' foray into the countryside begin by referencing the 1933 famine in light of the 1921 famine and attribute this news peg to Jones, while identifying him as the foreign affairs secretary (HK) or private secretary (EM) to David Lloyd George. Both reporters explain that Jones was basing his estimation "after a long walking tour through the Ukraine and other districts in the Soviet Union"[56] (HK) or "through the rural districts of the Ukraine"[57] (EM). While Knickerbocker notes that Jones spoke Russian fluently and was the first foreigner to visit the countryside since authorities forbade foreign correspondents from leaving Moscow, Mowrer writes that even though "foreign correspondents were forbidden to visit the famine regions of the Ukraine, Jones was allowed to do so."[58]

Mowrer's assertion was correct in that Jones had secured permission to travel from Umansky. Jones' status as a private individual and not a recognized member of the correspondents' corps may have played a role in securing Umansky's permission. Jones' status as a private individual also saved him after he was accosted in a small railway station by the secret police. Jones recounts the event twice: the first time in his second article for the *Western Mail*, titled "Starving Russians Seething with Discontent," published on April 4; and the second time on January 14, 1935, in an article syndicated in Hearst newspapers. In the first version, Jones frames the incident around the arrest of the six British engineers, four of whom were imprisoned in the headquarters of the OGPU, and then relates what happened to him.

I had narrowly escaped being arrested myself not long before at a small railway station in the Ukraine, where I had entered into conversation with some peasants. These were bewailing their hunger to me, and were gathering a crowd, all murmuring, "There is no bread," when a militiaman had appeared. "Stop that growling," he had shouted to the peasants; while to me he said, "Come along; where are your documents?"

A civilian (an OGPU man) appeared from nowhere, and they both submitted me to a thorough grueling of questions. They discussed among themselves what they should do with me, and finally the OGPU man decided to accompany me on the train to the big city of Kharkoff, where at last he left me in peace. There was to be no arrest.[59]

In the 1935 version Jones is confronted by "a red-faced, well-fed OGPU policemen in uniform," who then summons a member of the secret police to escort Jones to "the nearest city, Kharkov." Significantly, Jones develops this scene by highlighting his status as a journalist, not a private individual.

Throughout the journey I impressed him [secret police] with the fact that I had interviewed Lenin's widow, and a number of commissars and great panjandrums of the Soviet regime, and by the time we reached Kharkov I believed he was thoroughly convinced that any real arrest of myself would plunge Russia and Europe and the United States into a world war.

For he decided to accompany me to a foreign [German] consulate in Kharkov and he left me at the doorstep, while I, rejoicing at my freedom, bade him a polite farewell — an anti-climax but a welcome one.[60]

The second version, written almost two years after the fact when Jones had reason to feel as though he'd been abandoned by people like Lloyd George and Muggeridge, embellishes the incident. For example, only the second version refers to the interview with Lenin's widow (conducted during his 1931 visit) and that his arrest "would plunge Russia and Europe and the United States into a world war."[61] This mention of the United States makes sense because this article appeared in American newspapers for an American audience. Given the severity of the famine, one has to assume that only his status as adviser to the former prime minister, evidenced by his diplomatic passport (Illustration 15), enabled Jones to avoid arrest and be left off in Kharkov, on the doorstep of the German consulate. It should be noted that when Jones wrote the articles for the Hearst newspapers, he was en route to the Far East and was doubtlessly working from memory, which may account for the differences.

Another perplexing aspect related to this incident stems from the fact Jones did not record the arrest in his diary or discuss it in any personal correspondence. Not documenting his near arrest marks this episode as an extraordinary exception, but can be explained by the fact Jones knew his intention was to reveal the famine. Despite the discrepancy about Jones' being allowed to travel into the countryside, both Knickerbocker and Mowrer explain that Jones planned to use his address at the RIIA on March 30, to explain "the reasons for the [travel] prohibition"[62] (HK) and "the dislike of the Russian authorities to having conditions in the Soviet Union investigated"[63] (EM). In pointing to the famine as the reason why journalists had been banned from traveling and the charge that Soviet authorities bristled at any investigations of internal problems, Jones knew that he would be denounced by Soviet officials and never again be granted entrance into the USSR. What he might not have expected was to be denigrated by Western journalists and shunned by public officials like Lloyd George.

'A Crust of Bread and An Orange Peel'

Another significant difference revolves around the presentation of one of the most interesting and compelling anecdotes from Jones' journey into the countryside, one that occurred on the train as it headed toward Kharkov. Knickerbocker quotes Jones directly:

> In the train a Communist denied to me that there was a famine. I flung a crust of bread which I had been eating from my own supply into a spittoon. A peasant fellow-passenger fished it out and ravenously ate it. I threw an orange peel into the spittoon and the peasant again grabbed it and devoured it. The Communist subsided.[64]

Mowrer also quotes Jones directly but much more succinctly.

> I saw a peasant fish out a crust of bread and an orange peel which I had thrown into a cuspidor in the train.[65]

In the Knickerbocker version, the throwing of a crust of bread and an orange peel is not only grouped together but also done as a deliberate, calculated way of contesting the communist's denial of famine conditions. In this scenario, the communist's denial precipitates Jones' response. In the Mowrer version, there is no cause and effect. The incident is presented as independent action to illustrate the severity of the famine. Because Jones was acting as the source of this information and not the author of the articles in which this incident appears, he obviously did not have control over how the information was presented. Jones was reported to have held a press conference, not grant individual interviews or issue a press release. In this case, each journalist used the information differently. By the time Jones gave the press conference, he would have had time to process and to synthesize the information; it's certainly something he would have remembered quite clearly. What Jones recorded in his diaries are fragments, recorded either as events happened, after they happened, or whenever an opportunity presented itself. Comparing the newspaper versions with how the incidents appear in the diaries yields impressions, not composed, finished pictures of what was happening.

The throwing of a crust of bread appears in Diary 1, Part 3, immediately following a brief comment from a communist: "You must have a Cheka [secret police] in England. World revolution will come. Boy on train asking for bread. I dropped a small piece of bread on floor and put it in spittoon. Peasant came and picked it up and ate it."[66] Directly following this are several notes from peasants relating the lack of grain and cattle in the villages and *kolkhozy*. At the top of the following page, Jones wrote and underlined *Member Politotdel*. He then records what this member of a Moscow politotdel told him. He also notes comments from a train conductor, a young, disillusioned communist, a group of peasant women, and prices for a liter of milk and chicken before he mentions throwing away the orange peel. "I dropped orange peel into spittoon. Peasant picked it up and ate it. Later apple core. Man speaking German. Same story. 'Tell them in England we are starving. Bellies extended. Hunger.'"[67] In these entries, there is no cause and effect, but that does not necessarily mean there was none. While so much of what Jones wrote about the USSR during his three visits was certainly based on the information recorded in the diaries, it would be erroneous to conclude that everything published in the newspaper articles must have correspondence with what was recorded in the diaries. That Knickerbocker and Mowrer present this incident in different ways testifies to the hermeneutic nature of journalism.

Jones uses the scene from the train in the third article he wrote for the *Daily Express*, titled "Soviet Confiscate Part of Workers' Wages." His version gives a fuller treatment of the train ride without even mentioning the crust of bread or orange peel. The article begins with the warning he received from "a certain Embassy,"[68] that the starving peasants would steal anything they could get hold of. Doubtlessly, this warning came from the British Foreign Office, which he had visited on March 6. There is a brief note in his diaries, which articulates Jones' attitude about at least one consul member: "Ovey a fool."[69] The article explains about traveling by hard rather than soft class, if one wants to see "the real Russia." Jones had used this contrast about traveling in previous articles and in 1930 had titled his very first article for *The Times* "The Real Russia." Jones then presents a cast of characters he encountered on this slow train to Kharkov.

Jones begins these character sketches with a Communist Party member who not only believed that England was imprisoning all communists, but that Scotland Yard was also crushing the working class. When the idea of freedom in England came up, the communist says, "You have only freedom to chatter. But suppose you organized a military force to fight against the King, would you be allowed to do so? Certainly not. That is a proof that you have no freedom."[70] That is one of the earliest pieces of testimony from the train journey south, and on the very next page, Jones writes at the top of the page: "Member party. Lies**"[71] The word "lies" is accentuated with two large stars. Even though he did not use those lies in the article, Jones spells them out clearly in the entry as they pertain directly to the agricultural situation.

> There ought to be a good harvest this year because a lot of snow fell, the same as in 1923 when there was a lot of snow and a fine harvest. The government gave Ukraine 20 million poods. North Caucasus 12 million poods. Ukraine 87 % of seed is there. We filled the autumn sowing plan. Of course we did. We sowed more in the autumn of 1932 than in 1931.[72]

In response, Jones notes in the diary that hundreds of peasants were selling cakes and milk outside of a railway station in an attempt to secure grain and bread. He then records the communist's prediction about revolution eventually happening in England, "and then you must have a Cheka as ruthless as ours."[73] It is at this point in the diary that Jones notes a boy on the train asking for bread and then the episode of throwing the crust of bread into the spittoon. Rather than use that in the article, however, Jones chose a different way of countering the Communist Party member's assertions. "Two Russians listen intently to our conversation, but they do not say a single word. It is not safe for a Russian to argue in front of a Communist Party member."[74]

In the article, what follows are the accounts of three passengers: a peasant clinging to an empty sack who bought bread to bring back to his village but who had the bread taken away from him; a young communist who must give back part of his wages to pay for the Five-Year Plan; and a private trader who was going to look for work in Kharkov, having had to leave Leningrad when he was unable to secure an internal passport. "I sell things in the streets and because of that they deprived me of my rights."[75] Having established the peoples' desperation regarding conditions in the towns and villages, Jones recounts a conversation with a member of the politotdel or political department, one of 2,700 from the Moscow politotdel sent to the villages to force the peasants to work and to bring strict control to the *kolkhozy*. In the diary, Jones presents a description of him: "He clenched his fist and hit down with every word: resolute, ruthless, cruel."[76] In the article, this party member says, "We are semi-military. We'll smash the kulak and we'll smash all opposition. We are practically all men who served in the civil war. I was in the cavalry in the finest Red regiment."[77]

This attitude reflected what leaders like Kaganovich and Stalin said during the plenum of the party's Central Committee in January 1933. Kaganovich decried the idea that the kulaks had been eliminated when in fact many had not been exiled or had fled from exile and were in hiding with relatives. Stalin's speech, published as "Our Work in the Countryside," outlined five main deficiencies that resulted from the poor grain collection campaign in the fall of 1932. In the fourth point, Stalin points to the failure of local officials to recognize that the kulaks had gone from direct attacks on the *kolkhozy* to undermining them "on the sly..."

> The present-day kulak and kulak agents, the present-day anti-Soviet elements in the countryside are in the main "quiet," "smooth-spoken," almost "saintly" people. There is no need to look for them far from the collective farms; they are inside the collective farms, occupying posts as storekeepers, managers, accountants, secretaries, etc. They will never say, "Down with collective farms!" They are "in favour" of collective farms. But inside the collective farms they carry on sabotage and wrecking work that certainly does the collective farm no good.[78]

The party member that Jones records in the diary delineates this very type of subversive activity.

> The methods of the kulaks have changed. They used to murder. Now they are subtle. Now they say, 'Yes, we're for the kolkhozy, but they'll steal and they won't work and they'll make difficulties. They try to wreck by mean tricks, but they're not dangerous any longer.[79]

This description mirrors the plenum resolution published in the press on the need for vigilance by the political department. Jones recognized in this party member the ruthlessness with which the party approached this campaign. In the article, Jones writes, "He will not hesitate at shooting. He is filled with the doctrine of class warfare in the villages, and he is determined to carry on what he considers to be a holy war against all those who are against the Communist collective farms."[80] Jones effectively uses the final section of this article to not only have a German-speaking passenger make the desperate plea to people in England that they were starving and "getting swollen," but also to have the young communist warn him about leaving the train and tramping through the countryside. "Be careful. The Ukrainians are desperate."[81] With that warning, Jones created not only a picture of how desperate conditions were but also a feeling of suspense, illustrating his understanding about how to build interest in a series of articles. The diary and newspaper article also show Jones' ability to move from merely witnessing death and dying to humanizing the suffering involved, while encouraging readers to recognize their shared humanity. That he would challenge the communist's claim that there was no famine by throwing a crust of bread and an orange peel into a spittoon on the train clearly provides evidence of what Jones saw as his moral imperative to challenge oppression. It is one form of emotional commitment--the mode of denunciation, a perspective "in which compassion is combined with indignation and anger and turned into an accusation of the perpetrator."[82]

A Response to Shaw

In giving the Berlin press conference on March 29 that resulted in the articles by Knickerbocker and Mowrer, Jones reconfirmed reports that had begun appearing in European and American newspapers about famine conditions raging across the USSR beginning in January and February. Jones further developed this point the following evening in his speech at the RIIA in London, titled "Soviet Russia." In addition to what he had conveyed in his press conference, Jones aims part of his critique at the liberal press for hypocrisy and cowardice in railing about events in Eastern Galicia while remaining silent "when a hundred million peasants are condemned to hunger and serfdom."[83] Jones expresses particular disdain for a letter published in the *Manchester Guardian* on March 2 and signed by George Bernard Shaw and twenty others, a translation of which Jones had read in *Izvestia* while in Moscow. The letter decries attempts to discredit the experiment being conducted in Soviet Russia.

> We the undersigned are recent visitors to the USSR. Some of us travelled throughout the greater part of its civilized territory. We

desire to record that we saw nowhere evidence of such economic slavery, privation, unemployment and cynical despair of betterment as are accepted as inevitable and ignored by the press as having "no news value" in our own countries....

We would regard it as a calamity if the present lie campaign were to be allowed to make headway without contradiction and to damage the relationship between our country and the USSR. Accordingly we urge all men and women of goodwill to take every opportunity of informing themselves of the real facts of the situation and to support the movements which demand peace, trade and closer friendship with an understanding of the greater Workers Republic of Russia.[84]

Jones viewed the letter as farcical. In his speech, Jones decries the signatories' gullibility. "Viewed from Moscow it was a mixture of hypocrisy, of gullibility and of such crass ignorance of the situation that the signatories should be ashamed of venturing to express an opinion about something which they know so little."[85] In his press conference, Jones had made a point that Russians held Shaw in contempt. Mowrer quotes Jones, "After Dictator Josef V. Stalin, the hungry Russians most hate George Bernard Shaw for his accounts that they have plenty of food, whereas they are really starving."[86] Jones' willingness to confront cowardice on the part of liberals who turned a blind eye to the Stalinist regime's tyranny against the peasantry was not altogether surprising; nonetheless, he demonstrated his courage in criticizing someone as famous and popular as Shaw.

In exposing what he considered a catastrophic famine, Jones believed he was fulfilling the mission for which he had been so wonderfully prepared in his education and in his work experiences with Lloyd George and Ivy Lee. Upon graduating from Cambridge, he demonstrated a strong sense of what Himmelstein and Faithhorn call primary and secondary autonomous functioning, an ability "not to become overly dependent on his or her employers, official sources, or the perceived audience, for their approval."[87] Such functioning allows the reporter to tell his story as he witnessed it, resolute in knowing that what he has seen and heard must be communicated regardless of recriminations. Jones' independence, self-esteem and competence allowed him to interact with and affect his environment. Such "ego strength," coupled with his intellectual abilities and creative capabilities enabled him to enter a highly charged situation laden with considerable emotional stress and write newspaper articles that were informative, intelligent, and artistic. At this very point in his career Jones had, in effect, scaled a height to which few other journalists had dared to climb because of a loss of conviction, depression, or even a sense of impotence in not being able to effect change. With his superior coping mechanisms, Jones exhibited a strong conviction in his mission to expose the famine and assist his audience to enhance their awareness and understanding into the larger meaning of the events he had witnessed.

'A Big Scare Story' and 'A Particularly Nimble Mind'

Little did Jones know that as he delivered his RIIA speech at Chatham House, Duranty was preparing a piece for the *New York Times* in which he denies the famine and accuses Jones by name of distributing "a big scare story."[88] Editors at the *New York Times* created the main and secondary headlines that clearly deny the famine, providing irrefutable evidence that culpability for misrepresenting the famine goes well beyond Duranty. In his opening paragraph, Duranty calls Jones' claims "a big scare story...with 'thousands already dead and millions menaced by death and starvation.'"[89] Although no attribution is provided, this is the only direct quote that Duranty uses; however, Jones was not quoted in either Knickerbocker's *Evening Post* article or Mowrer's *Daily News* article as saying this. Knickerbocker quotes Jones as saying "Millions are dying of hunger."[90] In a summary of what Jones was planning to say at the RIIA, Knickerbocker writes about the "impending death of millions."[91] If Duranty had been working from a copy of Knickerbocker's article, he certainly allowed himself considerable laxity in presenting this information. Similarly, there is nothing in the Mowrer article that resembles Duranty's direct quote. In terms of fatalities, Mowrer quotes Jones about deaths in Kazakhstan: "A foreign expert [Otto Schiller] who returned from Kazakhstan told me [Jones] that 1,000,000 out of 5,000,000 inhabitants there have died of hunger."[92] The quote that Duranty uses appeared in none of the other articles that were syndicated in England and the United States. Duranty was most likely quoting Jones from the interview with him in Moscow. Furthermore, in the very next paragraph, Duranty identifies the quote's author as Jones, and then identifies him as Lloyd George's former secretary who spent three weeks in the USSR. Duranty then quotes Jones as saying that the country was "'on the verge of a terrific smash,' as he *told* the writer"[93] (emphasis added). In the next paragraph, Duranty again refers to their meeting.

> Mr. Jones is a man of a keen and active mind, and he has taken the trouble to learn Russian, which he speaks with considerable

fluency, but the writer [Duranty] thought Mr. Jones' judgment was somewhat hasty and asked him on what it was based. It appeared that he had made a forty-mile walk through villages in the neighborhood of Kharkov and had found conditions sad.

I suggested that that was a rather inadequate cross-section of a big country but nothing could shake his conviction of impending doom.[94]

Clearly, Duranty was basing his article on their interview and not on what had been published in the articles from the Berlin press conference. After a section about other scare stories, Duranty returns to their March interview. "He [Jones] told me there was virtually no bread in the villages he had visited and that the adults were haggard, gaunt and discouraged, but that he had seen no dead or dying animals or human beings."[95] Duranty was reporting the gist of their conversation without being completely truthful. In point of fact, while Jones did not record witnessing any dead animals or humans himself, he did record eyewitness testimony from peasants who had lost animals, neighbors, and family members. In his own Letter to the Editor, published in the *New York Times* on May 13, Jones takes up this very assertion of Duranty's. "Mr. Duranty says that I saw in the villages no dead human beings nor animals. That is true, but one does not need a particularly nimble brain to grasp that even in the Russian famine districts the dead are buried and that there the dead animals are devoured."[96]

Duranty then agrees with Jones' assessment about the mismanagement of collective farming. "I believed him because I knew it to be correct...."[97] However, that assessment was as far as Duranty went in agreeing with Jones. After admitting that agricultural commissariats made a mess of Soviet food production, however, Duranty reverts back to deploying stereotypes about Soviet indifference to the casualties involved in their drive toward the socialization of agriculture. Describing the Bolsheviks as being "animated by fanatical conviction," Duranty uses an expression that has become arguably the article's most oft cited line: "You can't make an omelette without breaking eggs..."[98] And it was only at this point in the article that Duranty decries Jones' "brief trip through any one area" and "hasty study" in favor of his "more trustworthy information" that led him to conclude in classic doublespeak. "There is no actual starvation or deaths from starvation, but there is widespread mortality from diseases due to malnutrition...."[99]

Duranty's article makes no direct reference to the March 29 articles; rather, every mention of Jones references their Moscow interview, which on the surface appeared to be cordial despite their differences of opinion. Jones did not initially record very much in his diary from the meeting except for one very telling sentence: "I don't trust Duranty. He still believes in collectivization. Said, Save face. Third international down & out. *Quiet*"[100] (Illustration 16) Several pages later, Jones recorded the substance of what they discussed over a few pages. In his letter to the *New York Times* editor [dated May 1 on the typescript and published May 13], Jones attacks Duranty's article but not the man, "whom I must thank for his continued kindness and helpfulness to hundreds of American and British visitors to Moscow...."[101] Duranty doubtlessly knew about the Jones press conference and perhaps even about Knickerbocker's article, but if Duranty had a copy, it seems reasonable that he would have directly attacked assertions in the article instead of the content of their interview in Moscow. That Duranty may not have had a copy of the article is a distinct possibility given the timing of these publications. As Nigel Colley notes:

> From considering international time zone differences between New York and Moscow, if Knickerbocker's article came out mid-afternoon in New York on the 29th, it would already be about midnight in Moscow, and this would have been before anyone in New York had chance to read it and then immediately disseminate its contents back to Moscow.[102]

Mr. Colley also explains that conceivably the Umansky-orchestrated party to throw down Jones occurred on the evening of March 30 and that Duranty was furnished with a complete copy of Knickerbocker's article "so as to counter Gareth's specific allegations"[103] and then still have time to cable his article to the *New York Times* in order for publication on March 31. Duranty, however, did not counter specific allegations from the Knickerbocker article; he countered specific points that Jones told him related to his tour of Ukraine. Had Duranty been furnished with a copy of Knickerbocker's article, he most likely would have used it. Lastly, Duranty's famine denial story was almost certainly his own doing. He was on his way to Berlin on March 30, having cabled another story from that city on March 31, meaning it is unlikely he attended the "vodka and *zakuski* party,"[104] described by Lyons, if such an event actually occurred.

Jones was not, as Lyons suggests, "... the most surprised human being alive when the facts he so painstakingly garnered from our mouths were snowed under by our denials."[105] Other than Duranty's story of March 31, the only other denial came from Fischer, who was on a book tour in the United States. When asked about the number of deaths in Kazakhstan, Fischer is quoted as saying, "Who counted them? How could anyone march through a country and count a million people? Of course people are hungry there—desperately hungry. Russia is turning over from agriculture to industrialism. It's like a man going into business on small capital."[106] Duranty's and Fischer's denials of famine hardly constitute an avalanche, raising further doubts about Lyons' version of that night's events.

Jones provided the world with ample evidence of the famine raging through much of the USSR, but particularly in Ukraine thanks largely to decisions made by Stalin to punish Ukrainian nationalist aspirations. Duranty's questioning of Jones' "hasty study" served as a prompt for Jones to explain how he collected his information, which was in sharp contrast to those journalists working under the strictures of censorship. What Jones reported about the famine was thoroughly researched, reasoned, and expertly reported. Rather than being snowed under by denials, Jones was silenced slowly, imperceptibly by a Red tide of indifference and collusion by British and American governments that had a completely different agenda, one which did not include saving the lives of peasants in a faraway land. What is amazing is that anyone could have remained indifferent after reading the articles Jones wrote in early 1933. In twenty-one articles, Jones created one of the most compelling accounts of human suffering in journalism history. That he was abandoned by those he should have been able to count on for support tested his resolve but did not deter him from doing what he considered his responsibility: Tell the world what he knew. Only slowly and imperceptibly was his lone voice pulled out to sea until it was all but inaudible.

Notes

1. Letter from Ambassador Ivan Maiskii to Comrade Neiman, Press Department of NKID, 25 January 1933, Arkhiv vneshnei politiki Rossiiskoi Federatsii (AVP RF) f. 056 (Otdel pechati), op. 18, pap. 38, d. 9, I. 27. Quoted in Teresa Cherfas, "Reporting Stalin's Famine: Jones and Muggeridege: A Case Study in Forgetting and Rediscovery," *Kritika: Explorations in Russian and Eurasian History*, 14:4 (Fall 2013), 775-804.
2. Letter from Neiman to I. M. Maiskii in London, 4 February 1933, (AVP RF) f. 056, op. 18, pap. 38, d. 9, I. 45. Quoted in Teresa Cherfas, "Reporting Stalin's Famine: Jones and Muggeridege: A Case Study in Forgetting and Rediscovery," *Kritika: Explorations in Russian and Eurasian History*, 14:4 (Fall 2013), 775-804.
3. Lyons, *Assignment in Utopia*, 575.
4. Ibid., 576.
5. Ibid., 572-574.
6. Ibid., 575.
7. Gareth Jones, "Mr. Jones Replies," *New York Times*, 13 May 1933, 12.

8. Gareth Jones, Letter dated March 27, 1933. Gareth Vaughan Jones Papers, National Library of Wales.
9. Gareth Jones, "My Russian Diary—III," *The Star*, 29 October 1930, 6.
10. Gareth Jones, Letter date December 21, 1932. Gareth Vaughan Jones Papers, National Library of Wales.
11. Gareth Jones, Letter dated October 25, 1932. Gareth Vaughan Jones Papers, National Library of Wales.
12. Quoted in Colley, *More than a Grain*, 197.
13. Ibid.
14. "Impressions of Russia: Mr. Jones' Lecture," *Manchester Guardian*, 24 January 1933, 3.
15. Gareth Jones, Letter dated January 27, 1933. Gareth Vaughan Jones Papers, National Library of Wales. File C1/1.
16. Ibid.
17. Davies and Wheatcroft, *The Years of Hunger*, 250-251.
18. Ibid., 206.
19. Lyons, *Assignment in Utopia*, 545.
20. Malcolm Muggeridge, *Like It Was: The Diaries of MM, Selected and Edited by John Bright-Holmes* (New York: William Morrow and Company, 1982), 53.
21. [Malcolm Muggeridge], "Russia's 'Plan,'" *Manchester Guardian*, 13 January 1933, 13.
22. Lyons, *Assignment in Utopia*, 545.
23. Ibid.
24. Ibid., 546.
25. Engerman, "Modernization from the Other Shore," 393.
26. Eugene Lyons, Dispatch 12152, folder 8, Box 28, Henry Shapiro Papers, Library of Congress, Washington, D.C.
27. Lyons, *Assignment in Utopia*, 551.
28. Ibid., 547.
29. Ibid.
30. Ibid., 546.
31. Ibid.
32. See Barbara S. Mahoney, *Dispatches and Dictators: Ralph Barnes for the Herald Tribune* (Corvallis: Oregon State University Press, 2002), 278, endnotes 16 and 18. The matter of whether or not the reporters were rounded up by the OGPU and returned to Moscow has only recently been disputed, calling into question assertions by Lyons and Harrison Salisbury. As Mahoney notes, Barnes never mentioned his being arrested in personal correspondence, and in March 1933, Stalin responded directly to his inquiry about the security of American citizens living in the USSR.
33. Davies and Wheatcroft, *The Years of Hunger*, 198.
34. Ibid.
35. Quoted in Davies and Wheatcroft, *The Years of Hunger*, 198.
36. See Davies and Wheatcroft, *The Years of Hunger*, 178, 180.
37. Gareth Jones, Letter dated February 26, 1933. Gareth Vaughan Jones Papers, National Library of Wales. Bundle 20.
38. Gareth Jones, Letter dated March 3, 1933. Gareth Vaughan Jones Papers, National Library of Wales. Bundle 20.

39. Gareth Jones, Diary of Tour of Russia, March 4-11, 1933. Gareth Vaughan Jones Papers, National Library of Wales. File B1/15. Diary 1, Part 2, 19.
40. Ibid.
41. Ibid.
42. Colley, *More Than a Grain*, 242.
43. Quoted in Paul D. Morris, *Representation and the Twentieth Century Novel: Studies in Gorky, Joyce and Pynchon* (Wurzburg, Germany: Königshausen & Neumann, 2005), 90.
44. Alexsey Bartoshevitch, "The Fortunes of Russian Hamlet." Accessed on 23 September 2012 from http://eng.1september.ru/2001/16/2.htm
45. Ibid.
46. Nigel Colley, Footnote 4, RE: 'See Hamlet.' Accessed on 23 September 2012 from http://www.garethjones.org/published_articles/st_patricks/litvinov_famine_denial2.htm
47. Gareth Jones, Diary of Tour of Russia, March 1933. Gareth Vaughan Jones Papers, National Library of Wales. File B1/13. Diary 3, Part 2, 7.
48. Gareth Jones, Diary of Tour of Russia, March 4-10, 1933. Gareth Vaughan Jones Papers, National Library of Wales. File B1/15. Diary 1, Part 1, 11.
49. Gareth Jones, Postcard dated March 7, 1933. Gareth Vaughan Jones Papers, National Library of Wales. Bundle 20.
50. Gareth Jones, Letter dated March 14, 1933. Gareth Vaughan Jones Papers, National Library of Wales. File B6/7.
51. Gareth Jones, Letter dated March 27, 1933. Gareth Vaughan Jones Papers, National Library of Wales. Bundle 20.
52. Letter from Brodovskii to Umanskii, 29 March 1933, AVP RF f. 056, op. 18, pap. 38, d. 9, I. 95. Quoted in Teresa Cherfas, "Reporting Stalin's Famine: Jones and Muggeridege: A Case Study in Forgetting and Rediscovery," *Kritika: Explorations in Russian and Eurasian History*, 14:4 (Fall 2013), 775-804.
53. Letter from S. J. [A.] Sylvester to His Excellency, the Ambassador of the USSR, 8 April 1933, [marked "copy] AVP RF f. 056, op. 18, pap. 38, d. 10, I. 5. Quoted in Cherfas.
54. Letter from M. Litvinov to the USSR Embassy in London, 16 April 1933, AVP RF f. 056, op. 18, pap. 38, d. 10, I. 19. Quoted in Cherfas.
55. Statement of the Resolution of the NKID Collegium, 2 April 1933, AVP RF f. 056, op. 18, pap. 39, d. 15, I. 28. Quoted in Cherfas.
56. H. R. Knickerbocker, "Famine Grips Russia, Millions Dying. Idle on Rise, Says Briton," *New York Evening Post*, 29 March 1933, 1.
57. Edgar Ansel Mowrer, "Russian Famine Now as Great as Starvation of 1921, Says Secretary to Lloyd George," *Chicago Daily News*, 29 March 1933, 2.
58. Ibid.
59. Gareth Jones, "Starving Russians Seething with Discontent," *Western Mail*, 4 April 1933, 1-2.
60. Gareth Jones, "Fate of Thrifty in USSR: Gareth Jones Tells How Communists Seized All Land and Let Peasants Starve," *Los Angeles Examiner*, 14 January 1935, 4.
61. Ibid.
62. Mowrer, "Russian Famine," 2.
63. Knickerbocker, "Famine Grips Russia," 1.

64. Ibid.
65. Mowrer, "Russian Famine," 2.
66. Gareth Jones, Diary of Tour of Russia, March 4-11, 1933. Gareth Vaughan Jones Papers, National Library of Wales. File B1/15. Diary 1, Part 3, 32.
67. Ibid., 35.
68. Gareth Jones, "Soviets Confiscate Part of Workers' Wages," *The Daily Express*, 5 April 1933, 8.
69. Gareth Jones, Diary of Tour of Russia, March 4-11, 1933. Gareth Vaughan Jones Papers, National Library of Wales. File B1/15. Diary 1, Part 1, 24.
70. Jones, "Soviets Confiscate," 8.
71. Gareth Jones, Diary of Tour of Russia, March 4-11, 1933. Gareth Vaughan Jones Papers, National Library of Wales. File B1/15. Diary 1, Part 3, 31.
72. Ibid., 31-32.
73. Ibid., 32.
74. Jones, "Soviets Confiscate," 8.
75. Ibid.
76. Jones, Gareth Jones, Diary of Tour of Russia, 1933, March 4-11, 1933. Gareth Vaughan Jones Papers, National Library of Wales. File B1/15. Diary 1, Part 3, 33.
77. Jones, "Soviets Confiscate," 8.
78. J. V. Stalin, "Our Work in the Countryside," *Works*, Vol. 13 (Moscow: Foreign Languages Publishers, 1954), 234-235.
79. Jones, Gareth Jones, Diary of Tour of Russia, 1933, March 11-25. Gareth Vaughan Jones Papers, National Library of Wales. File B1/15. Diary 1, Part 3, 33-34.
80. Jones, "Soviets Confiscate," 8.
81. Ibid.
82. Birgitta Hoijer, 'The Discourse of Global Compassion: The Audience and Media Reporting of Human Suffering', *Media, Culture & Society*, Vol. 26(4) p. 522. See also L. Boltanski, *Distant Suffering: Morality, Media and Politics*. (Cambridge: Cambridge University Press, 1999).
83. Gareth Jones, Lecture titled "Soviet Russia in March 1933," Royal Institute of International Affairs, 30 March 1933. Gareth Vaughan Jones Papers, National Library of Wales. File A/4. See also Colley, *More Than a Grain*, 229.
84. G. Bernard Shaw [and twenty others], "Social Conditions in Russia," Letters to the Editor, *Manchester Guardian*, 2 March 1933, 18.
85. Gareth Jones, Lecture titled "Soviet Russia in March 1933," Royal Institute of International Affairs, 30 March 1933. Gareth Vaughan Jones Papers, National Library of Wales. File A/4. See also Colley, *More Than a Grain*, 229.
86. Mowrer, "Russian Famine," 2.
87. Hal Himmelstein and E. Perry Faithorn, "Eyewitness to Disaster: How Journalists Cope with the Psychological Stress Inherent in Reporting Traumatic Events," *Journalism Studies*, Vol. 3, No. 4 (November 4, 2002), 551.
88. Duranty, "Russians Hungry but Not Starving," 13.
89. Ibid.
90. Knickerbocker, "Famine Grips Russia," 1.
91. Ibid.

92. Mowrer, "Russian Famine," 2.
93. Duranty, "Russians Hungry but Not Starving," 13.
94. Ibid.
95. Ibid.
96. Gareth Jones, "Mr. Jones Replies," *New York Times*, 13 May 1933, 12.
97. Duranty, "Russians Hungry but Not Starving," 13.
98. Ibid.
99. Ibid.
100. Gareth Jones, Diary of Tour of Russia, 1933, March 11-25. Gareth Vaughan Jones Papers, National Library of Wales. File B1/16. Diary 2, Part 2, 22.
101. Jones, "Mr. Jones Replies," 12.
102. Nigel Linsan Colley, "Paper Delivered at the James Mace Memorial Panel," IAUs Congress, Donetsk, Ukraine, 19 June 2005, 5.
103. Ibid.
104. Lyons, *Assignment in Utopia*, 576.
105. Ibid., 575.
106. "'New Deal' Need for Entire World, Says Visiting Author," *Denver Post*, 1 April 1933, 3.

7

'There is No Bread' (*'Hleba Nietu'*)

'A Marked Man'

On the very day that the *New York Times* published Walter Duranty's denial of famine in the USSR, Gareth Jones published the first of twenty-one articles that appeared over the course of three weeks in four different British newspapers: *The London Evening Standard* (1), *The Daily Express* (7), *The Western Mail* (10), and *The Financial Times* (3). Jones managed this ambitious project after having contracted with the three newspapers before beginning his salaried position with the *Western Mail* on April 1. All of the articles were published under his name, and Jones certainly realized that in exposing famine he would never again be granted a visa to enter the USSR. Fittingly, the last article he wrote for the *Daily Express* was titled "Goodbye Russia."

Knowing what had happened to Paul Scheffer for criticizing the Five-Year Plan, Jones could easily have gauged the gravity of his situation, especially considering that in his March 27 letter to Lloyd George, Jones notes, "M. Litvinoff asked me to treat this [arrest of the Metro-Vickers engineers] as particularly confidential."[1] Having breached that confidentiality by leaving the train bound for Kharkov and ultimately exposing the famine, Jones crossed a threshold and became "a marked man," as he explained more than a year later in a letter to Margaret Stewart, who was about to journey to the Soviet Union.

Alas! You will be very amused to hear that the inoffensive little 'Joneski' has achieved the dignity of being a marked man on the black list of the OGPU and is barred from entering the Soviet Union. I hear that there is a long list of crimes which I have committed under my name in the secret police file in Moscow and funnily enough espionage is said to be among them. As a matter of fact Litvinoff sent a special cable from Moscow to the

Soviet Embassy in London [Maisky] to tell them to make the strongest of complaints to Mr. Lloyd George about me.[2]

Part of journalism's moral responsibility invariably involves trust. As Matthew Kieran notes, "Without trust the news media cannot fulfill their function of conveying significant events and stories of human interest to the public."[3] And the public rightly demands that journalists tell the truth. But must a journalist always tell the truth? Can a journalist ever break promises? Should a journalist use deception in order to bring to light matters of public importance, or the distant suffering of others? Is it enough that the end justifies the means, or should we also consider the motives and intentions under which the journalist's actions and reports were created? Gareth Jones lied to the Soviet authorities, but he was doubtlessly justified in doing so.

It is also interesting that Jones made light of the situation of being a marked man of the OGPU and having a secret police file accusing him, as they had the Metro-Vickers engineers, of espionage, a serious charge that showed the extent of Litvinov's ire. In referring to himself as "Joneski," he borrowed a term that Jack Heinz II had coined in *Experiences*. That Maisky, the Soviet ambassador in London, had conveyed to Lloyd George Foreign Minister Litvinov's displeasure has been documented, evidenced by the fact that Lloyd George distanced himself from Jones. The three men—Litvinov, Lloyd George, and Jones—were brought together in June at the World Economic Conference held in London's Geological Museum. Dr. Colley speculates that "a meeting occurred between Gareth and the two senior statesmen ... and if they did meet, it would be certain that Gareth's Moscow interview [with Litvinov] was discussed."[4] Dr. Colley explains that Litvinov would have criticized Lloyd George directly for Jones' condemnation of the Five-Year Plan. Even if a meeting did not occur, Dr. Colley believes that the former prime minister may have shunned Jones in Litvinov's presence, sending a signal that Jones would be ostracized by the British political establishment.

'Grim Reality'

Whatever denials or recriminations Jones anticipated with the publication of his famine articles, he did not in any way show restraint or self-censorship, evidenced by the title of the first article published on that fateful day of March 31 in the *Evening Standard*, "Famine Rules Russia." The *Standard's* introduction was brief, describing Jones as "one of Mr. Lloyd George's private secretaries. He has just returned from an extensive tour on foot in Soviet Russia. He speaks Russian fluently—and here is the terrible story the peasants told him."[5] In the prior day's newspaper, the *Standard* had printed an advert titled "Russia as It Is," which used the same introduction, though it included the fact that Jones was "the first foreigner to visit the Russian countryside since the Soviets confined foreign correspondents to the city of Moscow."[6] Significantly, the *Standard's* editors referred to Jones in almost the same language as *The Times* editors had in 1930, highlighting his affiliation with Lloyd George, his fluency with the language, and his walking tour. The *Standard's* description of the walking tour as "extensive," in counterpoint to the very criticism leveled against the legitimacy of Jones' claims of famine by Duranty, points to the relativity of such an estimation because of the expansiveness of the USSR. Given the singular nature of this piece, it is not altogether surprising that Jones made extensive use of eyewitness testimony from peasants and workers to convey the article's thrust, which was articulated in the secondary headline, "The 5-Year Plan Has Killed the Bread Supply." This awkward trope fails to mention the people who were being starved to death.

Despite the clumsiness of the secondary headline, Jones organized his article around a series of encounters with ordinary citizens and excluded the interviews he conducted with commissariats and Party apparatchiks. The article serves as an example of how Jones employed his source material. He creates a sense of immediacy by dramatizing a confrontation between a father and his son, the former a skilled worker in a Moscow factory and the latter a member of the Young Communist League. Jones distills what is, in the diary, a fairly lengthy exchange between not only the father and son but also a woman, one of a family of ten people. In the article, the man "shouted at his son."

> It is terrible now. We workers are starving. Look at Chelyabinsk where I once worked. Disease there is carrying away members of us workers and the little food there is uneatable. That is what you have done to our Mother Russia.[7]

This last statement was not recorded in the diary, and the son's is limited to "But our gigants"; it is fleshed out much more fully in the article.

> The son cried back: But look at the gigants of industry which we have built. Look at the new tractor works. Look at the Dnieprostroy. That construction has been worth suffering for.[8]

The father turns the idea of construction into a rhetorical question, which

also ends the exchange in the diary. "What's the use of construction when you have destroyed all that's best in Russia?"[9]
In the diary, Jones describes their exchange as "a violent argument."[10] Only after the man tells the story of a friend saving his daughter by bringing her to a priest after two doctors said she would die within hours do we hear from the son about the "Terrible conditions before the Revolution."[11] When the boy complains that his father worked for an employer [kulak], the father turns that around.

> But we work for far greater slave drivers now. Now it's absolute slavery. And they've ruined the peasant.... Gigants, indeed; when they've robbed the whole country of bread, when people are dying of hunger everywhere, when the next winter will be worse still. The workers will be too hungry to work in those Gigants. They've cleared the country of horses.[12]

It is interesting to conjecture why Jones did not use this last indictment, for it conveys the essence of what Jones was attempting to communicate in this article, namely, that as a result of the rapid buildup of industrial might "all that was best in Russia has disappeared."[13] Jones then presents his own perspective on what the Five-Year Plan has left in its wake.

> This ruin I saw in its grim reality. I tramped through a number of villages in the snow of March. I saw children with swollen bellies. I slept in peasants' huts, sometimes nine of us in one room. I talked to every peasant I met, and the general conclusion I draw is that the present state of Russian agriculture is already catastrophic but that in a year's time its condition will have worsened tenfold.[14]

This paragraph captures the devastation in stark simplicity, and Jones effectively personalizes his experience by counting himself among "the nine of us in one room." Jones was not completely accurate in his prediction that things would worsen tenfold over the next year; in fact, the harvest of 1933 was considerably better than the previous two years, with several million fewer people to feed.[15] Nonetheless, conditions remained bleak through the summer of 1933, a fact substantiated by people like William Henry Chamberlin, Otto Schiller, and Whiting Williams, all of whom wrote about the famine later in 1933 and 1934. Despite the fact that the harvest of 1933 was an improvement over the previous two, the suffering of the peasants in Ukraine, North Caucasus, and the Lower Volga might have been alleviated had procurement quotas and exports been reduced the previous autumn.

In the next section, Jones establishes two sentences that serve as the leitmotiv of his Russian visit: "There is no bread" and "All are swollen." He then uses the testimony of four different peasants to document the conditions he found in the countryside and within miles of Moscow. Jones identifies the people as "women who were trudging with empty sacks towards Moscow."[16] The peasants tell him about having no food, no cattle, and very few horses. Jones explains the significance.

> The horse is now a question of life and death, for without a horse how can one plough? And if one cannot plough, how can one sow for the next harvest? And if one cannot sow for the next harvest, then death is the only prospect in the future.[17]

In the next paragraph, Jones poses a question about the gravity of the situation, speculating that "if millions are dying in the villages, as they are, for I did not visit a single village where many had not died, what will it be like in a month's time?"[18] This directly counters a contention Duranty made in his March 31 article in which he claimed that Jones told him that he had not seen anyone die. Jones may not have directly witnessed anyone dying, but that hardly discredits Jones' contention that people were dying in every village he visited. Without potatoes, without beets, previously used as cattle fodder but now needed human consumption, the situation was quickly approaching catastrophic proportions, far worse than the famine had been in 1921, which was more localized. "But today the famine is everywhere, in the formerly rich Ukraine, in Russia, in Central Asia, in North Caucasia—everywhere."[19]

Lack of food was not the only thing to dread, even for the people in the towns and cities, who for the most part were "warmly clad and … well fed." Moscow, Jones relates, "does not look so stricken."[20] However, for the vast majority of unskilled workers a new dread loomed, unemployment. Thousands were being dismissed from factories in many parts of the USSR. Jones uses the testimony from two workers to illustrate the new reality for many.

> It is terrible now. I get two pounds of bread a day and it is rotten bread. I get no meat, no eggs, no butter. Before the war I used to get a lot of meat and it was cheap. But I haven't had meat for a year. Eggs were only a kopeck each before the war, but now they are a great luxury. I get a little soup, but it is not enough to live on.[21]

Those who were dismissed, often for minor offenses like arriving minutes late, faced severe repercussions, including losing one's bread card and being expelled from the city. The internal passport system was introduced on December 27, 1932. The Central Committee and *Sovnarkom* issued the decree, titled "About establishment of the Unified Passport System within the USSR and the Obligatory *Propiska* of Passports." The declared purposes were the improvement of population bookkeeping in various urban settlements and "the removal of persons not engaged in industrial or other socially-useful work from towns and cleansing of towns from hiding kulaks, criminals and other antisocial elements."[22] Jones provides testimony related to the fate of these newly unemployed.

> We are treated like cattle. We are told to get away, and we get no bread card. How can I live? I used to get a pound of bread a day for all my family, but now there is no bread card. I have to leave the city and make my way out into the countryside where there is also no bread.[23]

Those banished to the countryside faced almost certain death if they could not find work or join a collective farm. Even when a worker was able to join a *kolkhoz*, life was difficult, as Jones notes in one diary entry. "I joined the kolkhozy three week ago. They made me pay so many taxes that life became a burden."[24] Jones ends the article by explaining that the Five-Year Plan's accomplishment of building factories came only with the destruction of agricultural, and "it is bread that makes factory wheels go round."[25]

'Charges of Espionage, Wrecking and Bribery'

The series of seven articles that ran in the *Daily Express* and the series of ten articles that ran in the *Western Mail* both began on April 3. The first six of the *Daily Express* articles ran on consecutive days through April 8, and the final article, titled "Goodbye Russia," was published a few days later on April 11. The first nine *Western Mail* articles ran on consecutive days except for April 9, when no article ran. The final article ran more than a week after the other nine on April 20. The three articles in the *Financial News* ran consecutively on April 11-13. Significantly, Jones published nothing further about the famine in Great Britain, although two additional articles were syndicated in American newspapers in June 1933.

The seven articles published in the *Daily Express*, a newspaper with a circulation of more than two million readers, follow in substance and style almost all of the articles that Jones had published previously. Except for the first article, which focuses on the arrest of the Metro-Vickers engineers, the series is organized chronologically, and makes ample use of material from the diaries. That first article's headline, "The Real Truth about Russia at Last," serves as an umbrella for the entire series rather than this specific article. A secondary headline, "Charges of Espionage, Wrecking and Bribery," articulates the article's main theme. Jones personalizes how he found out that the six British engineers had been arrested in Moscow and accused of wrecking the Soviet electrical industry and plotting against the Soviet government. At the time of the arrests, Jones was having tea with "a group of diplomats in a house in Kharkoff, 400 miles south of Moscow."[26] Presumably, this occurred when Jones was deposited there after his "near arrest" at a railway station somewhere in Ukraine. Members of the diplomatic corps at first did not believe the news of the engineers' arrest when it was first presented by one of the servants, who had read about it in the *Communist*, a Ukrainian newspaper. Jones immediately went looking for a copy of the newspaper, only to find them sold out.

Given the destitute conditions Jones experienced when he first arrived in Kharkov on March 13, it is interesting to note that newspapers were sold out. In his diary, he notes: "Heating very bad; lack of coal. Opera house in winter so cold that artists freezing; often joined the audience in order to have heat."[27] That contrasts with his description of the increased presence of the OGPU: "Women with fur coats. Probably wives of GPU. Few men ruling Kharkoff.... Streets—terrible condition, houses rotten, ice thawing, wet, dirty.... Many constructions were abandoned on account of financial difficulties. Rottenly built. Bricks not bad but huge gaps between. Then covered with plaster. Won't last."[28] In addition to the poor condition of the physical structures, Jones also notes the poor condition of livestock, especially horses. "Horses in very bad condition. They do not belong to any one person. So they do not trouble to look after. Lack of leather for harnesses, etc. Rub side of horse, blood, scruffy, diseased."[29] Jones also describes queues of 7,000 people lining up at three o'clock in the afternoon hoping to buy bread at seven the next morning.

Jones explains that the next morning he read about the arrests in *Izvestia*. "It was a plain, simple statement in a lower corner of the paper to the effect that the Ogpu had discovered a wrecking organization in the electrical industry, in which were involved six employees of Metropolitan-Vickers."[30] Jones then discovers that among the six was Alan Monkhouse, whom he had befriended on his 1931 trip. Relating his disbelief, Jones expresses admiration for Monkhouse's "frank, open bearing, his friendly welcome, and the honest conscientious impression which he made."[31] Three days later Jones renewed his acquaintance at the British Embassy in Moscow, noting that Monkhouse looked older than before. "He was nervous after the mental torture of continual questioning, but he smiled courageously."[32] Jones also notes Monkhouse's courage in returning to the Lubyanka prison in order to take clothes to another of those arrested, Leslie Thornton.

Jones then expands on the absurdity of the charges because "[s]abotage and counter-revolution are not British terms. Nothing is further from British mentality than underground plots for subversive purposes."[33] Jones finds an explanation for the arrests across the river where he sees the golden domes and ramparts of the Kremlin, which throughout its history, "has no respect for the life or rights of any, human individual."[34] Once occupied by Ivan the Terrible, the citadel is now occupied by Stalin, who is responsible for the policy of terror "which has changed the life of every man, woman, and child in Russia in the last five years."[35] But the Kremlin offers only one clue; the other Jones finds outside another building, the Lubyanka, headquarters of the OGPU. Jones asserts that the Kremlin was panic-stricken, fearing the wrath of a starving peasantry. "Seized with panic, they seek to find the foreigner on whom to put the blame when their promises fail."[36] Looking at the Lubyanka, Jones sees that too much power has been put into the hands of the OGPU, "the agents of fear," who dominate the Communist Party and show its power by arresting "on its own initiative six British engineers."[37]

Jones addressed this topic further in his series for the *Western Mail*, producing one of his best written pieces in an article titled "O.G.P.U.'s Reign of Terror in Russia," asserting that the Metro-Vickers trial serves as not only a symbol of the Five-Year Plan's collapse, but also as an indication of the control exercised by the OGPU over the entire life of the Communist Party. Jones points to the return of Genrikh Grigoryevich Yagoda, who oversaw construction of the White Sea-Baltic Canal 1931-1933 using forced labor from the *Gulag* system with huge casualties, as the person responsible for carrying out renewed terror on all fronts—party members, intelligentsia, peasants, and on Ukrainian, Georgian and Central Asian nationalists. Jones explains that the OGPU's power is also visible in material goods—the finest buildings and homes for offices and residences, the best stocked shops, and excellent foreign cars. "The wives of O.G.P.U. officials have the best dresses and the best fur coats."[38] Despite having distinct privileges, the OGPU overreached their power in arresting the six British engineers, which Jones describes as "the greatest mistake of its career," angering

even the Soviet Foreign Office and embittering its relations with Great
Britain and the United States, from whom it was seeking diplomatic
recognition.

> How the Soviet Foreign Office must curse the clumsiness which
> has so embittered their relations with Britain! But still more must
> they curse the spoke which it has put in the wheel of American
> recognition.[39]

Jones points out that the Soviets long sought recognition from the United
States, which had not had an ambassador or consul in Moscow since
the Revolution, and he correctly surmises that President Franklin D.
Roosevelt was favorably disposed toward recognition and "business men
were booming recognition with all the arts of American publicity."[40]
Having worked for Ivy Lee in New York City, Jones knew very well
how loudly the public relations machine could bellow once it supported
a cause, especially one likely to extend trade with the USSR. However,
as Jones explains, the arrest of the engineers "throws a vivid light
upon the difficulties which the Soviet Government is experiencing in
meeting payments abroad. Up to now it has met its obligations with a
punctiliousness which commands our respect."[41]

Additionally, orders from abroad were being cut drastically, and
Jones, like other observers, questions whether or not the trial was a
way of avoiding payment on foreign debt after having had to decrease
exportations of grain, something even Duranty pointed to as problematic
in his November 1932 series on the food shortages. Jones ends this article
by linking the arrest with the famine and the terror looming behind.
"For the mistaken policy which caused this visitation of famine British
engineers have to atone in the cells of the O.G.P.U. headquarters."[42]
Jones was usually quite insightful in his analysis of the Five-Year
Plan; remarkably, the increased work load did not affect his ability
to articulate so eloquently the implications of ongoing complications.
During this time period, it is reasonable to argue that the more Jones
wrote, the better he wrote.

As incisive as Jones was in analyzing the political implications of
the Metro-Vickers engineers' arrest, the core of his articles for the
Daily Express revolves around the famine, especially the little tragedies
visited upon the peasants and workers he encountered in Moscow and
the countryside. In the next five articles, Jones uses more than forty
such encounters to document the plight of peasants and workers. What
stand out in these articles are the techniques that Jones employs to
heighten the impact of what people told him. Not content to merely
replay these encounters, Jones utilizes what Mark Kramer describes

as an "intimate voice,"[43] one characterized as informal, frank, human, and ironic.

> It enables an author to step around acculturated views of relationships and issues that are usually guarded by walls of formal language and invisible institutional alliances. The powers of the intimate voice are many, and they bother people who insist on idealized versions of reality…. It is the voice in which we disclose how people and institutions really are. It is a key characteristic of literary journalism, and is indeed something new to journalism.[44]

Part of the power of this intimate voice stems from the writer's ability to create a sense of immediacy. For example, Jones places the reader directly in the scene in the second *Daily Express* article, titled "Bread! We are dying." After establishing that one cry haunts the streets, "*Hleba Nietu*," ("There is no bread"), Jones uses a second person point of view to put the reader in the scene. "As you walk through the Tverskaya-street in Moscow, a rough-bearded peasant in a sheepskin coat will lumber up to you and say…. Further on, a little girl, about eight years of age, with dark brown eyes, her little face wrapped in a shawl, sells you scented white spring flowers for a rouble a bunch."[45] Jones includes the questions he asked to give the encounters even more immediacy, as if the interview were being conducted in the present. He then shifts to the imperative voice, forcing the reader into the role of journalist. "Ask that pox-pitted youth who sells wooden bowls with burnt-in designs on the street corner where he comes from and what he is doing in the great city, and he will say…. Ask that peasant woman who stands in a side street and sells milk at three roubles (nominally six shillings) a litre why she is in Moscow, and she will reply…" Having created a sense of immediacy, Jones then shifts the point of view to first person plural to include himself. "Now we see a peasant enter a shop…. We shall follow the peasant and see…."[46]

Having achieved his goal to create a sense of wonder by integrating the reader into the scene, Jones offers what he calls "the solution to the mystery" of what these peasants are doing in Moscow, namely, attempting to buy bread with anything of value—gold, silver spoons, dollars sent by relatives who emigrated abroad, or even silver rubles from the days of the Czar Nicholas. Jones then returns to the first person point of view to keep the narrative flowing. "One night I saw a crowd on a street and heard piteous wails…." Jones then describes a peasant with three children begging for food being arrested by a policeman and driven away. "The unceasing cries of the children could be heard as the droshky trotted off."[47] Having engaged the reader's senses, Jones ends at a railway station, a place where there were always large numbers of peasants in transit. Jones allows a homogeneous, non-individualized group of peasant women to speak directly to the reader:

> We are starving. We have hardly had bread for two months. We are from the Ukraine and we are trying to go north for they are dying quickly in the villages. But we have come so far, and now they will give us no railway tickets. So we are stranded here without food and do not know what to do.[48]

In this wonderfully crafted piece, Jones creates a scene of tragedy by appealing to multiple senses, by subtly manipulating the point of view, and by ending with the central feature of ancient Greek drama—a chorus, this one composed of starving women. Kramer describes these techniques as the "breakable rules" for literary journalists, an attempt to comprehend subjects' felt lives by immersing oneself in detailed facts, creating narrative, and using the intimate voice. Jones invites the reader to demand not merely information, "but visions of how things fit together now that the center cannot hold.... And narratives of the felt lives of everyday people test idealizations against actualities. Truth is in the details of real lives."[49] Jones was able to combine these approaches effectively to document the tragedy that was unfolding as famine ravaged ordinary people.

'Nine to a Room'

In the next four articles, Jones reverts to the first person perspective, documenting his train ride (See Chapter 6), his tramping through the countryside, his stay in Kharkov, and his exploration into the side streets of Moscow. Each of these articles creates a sense of drama particular to what Jones wants to convey. His journey into the countryside is framed by a warning from "a certain Embassy,"[50] which took on considerable significance given the ban on travel outside of Moscow by Western correspondents, issued in February. By disregarding the ban and packing his rucksack "with many loaves of white bread, with butter, cheese, meat and chocolate,"[51] Jones not only risked arrest, confiscation of his passport, or deportation, but he also jeopardized access to important Soviet contacts to which he had been privileged thanks to his association with Lloyd George and the British Foreign Office. According to Andrew Gregorovich, "*all* travel by foreigners in Ukraine and especially all foreign correspondents"[52] was banned in early 1933, (emphasis added); despite having permission to travel, Jones certainly did not have permission to detrain and tramp through the countryside. Traveling in "the hard class compartment of the slowest rain which leaves Moscow for Kharkoff"[53] arguably provided Jones the anonymity he needed when it came time to detrain. Significantly, Jones uses the Embassy warning to begin this article, and he ends it with a terse warning from a young communist whom Jones describes as typical of the growing disillusionment becoming prevalent among this type: "Be careful. The Ukrainians are desperate."[54]

Jones takes up Ukrainian desperation in the next two articles, documenting his tramp through the villages of the Central Black Earth oblast and further southwest into Ukraine where he was finally rounded up and deposited in Kharkov. In what was once one of the most fertile agricultural areas in the world, Jones encounters absolute devastation from almost everyone he meets. Two sentences are repeated to him: "There is no bread." and "All are swollen."[55] Jones explains that the peasants have not had bread for more than two months. Reduced to eating a coarse beet normally used as cattle fodder, most people were already in various stages of starvation. In one of the first villages he enters, he see two children, "one of which [sic] had a large swollen stomach."[56] In another village, Jones relates that "we slept nine in the room. It was pitiful to see that two out of the three children had swollen stomachs."[57] Jones reports that collectivization of livestock was disastrous. "We used to have two hundred oxen but now, alas, there are only six."[58] Jones allows the peasants to describe conditions as being much worse than in 1921.

> In the old times we had horses and cows and pigs and chickens. Now we are dying of hunger. In the old days we fed the world. Now they have taken all we had away from us and we have nothing. In the old days I should have bade you welcome, and given you as my guest chickens and eggs and milk and fine, white bread. Now we have no bread in the house. They are killing us.[59]

This passage stitches together parts of a much longer conversation with a man Jones met shortly after crossing into Ukraine on March 10. In the diary, Jones describes the man as "a bearded peasant, who was walking along. His feet were covered with sacking." Rather than using the term "In the old days..." the man tells Jones, "Before the [civil] War..." and "If you had come before the Revolution..."[60] In the article, Jones creates impact with a concentrated contrast between the old days and now; in the diary, however, the impact comes from the accumulation of details.

Significantly, Jones explains that he gave the bearded peasant a lump of bread and cheese. Like the incident on the train in which Jones threw down a crust of bread and an orange peel, Jones' giving food to a destitute man certainly raises ethical questions about his actions throughout this tramp. Duty or de-ontological ethics is primarily related to the rights and duties of an agent. According to the Center for Journalism Ethics, "Rights and duties allow people to interact in responsible ways. Ethics is less about individuals seeking to maximize their goods and more about right relations among people. Therefore, concepts of justice and fairness figure prominently in duty theories."[61] Is giving food to a source who talks about the lack of food a way of mining for source material? Did Jones compromise his relationship with this source by giving him food? Sharing food with peasants is one thing; sharing his food with peasants to get them to talk about conditions is something else. At the time Jones was reporting, there were no ethical guidelines; a Code of Conduct was only adopted by the National Union of Journalists in Great Britain and Ireland in 1936.[62]

Immediately after receiving the food, the peasant tells him, "You couldn't buy that anywhere for 20 roubles. There just is no food."[63] Jones certainly did not provide food to everyone with whom he spoke or with those he stayed. In throwing down the crust of bread on the train ride, Jones precipitated a reaction, specifically to spite the communist's assertion that there was no famine. In the article, Jones mentions that the bearded peasant brought him to his hut where there was only "a very dirty watery soup, with a slice or two of potato, which all the family—and in the family I included myself—ate from a common bowl with wooden spoons."[64] Eating from the same bowl as a starving family certainly builds compassion, but there are those who would suggest that he should not have placed himself in that situation and that he should not be taking food from a family on the brink of starvation. Jones also explains that the family "had not enough potatoes to last until the next crop."[65] Even though Jones shares his bread with this family, it is clear that they would not have enough to eat in the coming weeks and months. Determining an ethical boundary in this situation is difficult.

It's important to remember that many of the villagers invited Jones into their homes, freely spoke with him, and shared whatever they had with him. The distinction that needs to be made is between agency— when Jones precipitates an action—and responsibility—which in this case means putting himself in the midst of a famine and reporting on it. Jones cannot be held accountable for the starvation conditions that the people he engaged were experiencing. Nor was he responsible for alleviating their suffering; Jones was not there to provide aid or assistance. The important question revolves around the use of food: To what ends did Jones share his food with the peasants—as an act of kindness or to elicit information? And it is not always clear how Jones negotiated that boundary in the newspaper articles. He notes, "When I shared my white bread and butter and cheese one of the peasant women said, 'Now I have eaten such wonderful things I can die happy.'"[66] Perhaps it is a distinction without a difference, but the fact that Jones does not try to hide the context of his having shared the food with this woman distinguishes this incident from throwing down the crust of bread to spite the communist. The former is an act of kindness and compassion; the latter an act of defiance.

Horses and Tractors

No such confusion emerges from his discussion of the transition from the use of livestock to mechanization in agriculture. While the peasants recognized that the *kolkhozy* and *sovkhozy* were becoming more mechanized, they did not readily accept the change. Jones quotes from a wall newspaper about the importance of the horse in the spring sowing campaign.

> The mechanization of the country is going rapidly ahead. In agriculture we must also go over to the machine, but this cannot be done immediately. Thus we must still pay attention to the horse. Now just look at how we treat horses in this village. Horses fall down and die of hunger and dirt. The collective farm members here must pay attention to the disgraceful perishing of our horses. The horse is the first helper for the spring sowing campaign.[67]

Such explicit criticism in a collective farm testifies to the urgency of the situation, revealing the sorry state that resulted from the collectivization of livestock. Surprisingly, Jones did not include one lament that the bearded peasant tells him about the difference between a horse and a tractor.

> A horse is better than a tractor. A tractor goes and stops, but a horse goes all the time. A tractor only works in certain times of the year, but a horse you can use all the time. A tractor cannot give manure, but a horse can.[68]

In his diary, Jones marked this quotation with several heavy pencil lines to make it stand out clearly, as if he wanted to make sure he could easily find it.

By the time Jones crossed the border into Ukraine, he had passed at least a dozen collective farms. He notes that while conditions on the *kolkhozy* are somewhat better than in the villages, collectivized peasants were reduced to eating horse flesh. "The peasants had eaten horseflesh in the next collective farm which I visited. This is significant, for the Russian peasant never ate horseflesh. It was only the Tartars who ate horses, and for this they were despised by other Russians."[69] In one village, two soldiers enter the hut where Jones is staying to arrest a peasant thief who was guilty of murder. "The thief had gone to steal potatoes from the hut of the other. The owner hearing the noise had come out to seize the intruder and the thief had stabbed him in the heart."[70] Not surprisingly, in almost every village where he stayed, Jones was warned not to travel alone or at night.

Significantly, the one crime that Jones did not mention in any of the twenty-one articles was cannibalism. As early as January 1933, reports from Ukraine, the North Caucasus, and the Lower Volga region were detailing murder for food (*lyudoedstvo*) and corpse-eating (*trupoedstvo*). Davies and Wheatcroft state that no comprehensive record of the number of acts of cannibalism is available, but throughout the spring and early summer until the next harvest, numerous examples were recorded in regions where famine conditions persisted.[71] During the time when Jones was in the USSR, the Kiev GPU documented more than seventy cases of cannibalism and more than sixty of corpse-eating. What Jones did encounter were villages with hundreds of empty cottages and people waiting for death, knowing that they had not enough food to last until the next crop. And because of the decree issued by Stalin and Molotov on January 22, 1933, borders had been closed and secured. People became immobilized, staying in their huts to await death. When the number of deaths began to increase dramatically, dead bodies were either not buried and left in the huts, piled on graves or in the yards of the cottages, or buried in common pits for a dozen or more corpses. Corpses were rounded up in carts that went through the villages. As he travelled further south, Jones encountered people who reported even worse conditions. In one village of three hundred huts, only a hundred had living people in them. Jones records in his diary that one woman told him, "We are looking forward to death."[72]

How Jones coped with these experiences during his roughly forty-mile tramp is not something he readily detailed in either the diaries or personal correspondence. As a journalist, Jones focused on what was happening around him, so he rarely provided insight into his emotional response to the tragedy. That, however, should not be construed as a lack of feeling, for even though Jones did not appear to suffer from what Keith Tester defines as compassion fatigue, there's no question that the experience left an indelible mark on him.

> Compassion fatigue means becoming so used to the spectacle of dreadful events, misery or suffering that we stop noticing them.... Compassion fatigue means being left exhausted and tired by those reports and ceasing to think that anything at all can be done to help.[73]

In fact, Jones appears to have been astutely aware of the moral significance of what he was attempting to communicate. By setting himself directly within the frame of his coverage and by using the eyewitness testimony of the suffering peasants and workers, Jones exercises a strong ethical obligation to tell readers exactly what was happening with the hope that his reports would induce a sense of moral outrage on the part of his readers. A care ethic gives priority to the problems, concerns and suffering of marginalized or oppressed people. As Linda Steiner and Chad Okrusch note:

> Indeed, the development and articulation of an ethic of care in journalism is less about radically changing journalists' behavior than revising journalism mythology in ways that give them permission and validation to do what they, as human beings, already may want to do and even try to do—to care about problems and to acknowledge that they care that their work has impact, produces care responses and actions, which is knowledge seeking grounded in and inspired by concrete, caring relationships.[74]

The fact that reader response was not translated into public pressure for action to mitigate the suffering of the Soviet people was arguably the most demoralizing aspect Jones experienced in the months following his return.

Part of his coping mechanism can be attributed to the opportunities Jones had to share his experiences; this he accomplished in the newspaper articles and speeches he delivered in the summer and autumn of 1933. Another part can be attributed to the "strength of his object relations."[75] His ability to bond with others at different levels—familial to professional to intimate relationships—provided Jones with the acknowledgment and emotional support to maintain an inner balance in the midst of chaos, suffering, and death. Lastly, bonding is related to another coping mechanism, that of being able to abandon social conventions, what psychoanalysts term adaptive regression in the service of the ego. This adaptive regression allows one to be open and adaptive to highly charged and volatile situations.

> This state of openness can be reinvigorating, releasing tension, and can often even lead to sudden *de novo* insights or conceptual configurations that are the foundation for creative inspiration or more profound understanding.[76]

Clearly, Jones had the ability to cope with suffering and death yet gain enough insight into the peasants' and workers' plight that he dramatized their experiences in a profoundly inspiring manner.

'The Last and Deepest Impression'

In the next two articles of his *Daily Express* series, Jones focuses his attention on conditions in the cities, Kharkov and Moscow. He begins by chronicling his view of Ukraine's new capital as he saw it on his three trips there. In 1930, the city was "a mast of scaffolding.... I could see thousands of men like ants hurry-scurrying here and there."[77] The following year Jones was impressed by "a spirit of adventurous construction among many of the young workers."[78] What he saw in 1933 was almost total collapse—dilapidated houses, new constructions lying idle, a church destroyed. In the same way that the physical aspect of the city was crumbling, so too were its people, forced to stand in queues before bread shops for hours on end only to be told by policemen: "There is no bread, and there will be no bread to-day."[79] The bread queues numbered between four thousand and seven thousand people. "They begin to assemble at about three or four o'clock in the afternoon and stand all night in the bitter Russian frost for opening of the shop at seven o'clock in the morning."[80]

Jones then uses an allegory about a louse and a pig that he heard to convey how the Russian people attempt "to laugh away their sorrow." The louse is leaving Germany because "people are so clean that I cannot find a single place to rest my head..." while the pig is leaving Russia because "people are eating what we pigs used to eat...."[81] Jones then catalogues "proof of the truth of this allegory" in the market where the "doomed" congregate, those who cannot get bread at the co-operative shops because they have lost their bread cards. Among this group Jones presents a private trader, a drunken peasant reeling from drinking vodka on an empty stomach, and a gypsy girl who sings "a *tzigane* song with all the dramatic emotion of an operatic contralto"[82] in the hope someone will give her a ruble for bread.

The group that made "the last and deepest impression" on Jones was the homeless children, the *bezprizorny*, a term originally used to describe orphans of the civil war. "With the foulest of rags and the most depraved of faces, they hover about.... They wander about the streets of the towns. I have seen some being captured by the police and taken away."[83] Jones again compares this group as he saw them in each of his three trips to the Soviet Union: in 1930 there were few, still fewer in 1931, but in 1933 he sees a resurgence of the boys. If Jones did not see many in 1931 it may have stemmed from the fact that many had been rounded up with their families and exiled during the second phase of dekulakization. As families broke apart, women and children of exiled husbands-fathers were often left to fend for themselves in often intolerable conditions, the children often becoming separated from parents. On August 5, 1931, a Politburo decision established OGPU homes for homeless children and approved measures to remove orphaned children "following the death or flight of their parents"[84] from re-settlement camps and transfer them to children's homes (Illustration 17). According to Wheatcroft and Davies, at the height of the famine in late spring and early summer of 1933, efforts were made to supply grain to hungry children, specifically to crèches and children's institutions in the badly hit districts. A report of June 3, 1933, recommended that "the People's Commissariat of Education should be obliged to decisively undertake and secure food assistance to the school and pre-school child population, and immediately establish a sufficient quantity of children's homes for the homeless (*bezprizorny*)."[85]

Jones ends this article at the Kharkov train station where he sees three hundred *bezprizorny* waiting to be taken away. Jones steals a look at them through a window, as if he were looking behind the curtain of a scene not intended for public inspection. Seeing these children yet being powerless to alleviate their suffering adds to the emotional impact. In four paragraphs Jones captures the devastation.

I peeped through the window. One of them near the window lay on the floor, his face red with fever and breathing heavily, with his mouth open. "Typhus," said another man who was looking at them. Another lay in rags stretched on the ground, with part of his body uncovered, revealing dried up flesh and thin arms.

I turned away and entered the train for Moscow. In the corridor stood a little girl. She was well dressed. Her cheeks were rosy. She held a toy in one hand and a piece of cake in the other. She was probably the daughter of a Communist Party member or of an engineer.

... These children are not the relics of the civil war. They are

the homeless children of hunger, most of them turned out from their homes to fend for themselves because the peasants have no bread.
The train rolled on to Moscow.[86]

The strength of Jones' work lies in his ability to contrast the privileged from those in privation. His description of the boy dying of typhus is unsparing and unrelenting. According to Dr. W. Horsley Gantt, who visited the USSR in the summer of 1933, the peak of the typhus epidemic coincided with the famine during the spring months of 1933. Factors contributing to the epidemic included increased poverty with under-nutrition, overcrowding, and the lack of soap and hot water for bathing.

The prevalence of typhus probably equaled that in the epidemic of 1921-2, which caused several million deaths, and the mortality rate was said to be higher; no official figures are available. In June, 1933, 400 new cases daily were admitted to the hospitals alone of Moscow and one-half as many in the Leningrad hospitals. In May, 1933, one of the large Moscow hospitals reported fifteen deaths per day from typhus. Accounts of the disease were prohibited, not only in the papers but in the medical journals, and officially it was reported as "Form No. 2."[87]

In his report, Dr. Gantt argues that death rates in the USSR were exacerbated because, unlike countries whose economies are based on a surplus, in the Soviet Union, "where the people have been existing on strictly limited rations, a slight reduction means severe deprivation."[88]

'Cruelly Strict'

In his description of living conditions in Moscow Jones was tempered by the fact that other than some peasants begging on the streets, Jones noted that on the main thoroughfares conditions appeared far better than they were in the countryside. He sees people dressed in warm clothes, walking briskly, able to buy goods in moderately well stocked shops. Skilled workers are well paid and "received plenty to eat in their factories. I learned that the children were given good meals in school."[89] On a visit to a packed theatre, he sees a crowd that was "exceedingly middle-class in its respectable clothing and nourished look. The brisk walk of many Muscovites had struck me. Hungry people do not walk like that, I reflected."[90] Jones poses a simple question to change the story's direction: "Would my visits to Soviet workers' homes confirm that impression?"[91]

By venturing beyond the center of the city and into the dark side streets, Jones found distinctly different conditions. In his diaries, he wrote that more than two million meals were being handed out a day and the number of new cases of typhus was approximately one hundred and fifty per day (significantly fewer than Dr. Gantt's estimate of 400 per day in June). Nonetheless, in this sixth article of the *Daily Express* series, Jones found hardship, crowded living conditions, and workers facing unemployment, loss of bread cards, and no passports. One woman tells him, "We have been refused passports, and we have to leave Moscow by March 30. We know no one in the world except in Moscow, but we have to go beyond sixty-five miles from Moscow. Where can we go? How will we have food there?"[92]

Jones relates that he became angry when a communist recited statistics about the need for the passportization system to remove almost 700,000 workers from Moscow, assuring him that "only crooks, speculators, kulaks, private traders, and ex-officers will have to go."[93] Jones counters those assertions by presenting the testimony of workers who complained about "cruelly strict" regulations. "If you are absent one day you are sacked, get your bread card taken away, and cannot get a passport. Life is a nightmare."[94] A worker could be dismissed for arriving at the factory a quarter of an hour late. What had been publicized as "The Land without Unemployment" had suddenly become a worker's hell. He ends with cold, hard statistics: "More and more workers are leaving the factory gates to face starvation. A vigorous economy drive is cutting down staffs in many offices, and in some factories from twenty-five to forty percent."[95]

It must be remembered that even though this tramp through the side streets of Moscow occurred on one night after having attended a reception given by the Soviet Foreign Office, Jones also spent a considerable amount of time in the districts around Moscow.

'Good-Bye Russia'

Jones ended his series for the *Daily Express* on April 11 with an opinion piece, titled "Good-bye Russia," in which he disentangles his early fascination with the USSR, impressed as he was with the Bolsheviks' courage, internationalism, and idealism grounded in equality, education, and industry "for the benefit of the workers."[96] Given the depressed state of capitalism and its system of tariffs and the rise of rampant nationalism in countries like Germany and Japan, "waving their banners of cheap patriotism,"[97] it is not surprising that Jones' liberal politics would draw him to what was being planned in the USSR. Jones then uses a succinct transition: *"Then I went to Russia."*[98] Despite the fact that Jones contrasts his early impressions with what he encountered when he saw "the real situation," he does not merely condemn the Five-Year Plan as a total mistake. In fact he notes what was being done "to care for the working class children in the towns,"[99] as well as the construction of housing for workers in Moscow, the motorcar factory in Nijni-Novgorod, and the Kharkov tractor factory. Moreover, Jones admits to liking "personally most of the Bolsheviks I knew,"[100] who exhibited tremendous enthusiasm, self-sacrifice, and non-aggression. He mentions in particular Lenin's widow [Nadezhda Krupskaya], who commanded his deep respect as one of the finest women he had ever met. He also acknowledges the courtesy extended to him by the Soviet Foreign Office, who "spared no trouble in their efforts to help me."[101] All of these aspects he puts on the "credit side" before turning his attention to the "debit side."

Jones delineated the debit side in nine succinct paragraphs in which he showed cause and effect. For example, he states, "Famine stalks the land. Surely the building of vast factories is no compensation for hunger."[102] Similarly, he differentiates class warfare as a literary slogan from its application as a program of terror, which has led "to the crushing of millions of innocent people whose only sin was that they were not of working class parentage."[103] Jones was, in a way, foreshadowing what became only four years later, Stalin's "Reign of Terror," in which hundreds of thousands of people were rounded up and summarily executed as "enemies of the people." It is hypocrisy that enables such duplicity, and he points to the destruction of the peasantry as the "greatest crime of which the Soviet regime is guilty."[104] Dekulakization and forced collectivization led to the displacement of six or seven millions of the better-off peasants, "sent away from their homes to exile. The treatment of the other peasants has been equally cruel. Their land and livestock taken away from them, they have been condemned to the status of landless serfs."[105]

This idea can be traced back to Eugene Lyons, whom Jones interviewed on March 7 in Moscow. As chronicled in the first 1933 diary, on the pages with Lyons' name, Jones notes several topics, including aspects of the new grain tax. "It's still a tax. After paying that and other taxes, they'll be lucky if they have enough to live on."[106] The idea of a free market after the tax is paid was academic, according to Lyons. In the diary, Jones writes, "New name for old system."[107] Jones also jots down six examples of the extension of force over the last six months. These include members of the politotdel establishing 7,000 new GPU stations in the villages, the passport system, commissars being sent to the grain regions with punitive powers and the right to enforce labor, factories depriving workers [bread] cards for one day's absence, death penalties for stealing, and extension of police power. Of the Party, Jones notes, "The fiction that the Party is not the government has disappeared. Force has come out into the open." And beneath that, he writes, "Serfdom for the peasants."[108]

The implication is clear: The Soviet experiment as a classless society has failed because the means employed to seek that end were based on hypocrisy and fear. Rather than employing justice to guarantee freedom for all, the OGPU has become "a weapon of the Communist Party to crush those who are not of working-class origin."[109] Any criticism of the Party or its Five-Year Plan is ruthlessly squashed, denying people the freedom to express their concerns and forcing everyone to live in fear. In the end, Jones praises British personal freedom and the rights of the individual, which "must be defended at all costs." That Jones ends this series with such an affirmation of Britain's ideals should not be considered surprising, for while he recognized capitalism's shortcomings, he understood that "a State cannot live upon the doctrine of class warfare...."[110]

Notes

1. Gareth Jones, Letter dated March 27, 1933. Gareth Vaughan Jones Papers, National Library of Wales. File C1/1.
2. Gareth Jones, Letter dated May 28, 1934. Gareth Vaughan Jones Papers, National Library of Wales. File B6/6.
3. Matthew Kieran, *Media Ethics: A Philosophical Approach* (London: Praeger, 1997), 65.
4. Colley, *More Than a Grain*, 300.
5. Gareth Jones, "Famine Rules Russia," *Evening Standard*, 31 March 1933, 7.
6. "Russia As It Is," *Evening Standard*, 30 March 1933.
7. Jones, "Famine Rules Russia," 7. See also Gareth Jones, Diary of Tour of Russia, March 1933. Gareth Vaughan Jones Papers, National Library of Wales. File B1/13. Diary 3, Part 1, 14.
8. Ibid. See also, Gareth Jones, Diary of Tour of Russia, March 1933. Gareth Vaughan Jones Papers, National Library of Wales. File B1/13. Diary 3, Part 1, 15.
9. Gareth Jones, Diary of Tour of Russia, March 1933. Gareth Vaughan Jones Papers, National Library of Wales. File B1/13.Diary 3, Part 1, 15.
10. Ibid.
11. Ibid.
12. Ibid., 15-16.

13. Ibid., 17.
14. Jones, "Famine Rules Russia," 7.
15. Davies and Wheatcroft offer an estimate of 70-77 million tons for the grain harvest of 1933, compared with 55-60 million tons in 1932 and 57-65 million tons in 1931. Tauger's numbers are slightly lower, but show an increase in the 1933 harvest.
16. Jones, "Famine Rules Russia," 7.
17. Ibid.
18. Ibid.
19. Ibid.
20. Ibid. See also Gareth Jones, Diary of Tour of Russia, March 4-11, 1933. Gareth Vaughan Jones Papers, National Library of Wales. File B1/15. Diary 1, Part 1, 10.
21. Ibid. See also Gareth Jones, Diary of Tour of Russia, March 4-11, 1933. Gareth Vaughan Jones Papers, National Library of Wales. File B1/15. Diary 1, Part 2, 1.
22. See Conquest, *Harvests of Sorrow*, 170; Davies and Wheatcroft, *The Years of Hunger*, 180; Snyder, *Bloodlands*, 45.
23. Jones, "Famine Rules Russia," 7. See also Gareth Jones, Diary of Tour of Russia, March 1933. Gareth Vaughan Jones Papers, National Library of Wales. File B1/16. Diary 2, Part 1, 3-4.
24. Gareth Jones, Diary of Tour of Russia, March 1933. Gareth Vaughan Jones Papers, National Library of Wales. File B1/13. Diary 3, Part 1, 13.
25. Jones, "Famine Rules Russia," 7.
26. Gareth Jones, "The Real Truth About Russia At Last," *Daily Express*, 3 April 1933, 1-2.
27. Gareth Jones, Diary of Tour of Russia, March 1933. Gareth Vaughan Jones Papers, National Library of Wales. File B1/16. Diary 2, Part 1, 13-14.
28. Ibid., 14-15.
29. Ibid., 15-16.
30. Jones, "The Real Truth," 1-2.
31. Ibid.
32. Ibid.
33. Ibid.
34. Ibid.
35. Ibid.
36. Ibid.
37. Ibid.
38. Gareth Jones, "O.G.P.U.'s Reign of Terror in Russia," *Western Mail*, 5 April 1933, 8. See also Gareth Jones, Diary of Tour of Russia, March 1933. Gareth Vaughan Jones Papers, National Library of Wales. File B1/16. Diary 2, Part 1, 14.
39. Ibid.
40. Ibid.
41. Ibid.
42. Ibid.
43. Mark Kramer, "Breakable Rules for Literary Journalists," in *Literary Journalism*, eds. Norman Sims and Mark Kramer (New York: Ballantine Books, 1995), 34.

44. Ibid., 35.
45. Gareth Jones, "'Bread! We Are Dying,'" *Daily Express*, 4 April 1933, 1-2. See also Gareth Jones, Diary of Tour of Russia, March 4-10, 1933. Gareth Vaughan Jones Papers, National Library of Wales. File B1/15. Diary 1, Part 1, 18.
46. Ibid.
47. Ibid.
48. Ibid.
49. Kramer, "Breakable Rules," 39.
50. Gareth Jones, "Soviet Confiscate Part of Workers' Wages," *Daily Express*, 5 April 1933, 8.
51. Ibid.
52. Andrew Gregorovich, "Genocide in Ukraine 1933," speech delivered at City Hall, Hamilton, Ontario, November 14, 1998. Accessed on 13August 2012 from http://faminegenocide.com/resources/genocide/genocide-speech.html
53. Jones, "Soviet Confiscate," 8.
54. Ibid.
55. Gareth Jones, "Nine to a Room in Slums of Russia," *Daily Express*, 6 April 1933, 8.
56. Ibid.
57. Ibid. See also Gareth Jones, Diary of Tour of Russia, March 4-11, 1933. Gareth Vaughan Jones Papers, National Library of Wales. File B1/15. Diary 1, Part 3, 39. In the diary, Jones notes, "Two of the smaller children were swollen."
58. Ibid.
59. Ibid. See also Gareth Jones, Diary of Tour of Russia, March 4-11, 1933. Gareth Vaughan Jones Papers, National Library of Wales. File B1/15. Diary 1, Part 3, 39.
60. Gareth Jones, Diary of Tour of Russia, March 4-11, 1933. Gareth Vaughan Jones Papers, National Library of Wales. File B1/15. Diary 1, Part 3, 38-39.
61. Stephen J. A. Ward, "Ethics in a Nutshell," Center for Journalism Ethics. Accessed on August 18, 2012, from http://ethics.journalism.wisc.edu/resources/ethics-in-a-nutshell/
62. Accessed from http://www.spj.org/ethicscode.asp; http://media.gn.apc.org/nujcode.html. The very first code of ethics for journalism was adopted by the American Society of Newspaper Editors in 1923.
63. Gareth Jones, Diary of Tour of Russia, March 4-11, 1933. Gareth Vaughan Jones Papers, National Library of Wales. File B1/15. Diary 1, Part 3, 38.
64. Jones, "Nine to a Room," 8.
65. Ibid.
66. Ibid.
67. Ibid.
68. Gareth Jones, Diary of Tour of Russia, March 4-11, 1933. Gareth Vaughan Jones Papers, National Library of Wales. File B1/15. Diary 1, Part 3, 38.
69. Jones, "Nine to a Room," 8.
70. Ibid. See also Gareth Jones, Diary of Tour of Russia, March 1933. Gareth Vaughan Jones Papers, National Library of Wales. File B1/16. Diary 2, Part 1, 2.

71. Davies and Wheatcroft, *The Years of Hunger*, 421-424. See also Conquest, *Harvest of Sorrow*, 257-258.

72. Gareth Jones, Diary of Tour of Russia, March 4-11, 1933. Gareth Vaughan Jones Papers, National Library of Wales. File B1/15. Diary 1, Part 3, 40.

73. Keith Tester, *Compassion, Morality and the Media* (Buckingham: Open University Press, 2001), 13. See also Susan D. Moeller, *Compassion Fatigue: How the Media Sell Disease, Famine, War and Death* (New York: Routledge, 1999).

74. Linda Steiner and Chad Okrusch, "Care as a Virtue for Journalists," *Journal of Mass Media Ethics*, Vol. 21(2&3), 115.

75. Himmelstein and Faithorn, "Eyewitness to Disaster," 550.

76. Ibid., 551.

77. Gareth Jones, "15 Hours to Wait for the Shops to Open," *Daily Express*, 7 April 1933, 11.

78. Ibid.

79. Ibid. See also Gareth Jones, Diary of Tour of Russia, March 1933. Gareth Vaughan Jones Papers, National Library of Wales. File B1/16. Diary 2, Part 1, 14.

80. Ibid. See also Gareth Jones, Diary of Tour of Russia, March 1933. Gareth Vaughan Jones Papers, National Library of Wales. File B1/16. Diary 2, Part 1, 16.

81. Ibid. See also Gareth Jones, Diary of Tour of Russia, March 1933. Gareth Vaughan Jones Papers, National Library of Wales. File B1/16. Diary 2, Part 1, 18.

82. Ibid. See also Gareth Jones, Diary of Tour of Russia, March 1933. Gareth Vaughan Jones Papers, National Library of Wales. File B1/16. Diary 2, Part 1, 22.

83. Ibid. See also Gareth Jones, Diary of Tour of Russia, March 1933. Gareth Vaughan Jones Papers, National Library of Wales. File B1/16. Diary 2, Part 2, 4-5.

84. Davies and Wheatcroft, *The Years of Hunger*, 43.

85. Ibid., 221-222.

86. Jones, "15 Hours to Wait for the Shops to Open," 11.

87. W. Horsley Gantt, "A Medical Review of Soviet Russia: Results of the First Five Year Plan," *The British Medical Journal*, July 4, 1936, 20. For a discussion of the identification of typhus as Form No. 2, see G. N. Kaminsky (Commissar of Health), *Health Protection in the Soviet Union* (Moscow: Biomedgiz, 1935).

88. Ibid., 21.

89. Gareth Jones, "Pitiful Lives of Soviet Factory Slaves," *Daily Express*, 8 April 1933, 7.

90. Ibid.

91. Ibid.

92. Ibid. See also Gareth Jones, Diary of Tour of Russia, March 1933. Gareth Vaughan Jones Papers, National Library of Wales. File B1/16. Diary 2, Part 2, 22.

93. Ibid.

94. Ibid. Gareth Jones, Diary of Tour of Russia, March 1933. Gareth Vaughan Jones Papers, National Library of Wales. File B1/16. Diary 2, Part 2, 22-23.

95.   Ibid.
96.   Gareth Jones, "Goodbye Russia," *Daily Express*, 11 April 1933, 12.
97.   Ibid.
98.   Ibid.
99.   Ibid.
100. Ibid.
101. Ibid.
102. Ibid.
103. Ibid.
104. Ibid.
105. Ibid.
106. Gareth Jones, Diary of Tour of Russia, March 4-10, 1933. Gareth Vaughan
      Jones Papers, National Library of Wales. File B1/15. Diary 1, Part 1, 29.
107. Ibid.
108. Ibid., 29-30.
109. Jones, "Goodbye Russia," 12.
110. Ibid.

8

'All Are Swollen' (*'Vse Pukhli'*)

'Master Gareth's Room'

As soon as Gareth Jones returned from the USSR and began employment with the *Western Mail* he moved back to his family's home in Barry where he "had a small bedroom at the top of the house which was always known as Master Gareth's room..."[1] Dr. Colley mentions that he was "unofficially" engaged to Jane Evans, although the couple never married, nor is there correspondence between them in the archives. Each day he took the bus from Barry to Cardiff and the offices of the *Mail's* newspaper office.

The *Western Mail* series began on the very same day, April 3, as the *Daily Express* series. While Jones explored some of the same topics for the Cardiff paper, he offered several original articles that did not duplicate those in the other series. That he published ten additional articles illustrates his creativity. While the series was given the overarching title, "We Are Starving," each article had its own headline. The first article, "Hunger and Slavery," is organized around an interview with Alexander Kerensky, who had taken over as prime minister of Russia's Provisional Government in July 1917 and promised elections for a constituent assembly only to have the Bolsheviks undermine that initiative after gaining only 168 of 703 seats in December. Jones begins by describing the end of his journey — his crossing the border from the USSR into Latvia with a group of American workers. "I saw the Red frontier soldiers with the fixed bayonets for the last time..."[2] That sense of relief at having safely departed the USSR was similarly described by Wells in his 1933 book, *Kapoot*.

> The moment the end of the train reached the middle of the bridge and crossed the red line, it stopped with a jerk. Everyone

climbed out of the carriages, and without any rehearsal at all, the passengers gave three cheers and at the same time placed their thumbs to their noses, pointing them at the Red soldiers who were slouching angrily away.[3]

Wells describes how the Finnish government placed a first-class restaurant within a hundred yards of the border, as well as the fact that every train leaving the Soviet Union had to be thoroughly fumigated. However, the most telling image Wells provides is eerily reminiscent of something Jones described as he rode the train to Kharkov. "The last thing I can remember about Russia was seeing a little ragged boy on the Red side of the river that divides Russia from Finland, trying to recover a piece of orange peel that was floating in the water."[4] While it may appear surprising that Jones had an orange in his rucksack when he departed Moscow aboard the train headed for Kharkov, he documents in his diary a young Crimean girl "selling scented spring flowers for one ruble."[5] In another brief entry, he mentions a man in Moscow selling a "tangerine from Tiflis for 3 rubles but he reduced it to 2.50."[6] The fact that fresh flowers and fruit were available on the streets of Moscow in March confirms that the incident on the train was no fiction.

'Captured Americans'

Jones' documenting the plight of foreign workers is significant. Having gone to the USSR expecting a workers' paradise but finding instead inefficiency, hunger, and near slavery, these foreign workers "breathed deeply with relief…"[7] after crossing the border into Latvia. That relief was attributable to their having escaped the USSR, as Jones explains in a later article. "Their American passports had been taken away from them in order to make it difficult for them to leave Russia."[8] Thousands of American workers were not as fortunate as those on the train with Jones; many ended up in the *Gulag* system, abandoned there by their government, even after the United States recognized the USSR in November 1933.

Jones was doubtlessly interested in the experiences of these American workers, having shared in the same idealism about the possibilities of a classless society before he made his first trip in 1930. He also befriended a number of Americans during his stint with Ivy Lee in New York. In the midst of the Great Depression in 1931, more than one hundred thousand Americans applied for emigration to the USSR through Amtorg—the Soviet trade agency based in New York—and through Intourist, the Soviet travel agency. Amtorg hired ten thousand Americans in 1931, and thousands more purchased one-way tickets with their tourist visas, believing they'd find jobs once they arrived. This wave of emigration marked the first time in American history that more people left than arrived.[9]

Even before the Great Depression left American workers desperate for hope of employment, the seeds for this migration had been sown in the mid-twenties when Henry Ford sent a party to investigate whether or not it was feasible to build a factory in the USSR. In May 1929, only months before the stock market crashed, Ford signed a forty-million dollar contract between the Ford Motor Company and the Soviet Supreme Council of National Economy for the Model-A plant that Ford was ready to scrap. Construction began in August 1930 and was completed by November 1931, one of the 521 factories designed by Detroit architect Albert Kahn and a staff of twenty-five architects and engineers headquartered in Moscow. Jones and Heinz interviewed members of the Kahn team during their 1931 journey, documenting the inefficiency and ineptitude of the Soviet way of doing things.[10]

In the last few pages of his final diary, Jones captures an exchange he had with some American workers, parts of which he used in his fifth article for the *Mail*. This article, reflective in nature as seen in the title, "My Thoughts on the Journey to Moscow," debunks the idea that the workers' journey was merely the crossing from the capitalist economic system to the communist classless society, for not every Western nation's version of capitalism was the same and the Soviet Union's quest for a communist classless society was still many years away. Rather, Jones describes the journey in more geographical terms; even though much of the USSR was territorially part of Europe, Jones characterizes it as "...Asiatic in the past and present poverty and in the fatalism of its peasants."[11] That attitude was typical of Western journalists covering the USSR at that time. Duranty, Lyons, Fischer, Chamberlin, and Barnes expressed similar views, especially in regards to the long-suffering character of the peasants.

However, Jones mentions that it was "through the efforts of an American journalist that they [American workers] had received their passports."[12] That journalist very likely was Lyons, who, in *Assignment in Utopia*, wrote about these workers having their passports confiscated after discovering that they were Soviet citizens. "I was constantly being maneuvered into interceding for Americans who had lost their passports, or were being forcibly detained on Soviet soil, or were trying to pull a Russian wife out of the country."[13] Lyons describes how he and other journalists helped some of the American workers secure visas for themselves and their families by threatening to bypass Soviet censorship and mailing their dispatches to London in diplomatic bags. From there the dispatches could be cabled to the newspaper offices in the United States. Although these threats occasionally worked, the sheer number of Americans seeking assistance to leave was beyond the scope of the journalists, not to mention the obstinacy of Soviet bureaucracy. "The fact is that none of us was a match for the devious and illogical ways of bureaucracy,"[14] Lyons writes.

Without recourse, the journalists coined the phrase "captured Americans"[15] to describe this growing group. Despite the lack of formal recognition, the U.S. government was apprised of what was happening in a military intelligence report that provided proof American passports were being stolen and re-used for espionage.

> Passports thus obtained by confiscation or theft are used for fraudulent entry of communists into the United States. The photograph is removed and a photograph of the communist user is substituted, who enters the United States under the name of the former owner.[16]

On the very first day the U.S. embassy opened in Moscow, two hundred Americans sought assistance with exit visas, and one member of the consular division noted in a memoir that he had helped five hundred people return home before the Soviets stopped granting exit visas completely.

Jones recognized that the plight of the American workers was akin to what had happened to the six British engineers. In "Starving Russians Seething with Discontent," he explains the arrests of foreigners as symbolic of the panic felt by Soviet leaders. To appease the starving peasants, "a sop must be provided for the wrath of the hungry mob. The wicked foreigner must be found on whom to put the blame."[17] He notes that the witch hunt was not confined to foreigners, for in the previous month, the Vice Commissar for Agriculture and more than thirty others had been arrested, tried, and executed for "counter-revolutionary wrecking in the machine-tractor stations [MTS] and in the State farms [*sovkhozy*] in the Ukraine, North Caucasia, and White Russia."[18] Jones ends the "Discontent" article by contrasting the "resounding slogans of the triumph of the Soviet electrical industry" with the reality of people sitting in darkness, unable to find food or fuel. "The great cities of Kharkoff and Kiev, the leading cities of the Ukraine, were often plunged for hours on end into darkness, and men and women and children had to huddle in blackened rooms, because it was difficult to buy candles and lamp oil."[19]

'Third-Degree Methods'

In two other articles for the *Mail*, Jones ties the arrest of the Metro-Vickers engineers to a worsening of Soviet economic fortunes, especially after the British Cabinet enacted an embargo on April 18 that prohibited eighty percent of imports from the USSR. This occurred after negotiations between Litvinov and Ovey broke down in late March. As Gordon W. Morrell notes, "In general it was thought that a trade embargo could not now prevent a trial, but that the extent of the enforcement of the powers to restrict Soviet exports to Britain might be directly connected to the treatment of the prisoners and the result of the trial."[20] For his part, Jones accuses the OGPU of committing this blunder as a natural extension of Russian history and of Russian mentality.

> The O.G.P.U.'s disregard of human life is also natural in view of Russian character. Human life has never been of much stock in Russia, and the rights of the individual have always been scorned by the ruling class, whether Tsarist or Bolshevik.[21]

Jones then provides three consequences of this blunder. No longer would foreign countries look upon the USSR as hospitable to its experts. "The third degree methods employed in the trial and the invalid nature of the evidence obtained by terrorizing Russians have also damaged the Soviet Government in foreign eyes."[22] The second consequence was the barrier to recognition by the United States, which was lifted as soon as the Soviets released the Metro-Vickers engineers. The third consequence was the aforementioned embargo, the impact of which was severe, given the fact that almost one-third of the Soviet exports in 1933 were destined for Great Britain. Additionally, Jones notes that the rapid decline in Soviet exports strained its ability to meet its foreign debt payments, which would have repercussions in Germany. Significantly, Jones asserts the arrest of the six British engineers must be seen in light of the famine and terror always looming behind. "For the mistaken policy which caused this visitation of famine British engineers have to atone in the cells of the OGPU headquarters."[23]

In successive articles, Jones took up the agricultural disaster, the increase in unemployment, Soviet military preparations, and religion, a topic with which Jones was obviously much fascinated given how often he mentioned it in the diaries during the 1931 and 1933 trips. In "Seizure of Land and Slaughter of Stock," Jones asserts that in 1932 "the weather was ideal. Climatic conditions have in the past few years blessed the Soviet Government. Then why the catastrophe?"[24] This question is significant in that it allows Jones to attribute causation to other factors—forced collectivization of the land into *kolkhozy* and *sovkhozy*, unrealistic grain procurements, and passive resistance by the peasants. Additionally, the loss of livestock and class warfare on kulaks had a deleterious effect on the entire nation. The question of climatic conditions in 1932 and whether or not weather played a role in the failed harvest that autumn has been vigorously debated by Sovietologists. However, absence of drought should not be construed as ideal growing conditions. Anecdotal information from observers like Andrew Cairns and Otto Schiller provides evidence that call Jones' assertion of the climatic conditions into question.

In the spring and summer 1932 Cairns travelled widely through the USSR, visiting Western Siberia (May 10-June 5); Ukraine, Crimea, and North Caucasus (June 15-July 30); and the Volga region (August 12-22). Not only did Cairns witness people starving from the famine conditions brought on by the drought of 1931, exacerbated by the large procurements that severely depleted stocks of seed, and by large grain exports, but he also noted large fields overrun with weeds, idle land, and whole fields ruined by rust. For example, on the way to Verblud, one of the large experimental state grain farms about 70 kilometers east of Rostov, Cairns notes:

> All the way out the crops were extremely poor—short, very thin and very weedy and many fields were not worth the cost of harvesting. What little summer fallow there was had a magnificent crop of weeds going to seed. There was practically no hay made and no cattle in sight.[25]

Additionally, as Tauger notes from Soviet sources, 1932 was a warm and humid year. "In several regions heavy rains damaged crops and reduced yields, particularly on the right bank of the Volga, in the North Caucasus, and in Ukraine.[26] Most of the fields Cairns inspected showed rot.

> One or two fields on summer fallow land looked fair but upon rubbing out the heads I found the kernels were badly shriveled with rust, bleached by the rain, and about two in each head eaten by bugs.... All the spring wheat I saw was simply rotten with rust.... The winter wheat was so full of weeds that the combines would not handle it, and they were using 300 old fashioned Russian reapers (one man drives the horses or tractor and another pushes the grain off the board with a fork), but needed twice as many more.[27]

Identifying rust was no easy task for the non-specialist. According to Tauger, this may in part account for the numerous claims in memoirs and testimonies that the 1932 harvest was a good one.[28] However, those claims are largely based on official estimates, which were routinely exaggerated by approximately ten percent.

Cairns travelled extensively with Otto Schiller, the German agricultural attaché in Moscow, whose reports corroborate what Cairns witnessed. For example, after passing through a section of the Central Black Earth district, they both were astonished at the amount of idle land; what is most significant is Schiller's description of how the Soviets compiled three sets of statistics. Cairns writes:

> Later he [Schiller] told me that he had been informed confidentially by an official of the Department of Agriculture in Moscow, a man in a position to know the facts, that the maximum spring sowing they expected this year [1932] was about 82 to 84 per cent of the plan and that a number of the officials thought that to expect even 82 percent was insane optimism, and that not more than 70 percent of the plan would be fulfilled. He said all Russian statistics are compiled in three sets—one for publication, one confidential set for the directors, and one very confidential set for the very high officials. The Government would not, he argued, weaken its prestige by publishing figures showing that the plan as a whole had not been carried out by less than about 90 percent no matter what the truth might be.[29]

The three sets of statistics point to the difficulties independent observers and journalists experienced in making sense of the disaster. Additionally, while in the Volga region, Cairns met a group of British journalists who were touring the country as guests of the Soviets. The group included among others Kingsley Martin, editor of the *New Statesman*; Mr. McGuire, a London stock broker who was representing the *Financial Times*; and Dr. Jules Menken, from the London School of Economics. Cairns describes being quizzed by them about conditions. When the chief tour guide tries to deflect the questioning, Cairns astutely comments:

> I am afraid the journalists' visit is going to be one more communist experiment gone wrong due to lack of adequate control. I'll be surprised if at least some of the guests don't fairly roast their hosts when they get home.[30]

Jones used parts of what Menken and Martin told him to write the two "Will There Be Soup?" articles in October 1932.

Other than climatic conditions, much of what Cairns observed corroborates what Jones reported seeing in March 1933. For example, in Voronezh, the capital of the Central Black Earth district, Cairns found conditions similar to what Jones saw in Kharkov. "The buildings and streets are all in a frightful state of dilapidation and, as nearly every place else I have been in the past two months, the work was apparently stopped on nearly all of the new buildings going up."[31] Most importantly, that Cairns witnessed famine conditions as early as May 1932 can be seen in his description of the bazaar in Slavgorod in Western Siberia where he and Schiller, having escaped their tour guide, were accosted by hundreds of people.

> I shall never forget the visit. We were not there five minutes before hundreds surged close around us to tell us all the people were hungry, that they (town workers, collective farm members, and individual peasants alike) worked and worked but got little bread, that people were eating all the dead horses and gophers, many were dying every day of hunger.... A small boy on the point of death was standing holding up his little skirt displaying thighs only about 3 or 4 inches thick. As Schiller took a photograph of him, two women with tears streaming down their face, said: "that is what is going to happen to all of us. Will you give that picture to the newspapers in America, so that they will send us food?"[32]

This description confirms what Jones had reported after his 1931 visit; namely, that famine conditions had already hit areas in Western Siberia and Kazakhstan, killing more than a million and a half people. In the very last diary entry during 1933, Jones documents meeting Schiller on a train, who not only confirms how horrible conditions were in central Asia, but expresses fears for his personal safety. "I am afraid that they may arrest me for sabotage."[33] Five months later, *The Daily Telegraph* anonymously published three articles by Schiller documenting the famine in the grain-growing areas, especially in the districts of the Northern Caucasus.

Lastly, that climactic conditions were anything but ideal can be seen in a speech, titled "Our Work in the Countryside," Stalin presented to the Central Committee plenum in January 1933 in which he acknowledged that "unfavorable climatic conditions" caused losses in the North Caucasus and Ukraine in 1932.

> This was by no means due to the bad state of the harvest; for in 1932 our harvest was not worse, but better than in the preceding year. No one can deny that the total amount of grain harvested

in 1932 was larger than in 1931, when the drought in five of the principal areas of the north-eastern part of the U.S.S.R. considerably reduced the country's grain output. Of course, in 1932, too, we suffered certain losses of crops, as a consequence of unfavourable climatic conditions in the Kuban and Terek regions, and also in certain districts of the Ukraine. But there cannot be any doubt that these losses do not amount to half those we suffered in 1931 as a result of the drought in the north-eastern areas of the U.S.S.R.[34]

While any discussion of climatic conditions is largely based on anecdotal information and therefore not completely reliable, it must be noted that the information from people like Cairns, Schiller, and others points to climate as a contributing but not determining factor to the famine that ravaged the Soviet countryside between 1931 and 1933.

As Jones notes at the end of his *Western Mail* article on agriculture, there were several reasons for the famine, all stemming from the Five-Year Plan's rapid industrialization. Among the four reasons that Jones delineates, the final reason was the Soviet export of food stuffs. In "Seizure of Land and Slaughter of Stock," Jones asserts that the Soviets were following the example of the Tsarist regime, "which used to export grain even in a year of food shortage."[35] The Soviets were exporting grain, butter, and eggs so they could purchase machinery. As Jones notes, the problem with this strategy was twofold: on the one hand exporting grain worsened the famine; on the other hand, grain prices fell precipitously in world markets, making it more difficult for the Soviets to meet its obligations and "causing western bankers and officials to consider seizure of Soviet property abroad and denial of future credits in case of Soviet default."[36] While the Soviets had been able to export 5.2 million tons of grain in 1931, the poor harvest of 1931 forced the regime to decrease that amount to 1.73 million tons in 1932 and then to 1.68 million tons in 1933. Most observers agree that even a limited amount of grain would have fed millions of people.

Jones explains that the Soviets were forced to export to forestall insolvency, which not only endangered the push to industrialize, but also left the ruling Politburo in a perilous position. "To export food at such a period has aggravated the hunger, and although the Soviet Government deserves praise for its habit of paying punctually it has by its policy harmed the health and endangered the life of a considerable section of its population."[37] Jones assessed the situation in a balanced manner.

'The Return of Unemployment'

In the same way that Jones affixed reasons for the ruin of Soviet agriculture, he organized "Why There Is Unemployment in Russia" by outlining the reasons for unemployment's return. He based this article on interviews he conducted with Gregory Grinko, the Commissar of Finance; the vice-commissar for Light Industry; as well as directors of specific factories that he visited. The first Five-Year Plan was supposed to abolish unemployment, and Jones credits the Soviets with having "successfully tackled that problem. Indeed their great problem was shortage of labor."[38] In the next paragraph, Jones asserts that the first Five-Year Plan was not an economic plan at all; it was primarily a military plan. While he described the Soviet Union's military preparedness in earlier articles, this is the first instance in which he characterizes the first Five-Year Plan as a military, rather than an economic, plan. He then contrasts it with the second Five-Year Plan, which "has seen the return of unemployment."[39] To illustrate this problem, Jones provides statistics, which he does not attribute to any official. He mentions that in Kharkov, more than 20,000 workers were recently released from factories, and in Moscow, "from 25 to 40 percent of the staffs have been dismissed, while in some offices up to 53 percent have lost their jobs."[40]

What Jones managed to find out likely came from directors involved in the daily operations of factories rather than commissariats in Moscow. That becomes evident from looking at the diaries. For example, in one of the entries from March 8, Jones provides quotations about unemployment; at the top of the page the name *Andreychin* is underlined, and the information is within quotation marks. The quotes rationalize what was happening. "Unemployment [was] according to plan. We are ejecting people from the offices in order to make the others work better.... The decree by which labour discipline is enforced is essential.... We are creating unemployment on purpose. The people understand."[41] Jones challenges this obvious propaganda by posing a question about whether or not the lack of food was also a part of the plan. This draws a denial. "No, the lack of food was not according to plan."[42] At the other end of the spectrum, he recorded an interview on March 15 while he was in Kharkov in which he lists three causes for unemployment, the same found in the article.

What was most important to Jones, however, was the toll these "exceedingly strict" policies were having on the workers, for whom there was no unemployment insurance. A worker could be dismissed for arriving at work fifteen minutes late. "When a man is dismissed his bread-card is taken away from him, or in some cases is left to him for a fortnight. Unemployment is thus a condemnation to starvation."[43] Refused a passport, the unemployed were forced to leave the city, and there was no bread outside of the cities.

In the second half of the article, Jones asserts that the reasons for unemployment were tied to shortages of raw materials, capital, and food, as well as an increased reliance on technology, decreasing the need for laborers. For example, shortages of coal led to long delays or stoppages in factories. To illustrate this, Jones quotes from the March 19 issue of *Pravda*, which criticizes the Southern Railway administration for failing to distribute metal to factories in Kharkov, Stalingrad, and Nijni-Novgorod. Food shortages also had a direct impact on factories. "A director is made responsible for the feeding [of workers].... In order to make the food supply go round workers are dismissed and are sent to the countryside."[44] This information, like the final reason, "was given to me by a director of the Kharkoff Tractor Factory."[45] That director is quoted in the diaries. "A factory is given a certain agricultural district from which to draw supplies.... Now it is most hard to get food, so workers are dismissed."[46]

To conclude, Jones offers a terse commentary. "The Five-Year Plan was intended to make Russia independent of the rest of the world. This aim has failed. Foreign specialists are leaving Russia. When they are gone woe betide the Soviet machines."[47] Jones' implication is clear: Without foreign specialists, Soviet inefficiencies and ineptitude would invariably lead to even more breakdowns of the machinery. In the short term, Jones' predictions proved accurate.

'An Army without Bread'

Jones understood Soviet foreign policy as well as anyone. He conducted thorough interviews with Litvinov, the Soviet Foreign Minister, and Karl Radek, editor of *Pravda*, which he used to write "Soviet Ready for War," for the April 11 issue of the *Western Mail*. Jones asserts that Soviet foreign policy was "emphatically one of peace." The USSR would not attack because it could not. "Russia will not attack because her internal position is too weak. An army cannot fight without bread.... Russia will not attack because the peasants would either rise or would refuse to deliver grain."[48] Additionally, there were national minorities "waiting for the war-drums to beat in order to gain independence."[49] Jones argues that the Soviet policy of Russification, which "began about two months ago will increase rebellious feelings of the Ukraine and will weaken Russia's military strength."[50] Jones states that nationalists in Ukraine, Georgia, and Central Asia were waiting for war in order to overthrow the Soviet regime.

Jones underestimated the severity of the repression enacted in Ukraine and the North Caucasus, where a large number of Communist Party members, senior officials, directors of *sovkhozy* and *kolkhozy* were either arrested or removed. In November 1932, the Politburo initiated a purge of party members with the intention of strengthening rural party organizations "by ensuring a satisfactory economic structure for the kolkhozy, the fulfillment of the grain plans, and the purging (*chistka*) of rural party organizations."[51] In the Kuban, 358 out of 716 party secretaries were expelled from the party, as well as almost half of the 25,000 party members.[52] As many as forty percent of the 120,000 rural party members in the North Caucasus were also expelled. On December 14, 1932, the Politburo approved another resolution which attempted to connect the policy of Ukrainization with the failure of grain collections. In the Poltava district, for example, any inhabitant identified as unsupportive of Soviet power was exiled to the North, and entire villages were resettled by units of the Red Army.[53] Little wonder that peasants warned Jones that things were much worse in that district. In the diary, Jones is told: "Go down to the Poltava district and there you'll see hundreds of cottages empty. In a village of 300 huts only about 100 will have people living in them. The others have died or gone away, but most died."[54]

Perhaps, the most telling indication that change was being effected was a diary entry in which Jones noted, "GPU men in the street. Supposed to be 250,000 men in the Ukraine, but this is an exaggeration. Peasants hate them like poison. We passed the GPU prison. A lot of Ukrainian nationalists sitting there. GPU certainly stronger than it was and has complete power." "The GPU is getting more and more powerful. Stalin & GPU now ruling Russia.... New Ukrainian policy. In the last few weeks there has been a beginning of Russification system. Moscovites have been placed in leading positions in Kharkov and now Russian is to be taught in the schools."[55] Moreover, nationalism was portrayed in Communist Party propaganda as part of a kulak web of anti-Soviet wrecking by counter-revolutionary non-Russian minorities that had to be stamped out. Even the attempted flight of people trying to find food was framed as the work of counter revolutionaries whose aim was to undermine Soviet authority. In the decree of January 22, Molotov and Stalin blamed enemies of the USSR.

> ... do not doubt that the flight of villagers and the exodus from Ukraine last year and this year is [being] organized by the enemies of Soviet government, S[ocial] R[evolutionarie]s and agents

of Poland with the goal of spreading propaganda "through the peasants" against collective farms and the Soviet government in the northern regions of the USSR. Last year, the Party, Soviet and Chekist structures of Ukraine missed that counterrevolutionary undertaking by the enemies of Soviet rule. Last year's mistakes cannot be repeated this year.[56]

Despite establishing a policy of non-aggression, fear of war helped to explain Soviet foreign policy. Jones reasons that the USSR feared an attack from capitalist nations. "To prevent this Russia has sought friendship with all the nations on her borders. She refuses to belong to any group of nations for fear she will be dragged into a conflict."[57] Disdaining entry into the League of Nations, the Soviets instead signed Pacts of Non-Aggression with Poland, France, and ultimately Germany. Japan was the one nation that refused to sign any pact with the Soviets, leading many to believe Japan was planning to attack the USSR. Even though Jones states that the arrest of the British engineers dimmed the hopes for recognition by the United States, close relations between the two countries were still possible "because both countries are united by fear of Japanese expansion."[58] This point was reinforced by both Litvinov and Radek. Jones interviewed Radek on March 8 in Moscow. Radek tells him, "We are on the crossways of two conflicts—France v. Germany and Japan v. China. We wish to remain neutral. We want to remain neutral and have no alliance with other nations. We're afraid that both parties will try to bring us in."[59] Jones did not interview Litvinov until March 23, well after having returned from his tramp through the countryside. Jones took ten pages of notes in his diary and transcribed those notes into a hand-written confidential letter that he sent to Lloyd George on March 27. In addition to foreign policy matters, Jones and Litvinov discussed the fate of the six Metro-Vickers engineers and unemployment in the USSR. Significantly, the only topic Jones did not broach with Litvinov was the famine conditions he had witnessed. Litvinov tells Jones that the only danger of war lies in the East.

There, Manchukuo is a Japanese province and Japan wants to go further. This expansion may lead to a conflict with the United States on one hand and with the U.S.S.R. on the other hand, if the expansion is towards our frontier.

The refusal of Japan to sign the pact of non-aggression with us means that war with the Soviet Union is within the practical plans of Japan. In this respect we must admire the sincerity of Japan. They don't veil their intentions. They say: "We don't want to tie our hands. We may attack you."[60]

In the article's final paragraph, Jones characterizes Soviet foreign policy as a paradox, combining a desire for peace with energetic preparations for war. He illustrated this preparedness in everything from propaganda posters to children in school given gas-mask demonstrations to increased enrollment in the Society for Aviation and Chemical Defense to improvements in military aviation and munitions factories. Litvinov, Lloyd George, and Jones all attended the London Economic Conference in June. Dr. Colley believes this was the occasion when the two statesmen orchestrated a deliberate shunning of Jones. She astutely notes, "Had he not been demonized by his honest reporting, he would have been in a strong position to contribute much of his learning to society at large from his profound knowledge when writing his future articles."[61]

Jones' article on religion, "Easter in Godless Russia," is arguably one of the strongest he wrote for the *Western Mail*. Jones recorded more than a dozen entries related to religion in the diaries, many of which he used to construct this article.[62] Some of the article's key ideas are based on an interview he conducted with Alexander Lukashevsky, deputy chairman of the League of the Militant Godless. Jones begins by establishing that holy days like Easter were used by the atheists to spread antireligious propaganda. "At Christmas and Easter time there are mocking processions in the streets which revile the beliefs and rites of Christianity."[63]

Jones then provides an overview of how antireligious methods changed through distinct time periods beginning with the Revolution, followed by periods of toleration and persecution, and in 1930 guided by more subtle methods of science and propaganda that were articulated at the Second Congress of the League of the Militant Godless in 1929. Significantly, by this time Yaroslavsky had achieved almost complete control of the antireligious propaganda machine, closely linked to the Communist Party but extending its influence far beyond it. In this way, he created a bureaucracy that mirrored what Stalin was achieving within the party. As Delaney notes, Yaroslavsky exhibited a sense of opportunism "which saw leadership of the antireligious movement as a promising fulcrum for personal power."[64]

Yaroslavsky's appeal to the Communist Party for support of his antireligious program provided Stalin with an opportunity to engage the party's influence into antireligious activity while pointing him in the direction of total control. Unfortunately, by conforming to the party's drive for collectivization, the League lost sight of its original mandate and left it vulnerable to the charged political context in which collectivization was being implemented. For example, during the drive for collectivization in early 1930, the League mobilized cadres that went out into the countryside to assist in collectivization, even attempting to form "Godless" collective farms. This drive led to excesses by overzealous local officials, which prompted directives from the Central Committee. One letter sent out in June 1930 was titled "On a Tactful Approach to Closing Churches," warning against activities that resulted in anti-Soviet attitudes and support for the clergy. Yaroslavsky published an article in *Pravda* on June 24, 1930, two days before the opening of the Party's Sixteenth Congress, in which he wrote that the antireligious campaign was also suffering from its own "dizziness from success," the result of overly ambitious leftist excesses. "Under the influence of the tremendous tangible successes of antireligious propaganda, people in some places have decided they can create 'districts of complete [*sploshnoe*] Godlessness,' and that in districts of complete collectivization, one can close every church, and so forth.... A special type of 'hurrah-atheists' have appeared, who believe that religion can be liquidated in a snap, who set a deadline for the liquidation of religion and set out to achieve it, causing great harm, antagonizing the peasants in some places."[65]

Jones focuses on the implementation of this policy grounded in science and education. As evidenced by the diary entry, Lukashevsky, who, though never named, was the source for the views of the atheists. In the article, Jones uses generic terms such as "the Atheists have now declared..." or "The Communists state..." and "According to the Communist...." Rather than using physical force, the atheists' new method was based on an "ideological form of struggle, for deep cultural propaganda."[66] Such propaganda claimed that religion was unscientific, superstitious, "symbolic of dirt, disease and drunkenness, while Atheism brings electric light, the aeroplane, and the tractor."[67] This polarity necessitates a class warfare that must be pursued with vigor because religion, Jones asserts, was being used as a "weapon to wreck the building of Socialism,"[68] including collectivization. Jones astutely captures the use of antireligious propaganda in consolidating the collectivization of agriculture.

The Lukashevsky interview provided examples of this wrecking by religious people who wrote letters and said "that these letters came from Heaven: 'I, God, tell you that the kolkhozy is Satan's work.' 'If you go into the kolkhozy, you will go to hell.'"[69] Another Lukashevsky example of kulak wrecking that Jones uses in the article related to religious peasants agitating against scientific methods by advocating for the three-field system because it was a reflection of the Holy Trinity. "Even God is for the three-field system, because God is for the Trinity, and the Trinity is symbolic for the three-field system."[70]

Moreover, religion is a tool of the old capitalist world whose missionaries are sent out for "Rockefeller, Ford, and Deterding."[71] The antireligious propaganda campaign was most successful with children, a fact Jones recorded several times in the diaries as he tramped through both the cities and towns. One little girl tells him, "Of course I don't believe in God. Only the silly, old people believe in God."[72] Jones also included the other side, quoting a girl who was going to join the Young Communist League despite the fact she believed in God. "I shall pretend to be a Communist and make wonderful Communist speeches, but all the time I shall believe in God.... For what my lips say, my heart need not believe."[73] This exchange bears a striking resemblance to one that Jones recorded during his 1931 trip on a train bound for Moscow. The second part of the quote was used almost verbatim in the third article Jones wrote for *The Times*, "A Blessed Word," in which a young girl studying to become a school teacher tells him. "If I do not become a Young Communist I shall not receive a good education, so I pretend to rejoice in their long-winded foreign words like 'industrialisation', but what my tongue says my heart does not believe."[74] That Jones recycled parts of earlier work is not altogether surprising, for he had done that with the 1932 "Will There Be Soup?" articles, although in that instance he had not been to the USSR when he wrote the articles. He certainly had fresher material he could have used. Jones ends his "Easter" article with a quotation from Hessell Tiltman, whom he met in 1932. "Long after the last anti-God poster has faded on the hoardings, the last lesson in Atheism been given in the schools, and the present Soviet leaders are no more, the love of God will be found in Russian hearts."[75]

What distinguish the *Western Mail* articles from the other series are his distinct appeals to his Welsh audience. In several articles, he related what was happening in the USSR to the Welsh experience. For example, in describing the journey into Russia as a trip back into time, he asserts that part of the backwardness could be attributed to the fact that "Russia never had the Reformation, which affected so deeply the life of Wales."[76] Similarly, when he describes the collectivization of agriculture where the land would be owned in common and run by tractors, Jones notes, "But the Russian peasant in one respect is no different from the Welsh farmer. He wants his own land, and if his land is taken away from him he will not work."[77] Nor would the Welsh farmer allow his cows to be taken away. "Imagine what would happen in the Vale of Glamorgan or in Cardiganshire if the county councils took away the cows of the farmers!"[78] Jones made certain his Welsh readers understood the implications of what was happening, making the distant seem very familiar.

'Balance Sheet of the Five-Year Plan'

The articles for *The Financial News* ran on three consecutive days, April 11-13. Titled "Balance Sheet of the Five-Year Plan," Jones analyzes the plan's impact on industrialization, the Soviet economy, and most importantly agriculture. Given the audience for these particular articles, Jones uses no anecdotal information from workers and peasants; rather, he provides hard data on factory output, prices of food products, and wages for skilled and unskilled laborers. In the article on finances, he notes, "The absence of [official] statistics upon the most vital sections of financial life makes it difficult to form a judgment concerning the currency."[79] Despite not having reliable figures, Jones still asserts that "there is a large-scale inflation..."[80] The proof he offers was based on prices of butter, meat, sugar, and bread. He also pointed to the fact that on the black market 50 to 70 roubles could be obtained for a dollar "instead of the legal 1 rouble 94 kopecks."[81]

In addition to statistical information, Jones provided reasons for the failures of industrialization and agriculture, using the very same reasons he outlined in the articles for the *Western Mail*. Even after explaining that the Five-Year Plan's emphasis on rapid industrialization and collectivization had ruined the country's agriculture, "its greatest source of wealth," Jones is cautious in predicting what might happen in the remainder of 1933. "The outlook for the next harvest is, therefore, black. It is dangerous to make any prophecy, for the miracle of perfect climatic conditions can always make good a part of the unfavourable factors."[82] Notwithstanding this caution, Jones states unequivocally that "there is a general famine threatening the lives of millions of people."[83]

In this last article for the *Financial News*, Jones points to the execution "of thirty-five prominent workers in the Commissariat of Agriculture,"[84] as symptomatic of the collapse of agriculture in the USSR. He quotes a March 5 *Pravda* article in which the accused men had "as their aim the ruining of agriculture and the creation of famine in the country."[85] Significantly, this mention of attempting to create famine, even within the context of an accusation against the thirty-five men, suggests that the Politburo was cognizant of the need to place blame for deteriorating conditions on someone, similar to blaming Ukrainian peasants for the catastrophic grain collections in November and December 1932. Jones asserts that "in the eyes of responsible foreign observers and of peasants, the famine in Russia to-day is far worse than that of 1921."[86] Jones utilizes arguments that he later included in his letter to the *New York Times*—written on May

1 but not published until May 13—responding to Duranty's March 31 article denying famine conditions. Jones asserts that he visited villages in the Moscow district, in the Black Earth district, and in North Ukraine, parts of which "are far from being the most badly hit in Russia."[87] He explains that his evidence was gathered by talking with hundreds of peasants and workers as well as foreign observers, journalists, and residents concerning the affected areas. Jones is tactful in explaining that the Politburo's attempts to conceal the famine by censoring foreign journalists have turned them into masters of euphemisms.

> The Soviet Government tries its best to conceal the situation, but the grim facts will out. Under the conditions of censorship existing in Moscow, foreign journalists have to tone down their messages and have become masters at the art of understatement. The existence of the general famine is none the less true, in spite of the fact that Moscow still has bread.[88]

At a time when Jones could easily have ridiculed Duranty, Fischer, and the others, he chose not to do so, naming no one in particular. He understood why they were forced to "give 'famine' the polite name of 'food shortage' and 'starving to death' is softened to read as 'widespread mortality from diseases due to malnutrition.'"[89] Rather than level accusations against these journalists working under duress, Jones instead sought to delineate the causes for the famine, pointing to the policies of forced collectivization, the massacre of livestock, dekulakization, and the export of foodstuffs.

Having seen firsthand the famine's devastating effect on the peasants and workers, Jones allowed his work to speak for itself. He was not attempting to spread a "big scare story"[90] or prophesize the demise of the USSR, which Duranty falsely accused him of doing. While it is difficult, if not impossible, to measure the direct impact Jones' reporting had in Great Britain and beyond, clearly there were forces at work that sought to mitigate what Jones was communicating. Those forces arguably included Hitler's rise to power in Germany in January 1933, the threat posed by Japan in the Far East, and the continuing worldwide financial crisis. That Jones' reporting of a devastating famine did not engender much of any response by Western governments remains one of the perplexing mysteries of twentieth century journalism history. And it points to why eighty years after this tragedy, we struggle to make sense of what happened, why it happened, and how we remember, or fail to remember, this famine.

Notes

1. Colley, *More Than a Grain*, 283.
2. Gareth Jones, "'We are Starving' cry from Russian Peasants," *Western Mail*, 3 April 1933, 7.
3. Wells, *Kapoot*, 243.
4. Ibid., 245.
5. Gareth Jones, Diary of Tour of Russia, March 4-10, 1933. Gareth Vaughan Jones Papers, National Library of Wales. File B1/15. Diary 1, Part 1, 28.
6. Gareth Jones, Diary of Tour of Russia, March 4-10, 1933. Gareth Vaughan Jones Papers, National Library of Wales. File B1/15. Diary 1, Part 2, 6.
7. Jones, "'We Are Starving,'" 7.
8. Gareth Jones, "My Thoughts on the Journey to Moscow," *Western Mail*, 7 April 1933, 8. See also Gareth Jones, Diary of Tour of Russia, March 4 1933. Gareth Vaughan Jones Papers, National Library of Wales. File B1/13. Diary 3, Part 2, 19.
9. Tim Tzouliadis, *The Forsaken: An American Tragedy in Stalin's Russia* (New York: Penguin Books, 2008), 6-8.
10. Ibid., 31-33.
11. Jones, "My Thoughts," 8.
12. Ibid.
13. Lyons, *Assignment in Utopia*, 519.
14. Ibid.
15. Tzouliadis, *The Forsaken*, 49; Lyons, *Assignment*, 519-523.
16. Quoted in Tzouliadis, *The Forsaken*, 49. Report no. 11,580, 7 August 1931, Berlin, RG 165, National Archives II, College Park, Maryland.
17. Gareth Jones, "Starving Russians Seething with Discontent," *Western Mail*, 4 April 1933, 1-2.
18. Ibid.
19. Ibid.
20. Gordon W. Morrell, *Britain Confronts the Stalin Revolution: Anglo-Soviet Relations and the Metro-Vickers Crisis* (Waterloo, Ontario: Wilfrid Laurier University Press, 1995), 89.
21. Gareth Jones, "O.G.P.U.'s Blow to Trade," *Western Mail*, 20 April 1933, 12.
22. Ibid.
23. Jones, "O.G.P.U.'s Reign of Terror in Russia," *Western Mail*, 5 April 1933, 8.
24. Gareth Jones, "Why People are Dying of Starvation in Russia," *Western Mail*, 8 April 1933, 7.
25. Andrew Cairns, *The Soviet Famine, 1932-33: An Eye-witness Account of Conditions in the Spring and Summer of 1932*, Tony J. Kuz, ed. (Edmonton, Alberta: Canadian Institute of Ukrainian Studies, University of Alberta Press, 1989), 81.
26. Tauger, "Natural Disaster," 11. See footnote 48 for Soviet sources.
27. Cairns, *The Soviet Famine*, 84-85.
28. Tauger, "Natural Disaster," 15.
29. Cairns, *The Soviet Famine*, 38.

30. Ibid., 113-114.
31. Ibid.
32. Ibid., 14.
33. Gareth Jones, Diary of Tour of Russia, March 1933. Gareth Vaughan Jones Papers, National Library of Wales. File B1/13. Diary 3, Part 2, 12.
34. Stalin, "Our Work in the Countryside," 220-221.
35. Jones, "Why People Are Starving," 7.
36. Mark B. Tauger, "The 1932 Harvest and the Famine of 1933," *Slavic Review*, vol. 50, no. 1 (Spring 1991) 88.
37. Jones, "Why People Are Starving," 7.
38. Gareth Jones, "Why There Is Unemployment in Russia," *Western Mail*, 10 April 1933, 11.
39. Ibid.
40. Ibid.
41. Gareth Jones, Diary of Tour of Russia, March 4-11, 1933. Gareth Vaughan Jones Papers, National Library of Wales. File B1/15. Diary 1, Part 2, 15.
42. Ibid.
43. Jones, "Unemployment," 11.
44. Ibid.
45. Ibid.
46. Gareth Jones, Diary of Tour of Russia, March 1933. Gareth Vaughan Jones Papers, National Library of Wales. File B1/16. Diary 2, Part 1, 23-24.
47. Jones, "Unemployment," 11.
48. Gareth Jones, "Soviet Ready for War," *Western Mail*, 11 April 1933, 5.
49. Ibid.
50. Ibid.
51. Davies and Wheatcroft, *The Years of Hunger*, 178.
52. Ibid., 178-179.
53. Ibid., 190-191.
54. Gareth Jones, Diary of Tour of Russia, March 1933. Gareth Vaughan Jones Papers, National Library of Wales. File B1/16. Diary 2, Part 1, 10.
55. Gareth Jones, Diary of Tour of Russia, March 4-24, 1933. Gareth Vaughan Jones Papers, National Library of Wales. File B1/15. Diary 2, 20.
56. J. Stalin, V. M. Molotov, "Order from the USSR SNK and CC AUCP(b) on preventing the mass flight of starving villagers in search of food," January 22, 1933. *Tragedy of the Soviet Countryside: Collectivization and Dekulakization, Documents and Materials in Five Volumes*. Vol. 3 (Moscow, 2001), 1007. *Top Secret: From Lubianka to Stalin on the State of the Country in Four Volumes* (Moscow, 2001, Vol. 4) 635. N. B. The document is signed by Stalin; Molotov's signature is missing.
57. Jones, "Soviet Ready for War," 5.
58. Ibid.
59. Gareth Jones, Diary of Tour of Russia, March 4-11, 1933. Gareth Vaughan Jones Papers, National Library of Wales. File B1/15. Diary 1, Part 2, 11.
60. Gareth Jones, Diary of Tour of Russia, March 1933. Gareth Vaughan Jones Papers, National Library of Wales. File B1/13. Diary 3, Part 2, 1-10. See also Gareth Jones, "Interview with Maxim Litvinow," Letter dated March 27, 1933, David Lloyd George Records. House of Lord's Office.
61. Colley, *More Than a Grain*, 301.

62. See Gareth Jones, Diary of Tour of Russia, March 4-11, 1933. Gareth Vaughan Jones Papers, National Library of Wales. File B1/13, 15, 16. Diary 1, Part 1, 20, 25, 27; Diary 1, Part 3, 10, 39-40; Diary 2, Part 1, 5, 8, 11, 15; Diary 2, Part 2, 10, 16-17; Diary 3, Part 1, 14-15.

63. Gareth Jones, "Easter in a Godless Country," *Western Mail*, 12 April 1933, n.p. Delaney notes that early *Komsomol* activities employed coarse mockeries of Easter celebrations in 1922, prompting warnings from the Central Committee.

64. Delaney, "The Origins of Soviet Antireligious Organizations," 126.

65. Peris, *Storming the Heavens*, 169-170.

66. Jones, "Easter in a Godless Country."

67. Ibid.

68. Ibid.

69. Ibid. See also Gareth Jones, Diary of Tour of Russia, March 1933. Gareth Vaughan Jones Papers, National Library of Wales. File B1/16. Diary 2, Part 2, 16-17.

70. Ibid. See also Gareth Jones, Diary of Tour of Russia, March 1933. Gareth Vaughan Jones Papers, National Library of Wales. File B1/16. Diary 2, Part 2, 18.

71. Ibid. See also Gareth Jones, Diary of Tour of Russia, March 1933. Gareth Vaughan Jones Papers, National Library of Wales. File B1/16. Diary 2, Part 2, 18.

72. Ibid. See also Gareth Jones, Diary of Tour of Russia, March 4-11, 1933. Gareth Vaughan Jones Papers, National Library of Wales. File B1/15. Diary 1, Part 3, 39-40.

73. Ibid.

74. Correspondent [Jones], "Youth," 13. See also [Heinz], *Experiences*, 55-56. See also Gareth Jones, Journal of Russian Travels, 1931, August 7-15. Gareth Vaughan Jones Papers, National Library of Wales. File B1/11. Diary 1, Part 1, 19.

75. Quoted in Jones, "Easter," n.p.

76. Jones, "My Thoughts," 8.

77. Jones, "Why People Are Dying," 7.

78. Ibid.

79. Gareth Jones, "Balance-Sheet of the Five-Year Plan: II Financial Impressions," *Financial News*, 12 April 1933, 6.

80. Ibid.

81. Ibid.

82. Gareth Jones, "Balance-Sheet of the Five-Year Plan: III Ruin of Russian Agriculture," *Financial News*, 13 April 1933, 6.

83. Ibid.

84. Ibid.

85. Ibid.

86. Ibid.

87. Ibid.

88. Ibid.

89. Gareth Jones, "Mr. Jones Replies: Former Secretary of Lloyd George Tells of Observations in Russia," *New York Times*, 13 May 1933, 12.

90. Duranty, "Russians Hungry," 13.

9

'Facts Are Stubborn Things...'

'So Much Worse'

In the months following the publication of his famine articles, Gareth Jones was anything but idle. On May 1, he responded to Duranty's article that denigrated his work as a "big scare story" while characterizing the famine as a "food shortage"[1] by writing a Letter to the Editor of the *New York Times*. The letter was published on May 17. By the end of the month Jones was back in Germany, reporting on the rise of Nazi militarism and the persecution of the Jews. During a visit with the Haferkorns in Danzig, he met the German consul stationed in Kharkov and his wife, who privately corroborated Jones' famine articles. In a letter to his parents dated May 28, Jones writes about conditions there.

> The German Consul in Kharkov and his wife thought that my Russian articles gave a wonderful picture, but that it was really much worse than I described it. Since March it has got so much worse that it is horrible to be in Kharkoff. So many dying, ill and beggars. They are dying off in the villages, he said, and the spring sowing campaign is <u>catastrophic</u>. The peasants have been eating the seed. To talk of a bumper harvest, as Molotoff did, was a tragic farce, and he only said that to keep up the spirits, but nobody believed Molotoff. Many villages are empty. The fate of the German colonists is terrible, [and] in some villages 25% have died off and there will be more dying off until August.[2]

Significantly, this evaluation of the famine by the German consul in Kharkov not only confirmed Jones' accurate reporting, but it also marked the famine as an ideological tool that Hitler used as a "condemnation of left-wing politics."[3]

Even though Jones published no additional articles about the famine for British newspapers, two famine articles were syndicated by Hearst-owned newspapers in early June. Significantly, the first sub-head used in the second article states: "The famine man made."[4] As he had in one of the articles for the *Western Mail*, Jones asserts that the famine was not caused by climatic conditions. "It is the result of the Soviet policy of abolishing the private farm and replacing it by large collective farms, where the land and cattle were owned in common."[5] Later, Jones continues this line of reasoning. "The Soviet leaders took everything into account except one thing—the human factor. They studied the soil, the tractor, science, fertilizers, but omitted—MAN."[6]

Jones' assertion that the famine was man-made may very well have come from having seen the same assertion published in a *New York Times* editorial on January 1, 1933, titled "The Five-Year Plan." The writer asserts that a mood of anxiety and anguish prevailed in Moscow despite completion of the Plan. Only one thing kept the Soviet Government from being able to boast about its accomplishments. "But there exists today the serious complication of a grave food shortage. The country is already on something close to a war-ration basis. What makes things harder for the Stalin Government is that hunger has not come upon the Russian land as an act of GOD; it is man-made. There has been no drought."[7] The *Times* editorial writer goes on to say that the "food shortage is the result of a nation-wide peasant strike precipitated by the rough-shod methods of the Soviet Government in hacking through to its industrialization objectives."[8] Placing the blame on a "nation-wide peasant strike" illustrates how distorted the *New York Times* viewed the situation. Rather than stating that the famine was a direct result of Stalin-orchestrated Politburo decrees, the writer couches the accusation within tempered phrases like "roughshod methods" and "hacking through to its industrialization objectives." Just how starving peasants could have organized such a nationwide strike is never explained. It must be remembered that this editorial was published only weeks after Duranty published his November series in which he pointed to harsh conditions but months before Duranty denigrated Jones' reporting, raising the question as to whether it was the *New York Times* following Duranty's lead in denying the famine or whether Duranty was following the editorial board's lead.

It's difficult to believe Jones would not have been aware of this editorial. In both of his syndicated articles for the American newspapers and his article for the *Western Mail* Jones writes, "The famine ... cannot be attributed to weather, for in the last few years climatic conditions have—with the exception of drought in some areas in 1931—*blessed* the Soviet government."[9] The *New York Times* editorial asserts, "The country indeed is said to have been *blessed* with the best planting and growing weather"[10] (emphasis added). It is highly unlikely this repetition was mere coincidence; more likely, it was Jones using the very language of the newspaper in which his good name and integrity as a reporter had been called into question by Walter Duranty to make his point.

'Striking Confirmation'

By August, Jones was cited by activists seeking to galvanize public opinion about the need for relief efforts by the International Red Cross and Western governments. On August 20, the *New York Times* published an appeal by Cardinal Theodor Innitzer, Archbishop of Vienna, who called on those governments "negotiating for the enlargement of economic relations with Soviet Russia ... [to] make those negotiations dependent on the comprehension of the necessity for help in the stricken districts of that country."[11] Cardinal Innitzer cites Andreas Scheeptyckyj, Metropolitan of Galicia; Jones; and Dr. Ewald Ammende, general secretary of the Nationalities Congress. Innitzer notes that Jones "confirms this [famine conditions] and has established by inquiries on the spot that in some districts already a quarter of the population have perished from hunger."[12]

On August 30, the *Western Mail* carried an edited version of Cardinal Innitzer's appeal. It begins the story with a note that "Striking confirmation of Mr. Gareth Jones' revelations in the *Western Mail & South Wales News* of the famine conditions in Russia is provided by the Cardinal Archbishop of Vienna, who has issued the following appeal to the world..."[13] When Jones visited Vienna in August, he was welcomed as something of a hero. In a letter to his family he writes, "I discover to my amazement that here in Vienna I am famous!! because of my Russian articles and also because the Cardinal referred to me. So I am in clover and am meeting most interesting people."[14] The article ends with an assertion that references Dr. Otto Schiller, the German Agricultural Attaché in Moscow, who published a three-part report in the *Daily Telegraph* on August 25, 28 and 30. "The report of Dr. Schiller, agricultural expert at the German Embassy, Moscow, fully bears out the tragic conclusions of Dr. Ammende and of Mr. Gareth Jones."[15] The *Western Mail* obtained an edited version of this report, which Schiller had written in May, despite the ban on travel in the Soviet Union by foreign newspaper representatives.

The *Telegraph* series provides an introduction in which it explains that even though "a permit has just been refused to a correspondent [Schiller] who wished to visit country places in the North Caucasus and Ukraine.... These articles consist of detailed report by an expert agricultural observer who has been in the habit of visiting these regions from time to time."[16] Further, the three articles are based on a report not intended for publication "but for the information of the writer's principals, and has been put into our hand because it reveals, with detail which only be gathered on the spot, conditions which may hitherto only been hinted at."[17] It is interesting that the *Western Mail* was quite determined to confirm Jones' reports about the famine to the point of naming Schiller as the author of the *Daily Telegraph* anonymous series, given the fact the *Western Mail* assigned Jones to cover anything but events in the Soviet Union.

'Trampled'

No further articles on famine in the Soviet Union were published in the major British newspapers beyond August 1933. Dr. Colley asserts that this was indicative of Jones being cast into the wilderness.

> No longer in the exciting milieu of London, he was trampled on by his political acquaintances; the establishment ostracized him for their own political ends, and his journalist colleagues shunned him, perhaps jealous of his international "scoop" of the exposing of the Soviet famine.[18]

By "trampled on," Dr. Colley may be referring to the fact that any mention of Jones is largely absent from the archives of David Lloyd George and from the biography of Lloyd George written by A. J. Sylvester, who worked for the prime minister during Jones' two stints with him. Nonetheless, Jones and Lloyd George came together in August 1933 at the Welsh Eisteddfod, "where poets and authors keeping the Welsh language alive..."[19] Jones reported on the event for the *Western Mail* and sent clippings to Lloyd George. Although the former prime minister did not reply directly, Frances Stevenson, his secretary, sent Jones a letter thanking him for the articles, noting that Lloyd George "read them with the greatest of enjoyment and he congratulates you on having collected such an interesting series."[20] Stevenson closes the letter by extending an invitation to Jones to visit. "Mr. Lloyd George would, I know, be delighted to see you."[21] On the surface, this cordial letter reveals no lingering animosity, even though the two men never saw each other again.

In June 1933 Jones covered the World Economic Conference in London, where Dr. Colley theorizes Lloyd George and Litvinov deliberately shunned Jones. In his letter Jones offers a different description of events and a markedly different reception by other journalists.

> I have thoroughly enjoyed the Conference and met a number of journalist friends. It is great fun and I am exceedingly happy in my work. All the journalists like Dewall and Scheffer and Cummings are most kind.
> A. J. Cummings has the same picture as I have on Russia. He says that practically everybody is hungry, that the spring sowing is rotten, that there's not even enough food in Moscow or Leningrad and that the workers are undernourished.[22]

Jones' upbeat demeanor belies any notion that he had been shunned by journalist colleagues. Additionally, Jones received several congratulatory letters on his articles from A. Beverley Baxter (*The Daily Express*), Sir Bernard Pares, and Professor Jules Menken from the London School of Economics. Baxter's letter was a mix of congratulations and business dealings since he alerted Jones that the business office would be sending him a cheque for the work. "First let me congratulate you on the first rate stuff you sent us. I am very pleased with you indeed and hope that this will not be the last time we shall be associated together."[23] In his letter, Menken lauded the articles as well as the courage Jones demonstrated in getting the information.

> I read your articles in the *Express* as they came out and wanted to write you before Easter but couldn't manage to do so. Now I have read them again and should like to send my very hearty congratulations on a splendid piece of work. What a dreadful situation Russia must be in! I immensely admire the articles you have done and still more the trip which lies behind them.[24]

More dubious was the official position taken by the British Foreign Office, which had firsthand knowledge of the famine but advised against making the information public. In July, William Strang sent several dispatches to Sir John Simon regarding evidence of the famine, even in Moscow. "The suffering and death inflicted upon the population are regarded as the normal casualties of a nation-wide operation in class warfare (a class war to end classes) in which the authorities are confident that victory will be theirs."[25] Despite such information, the Foreign Office adopted a policy of restraint. For example, Sir Laurence Collier, head of the Foreign Office Northern Department, furnished a reply to Sir Waldron Smithers, who had enquired the situation in the USSR.

The truth of the matter is, of course, that we have a certain amount of information about famine conditions in the south of Russia similar to what has appeared in the press, and that there is no obligation on us not to make it public. We do not want to make it public, however, because the Soviet Government would resent it and our relations with them would be prejudiced.[26]

Clearly, the British government avoided making public comments on the famine, fearing it would jeopardize its relations with the USSR after the six Metro-Vickers engineers were released on July 1, and the trade embargo was lifted soon thereafter. Advocating better relations with the Soviet Union became a matter of greater importance for Great Britain as National Socialism in Germany under Hitler took on more ominous, militaristic overtones. Whether or not the British government then "suppressed further reporting by Gareth fearing to give offence to the Soviet Union,"[27] as Dr. Colley suggests, is certainly an interesting possibility, even though it is not clear just how the government planned to implement such a reporting ban, perhaps indirectly by eliciting the support of publishers and editors. Dr. Colley does note that before his trip to the USSR, Jones had agreements to write articles on Russia for *The Economist* and *The Times*, neither of which came to fruition.

Despite these setbacks, Jones remained focused on world affairs. In early June after visiting Germany, Jones published several articles in the *Western Mail* that were critical of the Nazis. What Jones saw there reminded him of what he had seen in the Soviet Union—propaganda messages being communicated via film, wireless, stage, posters, and public demonstrations, all to arouse nationalistic fervor. Jones asserts that the Brownshirt in Germany resembled the Soviet Young Communist in having an idealism rooted in self-sacrifice, courage, selflessness, and a willingness to work tirelessly for the sake of a charismatic leader. Jones also recognized the dark side of such fanaticism.

But the idealism of the Nazis and of the Bolsheviks has its dark side of intolerance, and their faith is that of the fanatic who, driven by deep emotion, keeps his mind completely closed to another point of view.[28]

The British government took no direct action against Jones, and by mid-June he was back in London covering the World Economic Conference, where he reported on the speeches by Lloyd George and Litvinov. Jones describes Litvinov as being "mild and guarded.... The bright picture he painted of the Soviet Union was based on Soviet statistics, which are unreliable, and was intended to serve as propaganda rather than a real contribution to the Conference."[29] Jones' reporting on the conference was measured and balanced, hardly warranting action by the government to suppress him.

'The Dark Side of Intolerance'

Similarly, if indeed "journalist friends shunned him,"[30] it is not clear to what extent this impacted Jones personally or professionally. That Jones was stung by the Duranty denial is clear, evidenced by his request for support sent in a letter to Malcolm Muggeridge, to which Muggeridge responded on April 17 from Switzerland. In his response Muggeridge thanks Jones for his letter, which included praise for Muggeridge's series on the famine that had been published in March. "Duranty is, of course, a plain crook, though an amusing little man in his way,"[31] Muggeridge writes. Toward the end of the letter, Muggeridge adds, "If you send me a cutting of Duranty's piece, I'll gladly write to the NEW YORK TIMES a letter of protest."[32] Muggeridge ends the letter by apologizing that he wouldn't be back in England for some time because of the need to finish a book project and to earn some money. "When I am in England, however, I'll be delighted to come to Cardiff and lecture."[33]

Muggeridge did at least compose a Letter to the Editor of the *New York Times*, dated April 26 from Rossinières, Canton de Vaud, Switzerland. In this letter, which was never published, Muggeridge writes that it "has been brought to my notice that, in your March 30th [sic] issue, a message from your Moscow correspondent whose tendency was to discredit certain reports made by Mr. Gareth Jones on the conditions prevailing in agricultural districts in the Soviet Union."[34] Muggeridge then explains that his eight months as a correspondent in Soviet Russia and what he learned from agricultural experts in the impacted areas "led me to come to precisely the same conclusions as Mr. Gareth Jones."[35] Muggeridge outlines the causes for the famine, which he argues was worse than the famine of 1921, pointing to forced collectivization, the exporting of food products, and the establishment of politotdel in the machine-tractor stations, "which are under the control of, and to a large extent manned by, the Ogpu, and whose function is, to return to your correspondent's vivid, if cynical, metaphor, to go on cracking eggs in the hope that omlette may still be available in the Kremlin.... Though I have no doubts whatever about the Soviet Government's ability and preparedness to go on cracking eggs, every kind of egg, I am convinced that before very long there will be no omlette left for anything."[36] A carbon copy of this letter resides in the Jones archives, presumably furnished by Muggeridge. The length and rambling nature of the letter in part explains why the *New York Times* chose not to publish it, if it had been, in fact, ever sent. Perhaps having returned the favor by writing this letter was as much as Muggeridge felt he needed to do.

In the meantime, Jones wrote a Letter to the Editor of the *Manchester Guardian*, published on May 3, titled "The Peasants in Russia: Exhausted Supplies," in which he confirms Muggeridge's conclusions about the conditions in the Soviet countryside and congratulates him "on having been the first journalist to have informed Britain of the true situation of Russian agriculture."[37] Jones explains his own journey through the villages and the fate of the peasants, and expresses a wish "that something could be done to relieve the suffering of the peasants in Russia.... I hope that fellow liberals who boil at any injustices in Germany or Italy or Poland will express just one word of sympathy with the millions of peasants who are victims of persecution and famine in the Soviet Union."[38]

Even though Jones forwarded Muggeridge clippings of Duranty's reporting in early autumn, Muggeridge reneged on his promise, using the timing as his excuse. Not surprisingly, Duranty was the first Western journalist allowed to travel beyond Moscow when the travel restriction was lifted. In a letter dated September 29 Muggeridge was blunt in his assessment, but he shied away from a confrontation. "He [Duranty] just writes what they tell him to. At the same time, since his message refers to the new harvest I can't challenge him on first hand knowledge. That is to say, I know and you know that his description of things in the Caucasus is untrue; he can always retort, 'You haven't seen and I have.'" Muggeridge then proposes a project in which he would take specimens of Duranty's writings and write a satirical piece "that a paper like TRUTH might publish, and that might do some good."[39] By putting his own concerns before those of Jones, Muggeridge failed to support Jones, the one person who had gone out of his way to corroborate his work. Muggeridge published a number of books and articles in which he chronicles his journey from enthusiastic communist to disillusioned realist about the Soviet regime.

'Not a Soviet Apologist'

Despite their efforts, neither Jones nor Muggeridge was able to effectively counter the distinct advantage Duranty enjoyed by September 1933 when he travelled into the famine-stricken areas. Even before he ventured into the Caucasus, however, Duranty continued to denigrate any notion of a famine to describe conditions. In a front page story published on August 24 in the *New York Times* and titled "Famine Toll Heavy in Southern Russia," Duranty argues that any "report of a famine in Russia is today an exaggeration or malignant propaganda."[40] Conceding that food shortages had "caused heavy loss of life," he estimates that the death rate had trebled in the grain-growing areas, "not so much from actual starvation as from manifold diseases due to lowered resistance and to general disease in the last year…"[41] Employing the same type of double-speak that characterizes his March 31 article denigrating Jones' reporting, Duranty attempts to explain why the price of bread was doubled, rationalizing that this rise in price would end the rationing more quickly. Perhaps realizing how ridiculous this must have sounded, Duranty offers an explanation of his tortured logic.

> In any other country this explanation would sound fantastic, but the Soviet Union is not any other country, and in making this explanation, the writer is not a "Soviet apologist" but is stating facts….This may sound extraordinary to American readers but it happens to be true.[42]

Muggeridge and Lyons assert that Duranty told several people that the famine had killed many millions.[43] Additionally, William Strang sent Sir John Simon, the Foreign Secretary, a summary of what Duranty had told the British chancery in Moscow upon his return from the area in late September 1933. Strang writes:

> According to Mr. Duranty, the population of the North Caucasus and the Lower Volga has decreased in the past year by 3 million, and the population of the Ukraine by 4-5 million…. Mr. Duranty thinks it quite possible that as many as ten million people may have died directly or indirectly from lack of food in the Soviet Union during the past year.[44]

Nonetheless, in articles published in the *New York Times*, Duranty never uses such figures. In fact, he debunks the idea of famine in subsequent articles like "Abundance Found in North Caucasus." Duranty begins the article by saying any "use of the word 'famine' in connection with the North Caucasus is a sheer absurdity…."[45] Explaining that he recently completed an unaccompanied 300-mile automobile tour through Central Kuban without "an Intourist guide" or changes to his proposed itinerary, Duranty asserts that present conditions in no way compare with the 1921 Volga famine, "with which certain anti-Bolshevist elements abroad and some credulous American correspondents in Berlin and elsewhere have compared the present situation here."[46] Duranty relates that he saw only plump babies and husky women hoisting wheat to the threshing machines, the markets teeming with eggs, fruits, vegetables, poultry, milk and butter, all at prices lower than what could be found in Moscow. What surprises Duranty the most is the fact that the authorities had restricted the travel of foreign correspondents at all, even if they had written articles with distressing facts. "Maybe the facts were distressing then, and facts, as Lenin said, 'are stubborn things,' which even the Moscow censorship cannot overcome. For the writer's part, he believes the distressing facts were exaggerated."[47] Duranty even admits that he may have been guilty of exaggerating the death rate when saying it had trebled in the North Caucasus. Everything can easily be explained: empty villages, desolate fields, the loss of livestock provide evidence of a struggle, but those elements of kulak wrecking have been defeated. "So your correspondent reaches the conclusion that the 'good' peasants had a 'hardish' time last Winter... and that the 'bad' peasants, or kulaks, suffered the fate of the vanquished in any cruel war."[48]

In subsequent articles, Duranty's again uses the analogy of war to describe what happened in Ukraine where his estimates of the death rate he says were too low. "Here, too, in the Ukraine the Kremlin has won the battle with the peasant." That the Kremlin took too much grain from the area is one of those "blunt facts" necessitated by the threat of war in the Far East. After all, "this has been a struggle comparable in effect and intensity with Verdun. And victories cost lives."[49] What matters most to Duranty is that the Kremlin won its war with the peasant, regardless of the senseless and horrifying suffering people endured. Lyons relates that upon Duranty's return from his tour, he "gave us his fresh impressions in brutally frank terms and they added up to a picture of ghastly horror. His estimate of the dead from famine was the most startling I had as yet heard from anyone."[50] When one of the dinner guests suggests he doesn't mean the figure literally, Duranty responds, "Hell I don't...I'm being conservative. But they're only Russians."[51] The duplicity of Duranty's reporting can be seen in this cynical dismissal of the peasantry, whom he obviously despised, and in the fact that what he published publicly was so different from what he readily shared privately with friends, colleagues, and diplomats from Western governments. Only in his 1949 book *Stalin and Co.* did Duranty finally admit that "1932 was a year of famine in Russia...the mass migration of destitute peasants from the countryside to the towns and cities; epidemics of typhus and other diseases of malnutrition; great influx of beggars into Moscow and Leningrad."[52] It's not clear why Duranty changed his tune about the famine, for, as Taylor notes, he was incapable "of seeing any event in a light other than that dictated by the pattern he himself had created over the years. His stubborn adherence to his own pronouncements made him a slave to his former convictions."[53]

'A Shrug of the Shoulders'

Duranty was not the only dupe who willfully towed the famine-denying line. Édouard Herriot, the former Premier of France, visited Ukraine in August. In preparation of his visit to Kiev, food was shipped in and displayed in shop windows; police dispersed the crowds who could only stare and wonder since the shops had been empty all year.[54] When he arrived in Kharkov, he was taken to the Felik Dzerzhinsky Children's Commune, where he was shown children who were healthy, clean, nicely dressed, and well fed. Herriot's visit was reported by the *New York Times* in which Heriot is quoted as saying, "When one believes that the Ukraine is devastated by famine, allow me to shrug my shoulders."[55] Not surprisingly the September 13, 1933, issue of *Pravda* writes that Herriot "categorically contradicted the lies of the bourgeoisie press in connection with a famine in the USSR."[56]

That the Soviets could go to considerable lengths to impress and beguile foreign dignitaries with carefully choreographed exhibitions has been well documented by scholars and journalists. For example, in *Everything Flows*, Vasily Grossman recounts the Herriot visit. "He was taken to some village, to a collective-farm nursery school, and he asked the children what they'd had for lunch that day. 'Chicken soup with pies and rice croquettes,' came the answer. I saw those words with my own eyes, I can see that piece of newspaper [*Pravda*] even now.... Killing millions of people on the quiet and then duping the whole world."[57] Additionally, in *Forsaken*, Tim Tzouliadis shows how in 1944 U.S. Vice President Henry Wallace was taken on a twenty-five day tour of Kolyma and Far East Russia. The deceptions continued throughout the visit

> ...as the American vice president was walked through a charade designed to conceal the true nature of what was taking place around him. Like a moving stage set, everything in Kolyma had been carefully managed for Wallace's willing eyes. No beguiling detail was left untouched in the Soviet effort to convince Wallace that what lay before him was a vision of pioneers at work, not the reality of a network of death camps.[58]

'This Great Error'

Doubtlessly disappointed by the denials, Jones never abandoned his commitment to exposing the deleterious effects that the Five-Year Plan had on Soviet agriculture. In April 1933, he completed an academic-like study of Soviet agriculture, which may have been meant for Lloyd George and/or Ivy Lee. Additionally, in the autumn and winter of 1933-1934, Jones delivered a series of lectures in several cities within Great Britain and Ireland titled "The Enigma of Bolshevik Russia," (Illustration 18) with the objective of making public the failures of the Soviet regime. At some point, Jones created an outline for a book, titled *Bread Rules Russia*, which included nineteen chapters. The first six chapters deal with the importance and history of the peasant in Russian agriculture, with emphasis on the Revolution, NEP, and collectivization. The next six chapters deal with the effects of agricultural failure upon industry, foreign trade, worker rights, and justice. Subsequent chapters deal with bread and religion, bread and the army, bread and education, ending with bread and the future.

Jones wrote Chapter One, basing it primarily on an encounter he had with a peasant along the railway track when he first departed the train during his tramp through many villages in March 1933. Employing some of the same techniques he used in his newspaper articles, Jones invites the reader into an ordinary peasant's world.

> Let us call him Stepan Ivanovitch and follow him to his cottage, after leaving the railway track and penetrating a village which seems strangely silent and devoid of the sounds of cattle and of horses.[59]

Stepan Ivanovitch serves as a composite character for many of the peasants he encountered on his journey. Utilizing many of the anecdotes he recorded in his notebook diaries, Jones uses Stepan and his family to build a representative picture of starvation and hatred for the collectivized farm. Jones argues that it is "the land-hungry, individualistic bearded Stepan Ivanovitch"[60] who is the prototypical Russian, not the young communist shock-brigade worker. The peasant is a force, but a passive, unorganized force, unable to express his will; as a result, "he has been passed aside by foreign admirers of the Five-Year Plan. The aim of this book is to remedy this great error in the judgment of Russian events..."[61] Only by recognizing the importance of bread can one truly understand what "guides Russia's destiny during and after this century."[62] This brief manuscript illustrates the historical path Jones believed Soviet Russia had taken.

Even though Jones was assigned to cover stories about Wales, he published a book review in the *Western Mail* on September 20, 1933, titled "Opening the Door to Soviet Literature," in which he reviews a new anthology of Soviet writers translated into English. Praising both the translation and the introduction, Jones explains the book's value. "At last it is possible for the English critic or the English student of Soviet affairs to step into the new and little explored land inhabited by revolutionary writers."[63] Jones uses his March 20 interview with the writer Valentin Kataev, fully documented in his diary, to explain the role of the writer in the Five-Year Plan. Even though Jones says that he was impressed by Kataev for opening "an outlook which was fantastic to me, but real to him—the outlook of a writer whose heart has throbbed in the passionate days of a vast revolution," he concludes by noting that thousands of British readers can now experience "an adventure into revolutionary literary ideas."[64] Significantly, one part of the interview that Jones did not include in his review involved Jones asking Kataev: "If I were an artist and I wrote a play about real life in the village and did not end in success of collectivization, what would happen?" Kataev answers, "The Professional Trade Union and actors would not play it."[65] During his journey, Jones constantly probed his sources—whether they were involved in finance, agriculture, or art—about what was happening in the countryside.

If Jones could tolerate literary ideas, he was less tolerant of the Five-Year Plan's political agenda. Jones spoke out against the Five-Year Plan at the twelfth annual meeting of the Institute of World Affairs in Riverside, California, in mid-December 1934. He is quoted in a United Press report as saying, "The famine is a result of the Soviet policy of Collectivization, which takes the land from the Russian peasant and destroys his desire to work. The exile of five million Kulaks was one of the most brutal crimes in European history."[66] Even though he attributes the famine's cause to Soviet policy, his pointing to the exile of kulaks and not the millions of deaths by starvation as a brutal crime is noteworthy. Additionally, Jones ends his speech with a warning about another possible catastrophe resulting from the rapid development of armaments. "The final seed of catastrophe lies in the rapid development of the aeroplane as a military weapon. I have in the last few years been wandering in European countries and America and if I were asked: 'What sound do you recall most vividly after your travels?' I should reply: 'The burr of aeroplane propellers.'.... The burr of the aeroplane wings will be the first sound of the next war, if this war is to come."[67] Jones astutely predicted how World War II would be conducted, testimony to his thorough understanding of the political situation in Europe at this time.

The final series of famine articles that Jones wrote was for William Randolph Hearst, whom Jones had met in June 1934 at the newspaper magnate's Welsh estate of St. Donat's Castle at Llantwit Major a few miles southwest of both Cardiff and Barry, where the Jones family house was located. This was only months before Hearst visited Germany to take the waters at Bad Nauheim in September where he met with two of Hitler's most trusted Nazi propagandists to learn how Nazism could present a better image in the U.S. When Hearst went to Berlin later in the month, he was taken to see Hitler. Conspicuously absent from the article based on his initial interview with Hearst was any mention of the Soviet Union or Germany. Evidently, Hearst was impressed enough with Jones' understanding of world affairs to invite him to his ranch at San Simeon, California, when Jones travelled to the United States as part of his "Round the World Fact Finding Tour," which he wanted to begin upon completion of his employment with the *Western Mail* in the autumn of 1934. In July, he wrote to his parents outlining his options, including writing for International News, the *Daily Telegraph*, *Berliner Tageblatt* and the *Western Mail*, all of which would publish Jones' stories over the next year. Again, in September, he writes, "Now for really splendid news. Just imagine it. The Manchester Guardian wants a series of six articles on the Far East and two articles on America. That is a great compliment and augurs very well for the future."[68]

Before setting sail for the United States aboard the *S.S. Manhattan* on October 26, 1934, Jones wrote a number of articles about the worsening conditions in Germany—the Roehm revolt, the murder of Austrian chancellor Englebert Dollfuss, and the death of Paul von Hindenburg. During a visit to Germany he met with Paul Scheffer, for whom Jones agreed to cover the U.S. Congressional elections in early November. Upon arriving in the United States, Jones visited friends before completing the assignment, though not without difficulty. Jones intended on cabling his story from the offices of the *New York Herald Tribune*. Unable to use Commercial Cables to wire his story to Berlin, Jones sat in the crowded newspaper office until he noticed someone he recognized, Ralph W. Barnes, whom he had met in Moscow.

I went up and he gave me a wonderful welcome. He introduced me to all the political editors as a leading journalistic figure. (It is funny newspapermen know me here because I "scooped" the world on the Russian famine, and because all my stuff was confirmed by the most responsible American journalists later.)... It was one of the most exciting and enjoyable nights I've had. There is nothing like the thrill of sending the latest news from

New York to Berlin, and you see that Paul Scheffer was very pleased with my cable.[69]

Jones' parenthetical commentary reveals the extent to which he was still carrying the sting of the famine denials by Duranty and Fischer, as well as the lack of support from Lloyd George and Muggeridge. While it is not clear whom he meant by "the most responsible American journalists" and why he didn't include Barnes among those, Jones obviously relished in the attention, which probably contributed to this being "one of the most exciting and enjoyable nights" he'd had in a while. That this compared with his flight with Hitler, his interview with Lenin's widow, the RIIA lectures, or his news conference upon returning from the USSR suggests a real need for recognition of his famine articles. Jones didn't often gloat, even though he kept meticulous care of his clippings; in fact, he'd already created an album for his "Round the World Fact-Finding Tour" in anticipation of the articles he would write, as he'd often done before. In early February 1933, he wrote home asking for his clippings. "Please send me my articles—I always like to see them as soon as possible; because I do not know what I have written! Please also state whether 'leader page' or which. They are absolutely essential in helping me to write the next ones."[70]

In this same letter detailing his meeting with Barnes, Jones also mentions that in addition to meeting with the president of International News Service, for whom he was to write a series of articles on the Far East, he "was shown round the *New York Times* offices."[71] Although Jones offers no details about that visit, it's interesting to speculate what he thought upon seeing the plaque for the 1932 Pulitzer Prize with Walter Duranty's name on it.

Later in November, he met with the Japanese ambassador to the United States, Hiroshi Saito, perhaps to solicit information regarding the situation in Manchukuo, which was certainly one of the places Jones intended on investigating. In a letter to Ivy Lee, Jones writes, "I hope to go to Manchukuo and if there is a war somewhere I hope to get some experience as a war correspondent.... In the meantime I am looking around for any prospect of newspaper work I can do while going round the world."[72] By New Year's Day, Jones arrived at Hearst's San Simeon ranch where he contracted to write three short articles on the USSR for two-hundred and twenty-five dollars. The three-part series ran from January 12-14 and was syndicated in many Hearst newspapers. That the ultra-conservative, nationalist, Nazi-sympathizing Hearst commissioned Jones for these three articles is not surprising given the fact that Hearst had launched an anti-communist campaign focused on the Soviet famine of 1932-1933, according to Ewald

Ammende. "On January 5, 1935, William Randolph Hearst broadcast a speech based almost entirely on the account of the [Cardinal] Innitzer Committee.... The entire Hearst press next proceeded to deal with the Russian famine."[73]

'Such Ruthless Slaughter'

Despite not having been to the USSR for twenty-one months, Jones furnished Hearst with three articles that rehashed conditions he had found in March 1933, although Jones frames this series around a new wave of terror precipitated by the murder of Sergei M. Kirov, assassinated in the Smolny Institute, the headquarters of the Leningrad party *obkom*, on December 1, 1934. The assassin, Leonid Nikolaev, was a frustrated party apparatchik who had gained entry to Kirov's third-floor office and shot him on the spot.

Jones begins the first article by asserting that 1935 has dawned as a period of terror not seen for many years, and then he poses a question as to why Stalin should be unleashing "such ruthless slaughter upon Soviet citizens..."[74] The real reason for this new wave of executions can be traced to "a feeling of revolt and of hatred of the Communists that Stalin can only crush by terror and still more terror." This feeling, Jones asserts, he found when "I wandered alone on foot through a number of Russian villages, sleeping on hard floors of peasants' huts, and speaking to the rank and file of the real folk, to the 'forgotten men,' in their own language, Russian."[75] Jones then recounts his March 1933 journey, establishing the parameters by contrasting the luxury of a reception hosted by the Soviet Foreign Office where he is told about the "wonderful triumphs in the villages"[76] with the actual starvation conditions of the countryside. The remainder of this first article utilizes material from previous articles for the *Western Mail* and the *Daily Express*—the ban on journalists' travel, a warning from the embassy not to travel, the train ride "in a dark, smelling wooden train bound for the south,"[77] the hungry peasant devouring an orange peel and crust of bread, the gruesome refrain of "*Hleba Nietu*," and a disillusioned young communist's lament about broken promises. This member of the Young Communist League, or *Komsomol*, expresses disillusionment with the Five-Year Plan. "The Five-Year Plan is over and there is starvation throughout the land. No wonder there is a feeling of revolt."[78]

Significantly, this is the only mention of the Five-Year Plan in the three articles for Hearst. Arguably, the Five-Year Plan constituted the most important element of the articles Jones wrote from 1930-1933; however, the focus noticeably shifted to the Communist Party in the

1935 series. For example, the young communist makes a prediction of trouble for the party. "There'll be trouble within the Communist party, if the peasants and the workers in the small towns do not get more to eat, mark my words."[79] Why Jones used this "prophecy" when he certainly knew that conditions in the famine-stricken areas had improved since the harvest of 1933 is not clear. Further, Jones knew that the possibility of a revolt was remote. As early as July 1933, a Mr. Bailakoff from Australia had attempted to dissuade Jones of the notion that the famine had increased nationalist feelings. Bailakoff writes:

> It seems to me that your assumption that the famine has increased the nationalist feelings amongst the Ukrainians and other minor nationalities is entirely wrong and cannot be justified by facts…. Moscow is blamed not because it is a centre of the State which wants to subjugate the minor nations, but because it is a communist centre. There is no real separatist movement in the Ukraine or anywhere else. On the contrary, even those minor nations (Georgia, for instance) which formerly were decidedly separatist, have now realized the futility of the separatist idea from the point of view of their vital economic and political interests.[80]

While Bailakoff's point about the futility of a separatist movement in light of economic and political interests is cogent, there is no question that in December 1932 the Politburo enacted stringent decrees to punish Ukrainization, linking the long-established national policy with the failure of the grain collections. In effect, Ukrainization or any other type of nationalism was deemed anti-Bolshevik, punishable by exile to a concentration camp for five to ten years. Nationalism was portrayed in party propaganda as part of a kulak web of anti-Soviet wrecking by counter-revolutionary non-Russian minorities.

In effect, the young communist's "prophecy" is strategically used to remind Jones of the Kirov assassination and the revenge enacted on more than a hundred Soviet citizens executed as conspirators and provides him with a way to transition to the next article. "But more striking than that prophecy was what I saw during my tramp through Russian villages which began shortly after my talk with the disillusioned young Communist."[81]

'Golod'

The Hearst articles can be seen as digressions on the themes established in the 1933 series. Given that Jones was on a "Round the World Fact

Finding Tour," it is doubtful he had access to his diaries or copies of the published articles, except perhaps the two articles published in American newspapers during June 1933. If, indeed, he was working from memory, Jones understandably demonstrates less than perfect recall in delineating the details of his journey through the Russian countryside and his stay in Kharkov, which serve as the basis for the second and third articles respectively. For example, the young communist's "prophecy" appears in neither the diaries nor the *Daily Express* article of April 5, titled "Soviet Confiscate Part of Workers' Wages," in which this young Communist figures prominently. Nonetheless, Jones uses the same "gruesome refrains" — "There is no bread" and "All are swollen" — to convey the feelings of despair and desperation in the famine-stricken villages that he visited. To these, Jones introduces a word he had not used previously, "*golod*," which means "famine."[82] And the causes for this "man-made famine" are attributed to the communists "…because the Communists had demanded that they give up their cattle…" and "…because the Communists have cursed God…" and "Why should we allow the Communists to steal what is our own?" and "…the discussion continued of how the Communists had brought ruin to the countryside by their policy of taking the land and the grain and the cow away from the farmer…"[83] Jones clearly frames these articles around the peasants' hatred of the Communist Party.

The third article, "Fate of Thrifty in USSR," again lays the blame for the famine squarely at the feet of the communists. While ostensibly the article was intended to show how famine ravaged even the larger cities like Kharkov, Jones begins by describing the ruthlessness of the class warfare waged in the villages against the kulaks.

> The Communists I spoke to did not deny that they had ruthlessly exiled the hardest working farmers. On the contrary they were proud of it, and boasted that they would show no mercy to those who wanted to own their own land.
> "We must be strong and crush the accursed enemies of the working class," the Communists would say to me. "Let them suffer now. We have no place for them in our society."[84]

Children who denounce their parents to the secret police for stealing grain are elevated to the status of hero. When peasants refuse to form a collective farm, *Komsomolets* are called in "and THEY shot down all the peasants who would not give up their land and their cows."[85] Jones' own arrest in a small railroad station is dramatized, somewhat more sensationally than the way he dramatized the incident in the April 4 *Western Mail* article, "Starving Russians Seething with Discontent," in which he described it in two paragraphs. In the Hearst article, peasants are explaining that the famine is not the fault of nature but the fault of the communists when an OGPU policeman interrupts them and demands to see Jones' documents. Upon looking at his passport, the OGPU man turns Jones over to a member of the secret police. "He came to me and in the most polite and respectful terms bade me follow him. 'I shall have to take you to the nearest city, Kharkov.'"[86] That the secret police would speak to him with such respect is directly attributable to Jones' passport, which was stamped with the approval of the Foreign Minister's Office, granting Jones elite status and warranting the special treatment he received. Not content with this explanation, however, Jones indulges in a bit of self-aggrandizement.

> Throughout the journey I impressed him with the fact that I had interviewed Lenin's widow, and a number of commissars and great panjandrums of the Soviet regime, and by the time we reached Kharkov I believed he was thoroughly convinced that any real arrest of myself would plunge Russia and Europe and the United States into a world war.[87]

Could it be that Jones was still feeling the sting of Duranty's denunciation that his famine scoop was "a big scare story"? Did Barnes's identification of him as the man who broke the famine story awaken a desire for further recognition? Did Jones recklessly grab at the opportunity to support Hearst's anti-Communist campaign as a way to get back at the Soviets for having accused him of espionage, for having alienated him from Lloyd George and the British Foreign Office, and for having barred him from entering the Soviet Union? Had Jones, like Hearst, become more sympathetic toward the Nazis in Germany?

Toward the end of this third article, Jones writes, "Those have been some of the results of the Soviet régime which I witnessed MYSELF."[88] That he emphasizes his having witnessed the famine first-hand resonates with a sense of urgency, a final attempt to make up for the denials or even for the lack of recognition. On the same day that this last famine article was published in the *Los Angeles Examiner*, Jones could be heard on radio station KFWB (Illustration 19); the title of his talk was "What I Saw in Russia."

Unfortunately, within a month Jones' last series of articles about the famine would be undone not by Stalin apologists like Duranty or Fischer or "Friends of the Soviet Union," but by a bogus Hearst correspondent, Thomas Walker, who duped Hearst into publishing a series of articles and photographs purportedly documenting his 1934 trip into Ukraine. Described in the Hearst newspapers as "a noted journalist, traveler, and student of Russian affairs who has spent several years touring the Union of Soviet Russia,"[89] Walker was actually an escaped convicted felon whose real name was Robert Green. Green's materials were exposed as frauds by Louis Fischer of *The Nation*. Soviet authorities supplied Fischer with Green's actual USSR entry date (October 12 from Poland), his arrival in Moscow the next day, and his departure from Moscow on October 18 when he boarded a train headed for the Manchurian border. Rather than risking his life to cover the famine in Ukraine where he claimed he saw six million dead, Green never ventured there, took no photographs, and conjured up the details within the stories. Fischer suggests he concocted his stories by gathering information from "embittered foreigners the Ukrainian 'local color' he needed to give his articles the fake verisimilitude they possess."[90] Fischer also showed that Green's supposed photographs were clearly faked, evidenced by scenes of both winter and summer. Hearst's use of the Thomas Walker fake articles and photographs undermined the real reporting by journalists like Jones, Barnes, Stoneman, and Muggeridge. Even without mentioning Jones by name, Fischer managed to cast doubt on his honest reporting by exposing Walker.

In August 1935, Gareth Jones was kidnapped by bandits in China. Unfortunately, this time his being taken prisoner was unlike the kidnapping by young Welsh children that he described in a *Western Mail* article from September 1933. "It was here that I was for the first time in my life taken prisoner by bandits and ransomed. They were Welsh bandits, varying in age from seven to thirteen years, who seized me and took me to their tent. I have no complaints to make about my treatment by these outlaws and they speedily released me from my captivity when a supply of chocolate was forthcoming as ransom."[91] He would not be so fortunate when he was taken prisoner a second time. One of the many mysteries surrounding Jones' death is the fact that the vehicle he was kidnapped from belonged to the NKVD. One day before Gareth Jones would have turned thirty years of age, the most reliable eyewitness to the Soviet famine of 1932-1933 was eliminated and effectively silenced, his articles, like the famine itself, languishing in obscurity for more than seventy years.

Notes

1.   Duranty, "Russians Hungry," 13.
2.   Gareth Jones, Letter dated May 28, 1933. Gareth Vaughan Jones Papers, National Library of Wales. File B6/7.
3.   Snyder, *Bloodlands*, 61.

4. Gareth Jones, "Soviet Collective Farm Move Caused Famine in Russia, Says Gareth Jones," *Syracuse American*, 11 June 1933, E5.
5. Ibid.
6. Ibid.
7. "The Five-Year Plan," *New York Times*, 1 January 1933, E4.
8. Ibid.
9. Jones, "Soviet Collective Farm Move," E5.
10. "The Five-Year Plan," *New York Times*, 1 January 1933, E4.
11. "Cardinal Asks Aid in Russian Famine: Archbishop of Vienna Says Toll May Be Millions," *New York Times* (Wireless), 20 August 1933, 3.
12. Ibid.
13. "The Famine in Russia," *Western Mail*, 30 August 1933, 6.
14. Gareth Jones, Letter date August 5, 1933. Gareth Vaughan Jones Papers, National Library of Wales. File B6/5.
15. Ibid.
16. An Expert Observer [Otto Schiller], "Famine's Return to Russia," *Daily Telegraph*, 25 August 1933, n.p.
17. Ibid.
18. Colley, *More Than a Grain*, 301.
19. Ibid., 307.
20. Quoted in Colley, *More Than a Grain*, 309.
21. Ibid.
22. Gareth Jones, Letter dated June 11, 1933. Gareth Vaughan Jones Papers, National Library of Wales. File B6/7.
23. A. Beverley Baxter, Letter date April 7, 1933. Gareth Vaughan Jones Papers, National Library of Wales. File B6/8.
24. Professor Jules Menken, Letter dated April 20, 1933. Gareth Vaughan Jones Papers, National Library of Wales. File B6/8.
25. Carynnyk, ed., *The Foreign Office and the Famine*, 257.
26. Ibid., 397.
27. Colley, *More Than a Grain*, 305.
28. Gareth Jones, "Methods of Nazis, Fascists, and Bolsheviks," *Western Mail*, 10 June 1933, 11.
29. Gareth Jones, "Britain's Policy before the World Economic Conference," *Western Mail*, 15 June 1933, 5.
30. Colley, *More Than a Grain*, 301.
31. Malcolm Muggeridge, Letter dated April 17, 1933. Gareth Vaughan Jones Papers, National Library of Wales. File B6/8.
32. Ibid.
33. Ibid.
34. Malcolm Muggeridge, Letter dated April 26, 1933. Gareth Vaughan Jones Papers, National Library of Wales. File 47.
35. Ibid.
36. Ibid.
37. Gareth Jones, [Letter to the Editor] "The Peasants in Russia: Exhausted Supplies," *Manchester Guardian*, 3 May 1933, 18.
38. Ibid.
39. Malcolm Muggeridge, Letter dated September 29, 1933. Gareth Vaughan Jones Papers, National Library of Wales. File B6/8.

40. Walter Duranty, "Famine Toll Heavy in Southern Russia," *New York Times*, 24 August 1933, 1.
41. Ibid.
42. Ibid.
43. See Lyons, Assignment in Utopia, 579-580; See Malcolm Muggeridge, *Chronicles of a Wasted Time*, Vol. I. *The Green Stick* (London: Collins, 1972), 254-255.
44. Carynnyk, ed., *The Foreign Office and the Famine*, 313.
45. Walter Duranty, "Abundance Found in North Caucasus," *New York Times*, 14 September 1933, 14.
46. Ibid.
47. Ibid.
48. Ibid.
49. Walter Duranty, "Big Soviet Crop Follows Famine," *New York Times*, 16 September 1933, 14.
50. Lyons, *Assignment in Utopia*, 580.
51. Ibid.
52. Walter Duranty, *Stalin and Co.: The Politburo—the Men Who Run Russia* (New York: William Sloan and Associates, 1949), 78.
53. Taylor, *Stalin's Apologist*, 337.
54. See Snyder, *Bloodlands*, 57-58.
55. "Herriot Scoffs at Famine Talk," *New York Times*, 18 September 1933, 8.
56. Quoted in Étienne Thevenin, "France, Germany and Austria: Facing the Famine of 1932-1933 in Ukraine," James Mace Memorial Panel, IAUS Congress, Donetsk, Ukraine, 29 June 2005, 8.
57. See Vasily Grossman, *Everything Flows*, trans. by Robert Chandler, Elizabeth Chandler, and Anna Aslanyan (New York: New York Review of Books, 2009), 132.
58. Tzouliadis, *Forsaken*, 220-221.
59. Gareth Jones, "Chapter One," *Bread Rules Russia*. Gareth Vaughan Jones Papers, National Museum of Wales. File 24.
60. Ibid., 8.
61. Ibid.
62. Ibid., 9.
63. Gareth Jones, "Opening the Door to Soviet Literature," *Western Mail*, 20 September 1933, 11.
64. Ibid.
65. Gareth Jones, Diary of Tour of Russia, March 1933. Gareth Vaughan Jones Papers, National Library of Wales. File B1/13, 9-10.
66. Gareth Jones, Speech Delivered at the Institute of World Affairs, Riverside, 14 December 1934. Gareth Vaughan Jones Papers, National Library of Wales. File 47.
67. Ibid.
68. Gareth Jones, Letter dated September 19, 1934. Gareth Vaughan Jones Papers, National Library of Wales. File B6/5.
69. Gareth Jones, Letter dated November 6, 1934. Gareth Vaughan Jones Papers, National Library of Wales. File B6/5.
70. Gareth Jones, Letter dated February 12, 1933. Gareth Vaughan Jones Papers, National Library of Wales. File B6/5.

71. Gareth Jones, Letter dated November 6, 1934. Gareth Vaughan Jones Papers, National Library of Wales. File B6/5.

72. Gareth Jones, Letter dated January 25, 1934. Series 1: Correspondence; 1905-1938; Ivy Ledbetter Lee Papers, Public Policy Papers, Department of Rare Books and Special Collections, Princeton University Library.

73. Ewald Ammende, *Human Life in Russia* (Cleveland: John T. Zubal, 1984), 274-275.

74. Gareth Jones, "Russia—Land of Starvation," *Los Angeles Examiner*, 12 January 1935, 2.

75. Ibid.

76. Ibid.

77. Ibid.

78. Ibid.

79. Ibid.

80. A. Bailakoff, Letter dated July 4, 1933. Gareth Vaughan Jones Papers, National Library of Wales. File B6/8.

81. Jones, "Russia—Land of Starvation," 2.

82. Gareth Jones, "'There Is No Bread,'" *Los Angeles Examiner*, 13 January 1935, 8.

83. Ibid.

84. Gareth Jones, "Fate of Thrifty in USSR: Gareth Jones Tells How Communists Seized All Land and Let Peasants Starve," *Los Angeles Examiner*, 14 January 1935, 4.

85. Ibid.

86. Ibid.

87. Ibid.

88. Thomas Walker, "6,000,000 Starve to Death in Russia," *New York Evening Journal*, 18 February 1935, 1.

89. Louis Fischer, "Hearst's Russian Famine," *The Nation*, 13 March 1935, 296-297.

90. Ibid., 297.

91. Gareth Jones, "Tramping in Three Welsh Counties: Mining Town Brimming Over with Music," *Western Mail*, 13 September 1933, n.p.

10

'Hero of the Ukraine'

'In Touch with People'

This textual analysis of the newspaper articles, correspondence, and diaries of Gareth Jones reveals much about his development as a journalist. That he witnessed one of the most tragic historic events of the twentieth century makes that development even more significant. Through most his brief career, Jones was primarily known as the foreign affairs adviser to David Lloyd George, even after he left the former prime minister's employ. There is no denying that, thanks to his relationship with Lloyd George, Jones was afforded access to some of the most important and influential politicians of that time. Access alone, however, does not necessarily translate into incisive journalism. What Jones accomplished in his work was the direct result of his linguistic abilities, courage, and "nimble mind," a phrase he used in his letter to the *New York Times* in response to Walter Duranty's famine denying article. That scholars continue to label Jones as foreign affairs adviser rather than seeing him as a journalist is one of the many unfortunate circumstances that dilute appreciation for him and his work. His desire for "a good and interesting career" rather than the safety and security of a university position compelled him forward, even if it left him at odds with his parents.

> Tell me why you have no confidence in my future? Why do you want a son of yours to have no courage and just stick in the mud, for the feeling of security? ... You may not think much of my job, but in the view of people in Cambridge and in the R.I.I.A. it is most important. It brings me in touch with people of international repute.[1]

The list of people of international repute he interviewed is nothing short of dazzling: David Lloyd George, Ivy Lee, Adolph Hitler, Maxim

Litvinov, Nadezhda Krupskaya, Alexander Kerensky, and Éamon De Valera. Jones knew many of the leading journalists and writers of his time, including Paul Scheffer, Kingsley Martin, Hessel Tiltman, Malcolm Muggeridge, Ralph Barnes, W. H. Chamberlin, Walter Duranty, Eugene Lyons, H. R. Knickerbocker, Edgar Ansel Mowrer, William Stoneman, W. M. Aitken (Lord Beaverbrook) and Karl Radek. Lastly, Jones knew influential scholars and experts in various fields who certainly influenced and informed him on important world developments, including Sir Bernard Pares, Professor Jules Menken, Dr. Bruce Hopper, Otto Schiller, and Prince Dmitri Petrovich Mirsky.

Given his education and facility with languages, Jones was uniquely qualified to report on international affairs. That he was willing to travel "hard class" through the USSR testifies to his understanding and courage about how to acquire unadulterated source material. Even though Jones could easily have settled for interviews with ministers, deputy ministers, and commissars, what is often referred to as "access upward," Jones used his facility with language to interview countless peasants, workers, and members of the Communist Party, what is referred to as "access downward."[2] From the very first series of newspaper articles he wrote in 1930, Jones used source material to show exactly what everyday people in the USSR were experiencing. Jones' development as a journalist over the course of five years can be seen in the techniques and tropes he utilized in his stories. In many ways, Jones employed many of the techniques that now characterize new journalism. Shortly after his return from the 1933 trip, he writes to Margaret Stewart, a Cambridge student, "This is a great life. I've become a journalist and it is wonderful fun."[3]

Arguably, the most significant aspect of his work can be seen in the correspondence between his diaries and newspaper articles. Jones used the diaries to record many eyewitness accounts that serve as the bulwark of his reporting, and they served as the source material for *Experiences in Russia 1931—A Diary*, the book written by Jack Heinz II. Additionally, his personal correspondence provides considerable insight into his personal and professional goals and growth. Eugene Lyons' description of Jones' inveterate note-taking illustrates how seriously he took his work, and that attitude is also evidenced in how meticulous he was about keeping his clippings, his appointment books, and his correspondence. Jones left a veritable treasure trove of source material that includes not only the things analyzed in this book but also a collection of Soviet propaganda posters, drafts of speeches and presentations, and unpublished manuscripts.

What Jones accomplished as a journalist can be traced to his fascination with the Soviet Five-Year Plan and the disasters that accompanied the socialization of agriculture through the forced collectivization beginning in 1929-1930. Jones did not travel to the USSR in search of a famine; in fact, as a staunch Liberal, Jones was sympathetic to the internationalism and idealism he associated with the goals of the Bolsheviks and their Five-Year Plan—education for all, industry for the benefit of the workers, and rights to the smaller nations to speak their own languages. In "Good-bye Russia," he writes, "They abhorred pogrom.... They were not guilty of the narrow nationalisms of post-war days."[4] Jones readily admits to liking personally most of the Bolsheviks he knew. "The Soviet Foreign Officials were on every occasion courteous, and spared no trouble in their efforts to help me."[5]

Despite the courtesy he was afforded, what Jones discovered in his travels across the republics of Russia and Ukraine certainly challenged his idealism. Even while recognizing the accomplishments of the Five-Year Plan, including vast building projects, fine art galleries and museums, and a campaign against illiteracy, Jones also witnessed the devastating effects of forced collectivization, a policy that robbed the peasants of livestock and land. Compounding the peasants' suffering was the imposition of unrelenting, unrealistic grain requisitions, savage class warfare against the most successful farmers [kulaks], and a stifling oppression of religion. Jones' sensibilities were thoroughly assaulted by the deprivation and despair he witnessed when he traveled through the countryside in 1930, 1931, and 1933. Because of what he and Jack Heinz II documented during their 1931 trip, Jones was arguably the first journalist to recognize that famine was beginning to ravage the Soviet countryside, evidenced by the fact that in that year more than a million Kazakhs died as a direct result of the collectivization of livestock, which undermined their nomadic and semi-nomadic way of life.

In March 1933 Jones traveled to the Soviet Union because people like Menken, Hopper, and Pares had informed him that the harvest of 1932 was a dismal failure, and famine was afflicting Ukraine, North Caucasus, and the Lower Volga. After arriving in Moscow and interviewing Soviet officials and Western journalists, Jones set out to visit a tractor factory in Kharkov as a guest of the German consulate, having secured permission from Konstantin Umansky.[6] Before crossing into Ukraine, Jones got off the train and walked forty miles through more than a dozen villages and farms, knowing full well that he was violating the trust of powerful men like Umansky and Litvinov, who were certain to complain to Lloyd George. Nonetheless, Jones had to witness for himself whether or not famine conditions were ravaging the countryside, and what he documented was the plight of peasants who had no bread, children with swollen stomachs, and empty villages.

At a small station, Jones was rounded up and deposited at the German embassy in Kharkov, a city that only two years earlier had been teeming with growth, but where now he witnessed dilapidated buildings, unfinished projects, queues of thousands of people waiting for bread, and jails packed with Ukrainian nationalists. There he learned about the arrest of the six British engineers charged with espionage. After his return to Moscow, an interview with Litvinov, and a tour of the outskirts of Moscow where he met Otto Schiller, Jones departed the USSR, knowing full well that when he reported what he had seen he would never be allowed to return.

Denigration

Even though he was neither the first nor the only journalist to document the famine, Jones, by virtue of his press conference in Berlin, confirmed publicly to the world that famine was ravaging the countryside and impacting the major cities. His first article, "Famine Rules Russia," published on March 31 in the *London Evening Standard* coincided with Duranty's *New York Times* famine-denying story in which he denigrated Jones' reporting as a "big scare story." Louis Fischer of *The Nation* was on a speaking tour of the American West when he learned about Jones' claims. Asked about the million who had died since 1930 in Kazakhstan, Fischer scoffed at the number, asking derisively who counted them.

This controversy involving Duranty's and Fischer's denigration of Jones' honest reporting did not end with their denials of the famine. Even Malcolm Muggeridge, whom Jones had supported by writing a Letter to the Editor of the *Manchester Guardian* praising his three articles about the famine, failed to acknowledge Jones' work when Jones asked him for a letter of support. Additionally, Muggeridge misrepresented Jones in his 1934 novel *Winter in Moscow* through the character Pye, who is depicted as almost the exact opposite of Jones. Martin Sieff notes:

> He [Pye] is old where Jones was young, cynical where Jones was idealistic and a hard drinker and chain smoker where Jones was a teetotaler. It is as if Muggeridge, a cynic, smoker and chronic drinker himself, was driven to expurgate the very image of Jones, even though he had written him a letter of support during the controversy.[7]

And forty years later, Muggeridge almost totally eviscerated Jones' record of reporting on the famine by misrepresenting Duranty's March 31 article to suggest that Duranty was attempting to rebut his *Manchester Guardian* articles.

Commemorating a Hero

How we come to know, understand and remember the reporting of the famine of 1932-1933 is important because of what scholar Barbie Zelizer refers to as journalism's usability, "its invocation as a tool to defend different aims and agendas."[8] Journalists develop a repertoire of preferred practices through a recycling of informal associations around shared experiences. In this case, the famine is the key event through which journalists set up and negotiate these preferred practices. Journalists come together as an "interpretive community"[9] by creating stories about their past that they routinely and informally circulate to each other—stories that contain certain constructions of reality, certain kinds of narratives, and certain definitions of appropriate practice. Armed with the knowledge of what famine reporting has been, various publics can attend to representing this key event by fitting it within their collective memory, validating themselves as well as the memories they invoke. However, it's also important to understand that all collective memories are partial, and at times "hide as much as they reveal."[10] Memories, in this way, act like mythologies; no one memory can bring forth all that is known about an event, nor can an event rely upon a single source.

   What has happened to the legacy of Gareth Jones' reporting further illustrates this concept of usability. In 2003, three of the many articles published link Jones with the *Holodomor*. Roman Revkniv wrote an article for the *Ukrainian Archive & News* titled "Welsh Journalist Gareth Jones—Hero of Ukraine." The *Ukrainian Weekly* published "Gareth Jones: Correspondent Who Reported the Great Famine." And Martin Sieff, senior news analyst for UPI, wrote a commentary titled "Gareth Jones, Hero of Ukraine." That Jones has been elevated to the status of hero is not altogether surprising. At the University Wales, Aberystwyth, where Jones earned a "First Class Honours Degree" before moving on to Trinity College at Cambridge, a bronzed bas relief of Jones' torso adorns a memorial plaque erected in 2006 (Illustration 20). In English, Welsh and Ukrainian, the plaque reads: "In Memory of Gareth Richard Vaughn Jones...One of the first journalists to report on the *Holodomor*, the Great Famine of 1932-33 in the Soviet Ukraine." Attending the ceremony were members of Jones' family and the Ukrainian ambassador to Great Britain, Ihor Kharchanko, who lauded Jones as an "outstanding figure who should be noted. He should be seen as a hero for what he did and for the way he put his life on the line."[11]

In addition to the plaque commemoration, Jones was honored by the Ukrainian government in November 2008 with the Order of Merit, which was presented to Dr. Colley at the British 75th *Holodomor* Commemorations at Westminster Central Hall, London. Fedir Kurlak, chief executive of the Association of Ukrainians in Great Britain, said, "As far as the Ukrainian community is concerned, anyone who has heard of Gareth's exploits will quite simply take his hat off to him, and regard him as an exemplary journalist."[12] Commemoration of Jones' reporting of the *Holodomor* has not been the only symbolic campaign. An effort to have Duranty stripped of his 1932 Pulitzer Prize has also accompanied how the famine is remembered. Calls in the early 1990s to rescind Duranty's Pulitzer Prize were not accepted by the Pulitzer Prize Board, who revisited the issue again in 2003. In July of that year the board notified the *New York Times* that it was reconsidering the request, but ultimately decided that no action was warranted. In its statement the board argued that there was no evidence of "deliberate deception" by Duranty.

> Revoking a prize 71 years after it was awarded under different circumstances, when all principals are dead and unable to respond, would be a momentous step and therefore would have to rise to that threshold.... A Pulitzer Prize for reporting is awarded not for the author's body of work or for the author's character, but for the specific pieces entered in the competition.... The board extends its sympathy to Ukrainians and others in the United States and throughout the world who still mourn the suffering and deaths brought on by Josef Stalin.[13]

Even though the board can argue that Duranty's 1931 articles did not deliberately deceive the reading public, the same can certainly not be said about his articles written in 1933. Given the evidence Duranty himself supplied to the British Foreign Office as well as to Lyons, Muggeridge, and Anne O'Hare McCormick, Duranty willfully and deliberately deceived readers into believing that there was no famine, just as he had deliberately denigrated the reporting of Gareth Jones. Arthur Sulzberger Jr., publisher of the *New York Times*, commended the board's decision, noting the "many defects"[14] in Duranty's journalism without acknowledging its own culpability in publishing Duranty's work, as well as in its editorial decisions in terms of assigning headlines and placement of his famine-denying story. Additionally, *New York Times* editorials clearly followed the same pattern of denials found in Duranty's articles. Even though the newspaper may "regret his [Duranty's] lapses,"[15] until it fully acknowledges its own part in disseminating famine denial stories, that newspaper remains every bit as guilty as Duranty. The company ended a statement at its website explaining the 1932 Pulitzer Prize awarded to Duranty by noting that the *New York Times* "does not have the award in its possession."[16] Presumably, that absolves the newspaper of meeting its ethical obligation and returning the 1932 Pulitzer Prize.

Rather than commending the Pulitzer Prize board's decision not to rescind Duranty's prize, the *New York Times* should voluntarily return the prize, even if only symbolically, for the newspaper clearly knew that Duranty's reporting reflected Soviet policy. Evidence shows that the newspaper was itself complicit in duping the public. In a memorandum dated June 4, 1931, A. W. Kliefoth, a member of the U.S. Berlin Embassy, summarized a meeting he had with Duranty (Illustration 21). The final sentence of the memorandum reads: "In conclusion, Duranty pointed out that 'in agreement with NEW YORK TIMES and the Soviet authorities,' his dispatches always reflect the official position of the Soviet regime and not his own."[17] The series that Duranty wrote about the Five-Year Plan for which he was awarded the Pulitzer Prize ran from June 14-27, 1931, only ten days after this meeting. Significantly, Kliefoth was careful to quote Duranty directly regarding the crucial point about this agreement between the *New York Times* and Soviet authorities. Given this agreement and having abrogated the trust placed in it by the public, the only ethical course for the *New York Times* to follow is to return the 1932 Pulitzer Prize awarded to Walter Duranty, regardless of whether or not the prize is in its possession.

Publication of the book *Not Worthy* illustrates how inimical a figure Duranty remains for Ukrainians and anyone impacted by the tragedy. As Lubomyr Luciuk argues, "That Walter Duranty was not worthy of his Pulitzer Prize is certain. Why the *Holodomor's* murdered millions are not worthy of justice remains unexplained."[18] Both of these statements are perfectly logical; unfortunately, the Pulitzer Prize board's decision not to revoke the prize and the *Times'* recalcitrance in voluntarily returning it means that the *Holodomor's* victims are left without meaningful justice and the famine deniers are not impugned as Soviet stooges. Justice can only occur when journalists like Gareth Jones "who dared expose the Stalinist regime for what it was"[19] are afforded their rightful place in journalism history. Duranty's reporting of the Soviet Union in general and of the famine in particular has received critical scrutiny by media scholars, and he serves as the most obvious example of how governments can and still do manipulate journalists.

Stripping him of the Pulitzer Prize is a necessary symbolic gesture, one that might clear the clutter that clouds our understanding of why we continue to look away when confronted with what the political theorist Judith Shklar has called the *summum malum*,[20] the ultimate evil, not merely a manifestation of evil.

Recognition

After more than eighty years, the *Holodomor* continues to struggle for recognition. That struggle stems in part from the idea that our understanding of evil is rooted in using the word to refer to both acts of human cruelty and instances of human suffering. Because the *Holodomor* is indelibly associated with famine and often referred to as "The Great Famine," its acceptance has arguably been inhibited from being considered "all that is meant when we use the word *evil* today: an absolute wrongdoing that leaves no room for account or expiation."[21] Famines, like earthquakes, floods, hurricanes and other natural disasters, are often labelled "acts of God," and responsibility for such acts often becomes mired in theological and philosophical principles. We want to understand them in order to continue to believe that there is meaning in the human condition. However, as Susan Neiman argues in her Preface to *Evil in Modern Thought*, while genocide and torture have no general principle that proves them to be wrong, that should not prevent us from seeing them as paradigmatic of evil.

Nineteen nations have recognized the *Holodomor* as genocide, yet this most monstrous crime against humanity has not the same connotative resonance that Auschwitz or the Holocaust has. Perhaps that is because from the very beginning the Soviets and Stalin denied that there even was a famine, and those denials were parroted by Western journalists. Stalin's second October revolution, a revolution from above, became conflated with the drive for industrialization through collectivization and the socialization of agriculture. Conditions that existed eighty years ago should not confuse us today. As many scholars have pointed out, there is still considerable disagreement on not only the nature of the crime and the identity of the victims, but also as to whether or not the *Holodomor* ought to be considered genocide. Partisan feelings related to interpretations of motives, geo-political conditions, agricultural yields, and other factors in which memory and meaning confront demographic data are all open to continuing shifts in perspective. As Roman Serbyn has noted, "Traditional *famine-denial* has been updated to *famine-genocide denial*, but the essence of the ideological trappings is the same. Today's famine-genocide deniers are the spiritual heirs of the first famine deniers, Stalin and those who helped him carry out the most heinous of crimes against the Ukrainian nation or to deny its existence."[22]

Despite the varied positions scholars have taken, the historicity of the Ukrainian genocide of 1932-1933 is invariably tied to the moral responsibility of Stalin and his regime for knowingly and deliberately starving millions of innocent people by creating and implementing policies that they knew would culminate in the loss of lives. What happened in Ukraine in 1932-1933, meets not only the criteria of genocide, but provides one of the clearest examples of ultimate evil. It illustrates how evil operates as not only the individual actions of a Stalin, but also becomes intertwined with impersonal ideological processes, in this case Soviet Communism. Certainly, as Hannah Arendt has pointed out, "no man, however strong, can ever accomplish anything, good or bad, without the help of others."[23] When evil is sufficiently large-scale, not everyone involved will share the same intentions; people will act for a variety of reasons, many of them having nothing to do with the criminal nature of the enterprise itself. That, Arendt argued, is the aim of a totalitarian regime: to make the individual—whether victim or bystander, collaborator or perpetrator—superfluous, to render his actions pointless, his contribution to society meaningless. Evil actions, we know today, do not require evil intent. Propaganda campaigns were used to override moral objections that might have functioned and "to convince people that the criminal actions in which they participated were guided by acceptable, even noble motives."[24]

In this way, it is possible to trace the trajectory of Stalin's revolution as an example or radical evil against Ukrainian sovereignty without the ideological trappings that began as famine denial and in many ways continues as famine-genocide denial. There can be no denying that what happened throughout the USSR (the pan-Soviet famine) and the deliberate mass starvation that dominated Ukraine, the Kuban region of North Caucasus and the Lower Volga was a consequence of political choices. Those political choices were not only aimed at peasants, whom Stalin had long despised, but also directed toward Ukrainian nationals, who, Stalin determined, had undertaken a "nationalist deviation" and were thus counter-revolutionary and had to be stopped. As Liber posits, "The equating of Ukrainian national communists with the Ukrainian nationalists (bourgeois nationalists) was false. But Stalin's entourage, men who were not known for their theoretical or political subtlety, claimed to see an alliance between these two groups and tried very hard to discredit both in the eyes of the Soviet Ukrainian public, the rest of the USSR, the world, and posterity."[25] It is our responsibility to recognize that the *Holodomor* was an act of evil in which epic action and impersonal organization were not in opposition. Recognition of this genocide is a necessary step in understanding the problem of evil, which ultimately reveals changes in our understanding of ourselves, and of our place in the world.

Limitations and Future Research

This work is not without limitations; it analyzes only those texts that are relevant to Jones reporting on the Soviet Union. Further research of Jones' work might include an analysis of his coverage of Nazi Germany, Ireland, the United States, and Wales. Work has begun in transcribing the diaries, for there is a wealth of material within them.[26] Having transcriptions of them may alleviate some of the difficulties they currently present. Translations of those passages in Welsh and Russian would also contribute to our understanding of the contents. Showing correspondence between the diaries and the published articles has been a small part of this project, and there is more that can be done in this realm. Finally, there are a number of unanswered questions relating to his death, who was responsible, and what, if any, part the Soviet Union played; those questions persist as long as any of Jones' files in Russia's archives remain closed to scholars.

This is but one interpretation of Jones' work related to the policies enacted by the leaders of the Soviet Union. Other interpretations would doubtlessly add to our understanding of these important texts, for they cover a period of history in which starvation on a mass scale resulted in millions of people dying. It is our moral duty to make sure that the work of Gareth Jones is not airbrushed from history and that the victims of the *Holodomor* are not forgotten.

Notes

1. Gareth Jones, Letter dated February 5, 1930. Gareth Vaughan Jones Papers, National Library of Wales. Bundle 18.
2. Kramer, "Breakable Rules," 34.
3. Gareth Jones, Letter dated May 12, 1933. Gareth Vaughan Jones Papers, National Library of Wales. File 18.
4. Jones, "Good-bye Russia," 12.
5. Ibid.
6. George Carey, "Hitler, Stalin & Mr. Jones," BBC Four Storyville Series, 5 July 2012.
7. Martin Sieff, "Commentary: Gareth Jones, Hero of Ukraine," United Press International website, 12 June 2003.

8.   Barbie Zelizer, "Reading the Past Against the Grain: The Shape of Memory Studies," *Critical Studies in Mass Communication*, vol. 12, no. 2, (June 1995), 226.

9.   Barbie Zelizer, "Journalists as Interpretive Communities," *Critical Studies in Mass Communication*, vol. 10, (1993), 223.

10. Ruth Teer-Tomaselli, "Memory and Markers: Collective Memory and Newsworthiness," in Ingrid Volkmer, ed., *News in Public Memory: An International Study of Media Memories across Generations* (New York, Peter Lang, 2006) 226.

11. "'Unsung hero' reporter remembered," BBC News. 2 May 2006. Accessed from http:// http://news.bbc.co.uk/2/hi/uk_news/wales/south_east/7742330. stm.

12. "Ukraine honour for Welsh reporter," BBC News. 22 November 2008. Accessed from http://news.bbc.co.uk/go/pr/fr/-/2/hi/uk_news/wales/south_east/7742330. stm.

13. David D. Kirkpatrick, "Pulitzer Board Won't Void '32 Award to *Times* Writer," *New York Times*, 22 November 2003, A13.

14. Ibid.

15. Ibid.

16. "New York Times Statement About 1932 Pulitzer Prize Awarded to Walter Duranty." Accessed from http://www.nytco.com/company/awards/statement. html.

17. A. W. Kliehoth, "Memorandum," US Embassy in Berlin. Accessed from http:// http://www.garethjones.org/Embassy-1.pdf.

18. Lubomyr Y. Luciuk, "Not Worthy?" in Lubomyr Luciuk, ed., *Not Worthy: Walter Duranty's Pulitzer Prize and the* New York Times (Kingston, Ontario: Kashtan Press, 2004), vii.

19. Ibid., vi.

20. Judith Shklar, "The Liberalism of Fear," in *Liberalism and the Moral Life*, ed. Nancy L. Rosenblum (Cambridge: Harvard University Press, 1989) 29.

21. Susan Neiman, *Evil in Modern Thought: An Alternative History of Philosophy* (Princeton: Princeton University Press, 2002), 3.

22. Roman Serbyn, "The Last Stand of the Famine-Genocide Deniers," *The Ukrainian Canadian* (February 1989) 7.

23. Hannah Arendt, *Responsibility and Judgment* (New York: Schocken Books, 2003) 47.

24. Neiman, *Evil in Modern Thought*, 275.

25. Liber, *Soviet Nationality Policy*, 172-173.

26. Lubomyr Y. Luciuk, ed.,"*Tell Them We Are Starving*": The 1933 Soviet Diaries of Gareth Jones (Kingston: Kashtan Press, 2015).

Bibliography

Primary Sources

Baikaloff, A. Letter dated 4 July 1933. Gareth Vaughan Jones Papers, National Library of Wales. File B6/8.

Barnes, Ralph W. "Million Feared Dead of Hunger in South Russia," *New York Herald Tribune*, 21 August 1933, 7.

Baxter, A. Beverley. Letter date 7 April 1933. Gareth Vaughan Jones Papers, National Library of Wales. File B6/8.

Cairns, Andrew. *The Soviet Famine, 1932-33: An Eye-witness Account of Conditions in the Spring and Summer of 1932*. Edited by Tony J. Kuz. Edmonton, Alberta: Canadian Institute of Ukrainian Studies, University of Alberta Press, 1989.

"Cardinal Asks Aid in Russian Famine: Archbishop of Vienna Says Toll May Be Millions." *New York Times* (Wireless), 20 August 1933.

Chamberlin, W. H. *Russia's Iron Age*. Boston: Little, Brown, 1934.

"Declares Germany Can Pay No More," *New York Times*, 25 November 1931.

Duranty, Walter. "All Russia Suffers Shortage of Food; Supplies Dwindling." *New York Times*, 25 November 1932.

— —. "Food Shortage Laid To Soviet Peasants." *New York Times*, 26 November 1932.

— —. "Soviet Industries Hurt Agriculture." *New York Times*, 29 November 1932.

— —. "Russians Hungry But Not Starving." *New York Times*, March 31, 1933.

— —. "Famine Toll Heavy in Southern Russia." *New York Times*, 24 August 1933.

— —. "Abundance Found in North Caucasus." *New York Times*, 14 September 1933.

— —. "Big Soviet Crop Follows Famine." *New York Times*, 16 September 1933.

— —. *I Write as I Please*. New York: Simon & Schuster, 1935.

— —. *Stalin and Co.: The Politburo—the Men Who Run Russia*. New York: William Sloan and Associates, 1949.

Fischer, Louis. Letter dated 16 February 1930. Ivy Ledbetter Lee Papers; 1881-2003, Public Policy Papers, Department of Rare Books and Special Collections, Princeton University Library.

— —. "Soviet Poverty and Progress." *The Nation*, Vol. 135, No. 3518, 7 December 1932, 552-555.

— —. "Private Profits in Russia." *The Nation*, Vol. 135, No. 3503, 24 August 1932, 159-161.

— —. "Hearst's Russian Famine." *The Nation*, 13 March 1935, 296-297.

Gantt, W. Horsley. "A Medical Review of Soviet Russia: Results of the First Five Year Plan." *The British Medical Journal*, 4 July 1936, 19-22.

House of Lords Archives, David Lloyd George files. Gareth Jones, "Soviet Russian and the Caucasus." 9 December 1930.

Heinz, Howard. Letter dated October 1931. Ivy Ledbetter Lee Papers. Seeley G. Mudd Manuscript Library, Princeton University. Box 2, Folder 27.

[Heinz II, Jack]. *Experiences in Russia 1931 — A Diary*. Pittsburgh: Alton Press, 1932.

"Herriot Scoffs at Famine Talk." *New York Times*. 18 September 1933.

Jones, Annie Gwen. "Impressions of Life on the Steppes of Russia." Unpublished manuscript essay. Gareth Vaughan Jones Papers. National Library of Wales. File A/2.

Jones, Gareth. "Chapter One." *Bread Rules Russia*. Gareth Vaughan Jones Papers, National Museum of Wales. File 24.

— —. Diary of Service with Lloyd George, 1929-1930. Gareth Vaughan Jones Papers, National Library of Wales. File B1/3.

— —. Itinerary of Tour in Russia, August 1931. Gareth Vaughan Jones Papers, National Library of Wales. Bundle 24.

— —. Journal of Russian Travels, 1931, August 21-September 4. Gareth Vaughan Jones Papers, National Library of Wales. File B1/11.

— —. Journal of Russian Travels, 1931, August 21-September 4. Gareth Vaughan Jones Papers, National Library of Wales. File B1/12.

— —. [Diary 3] Journal of Russian Travels, 1931, August21-September 4. Gareth Vaughan Jones Papers, National Library of Wales. Folder 35.

— —. Diary of Tour of Russia, March 4-11, 1933. Gareth Vaughan Jones Papers, National Library of Wales. File B1/15.

— —. Diary of Tour of Russia, March 11-25, 1933. Gareth Vaughan Jones Papers, National Library of Wales. File B1/16.

— —. Diary of Tour of Russia, March 1933. Gareth Vaughan Jones Papers, National Library of Wales. File B1/13.

— —. Lecture titled "Soviet Russia in March 1933." Royal Institute of International Affairs, 30 March 1933.

— —. Letter dated 15 September 1932. Ivy Ledbetter Lee Papers, Seeley G. Mudd Manuscript Library, Princeton University. Box 2, Folder 27.

— —. Letters from New York 1931. Gareth Vaughan Jones Papers, National Library of Wales, File B6/3.

— —. "Interview with Maxim Litvinow." Letter dated 27 March 1933. David Lloyd George Records. House of Lord's Office.

— —. "Glimpses of Soviet Russia." *The Liberal Woman's News*, 18 September 1930.

— —. "Famine Rules Russia." *Evening Standard*, March 31, 1933.

— —. From a Correspondent. "Rulers and Ruled." *The Times*, 13 October 1930.

— —. "The Snobbery of Soviet Russia." *News Chronicle*, 3 October 1930.

— —. From a Correspondent. "Fanaticism and Disillusion." *The Times*, 14 October 1930.

— —. From a Correspondent. "Strength of the Communists." *The Times*, 16 October 1930.

— —. "My Russian Diary—I." *The Star*, 22 October 1930.

— —. "My Russian Diary—II." *The Star*, 27 October 1930.

— —. "My Russian Diary—III," *The Star*, 29 October 1930.

— —. "Russia's Man of Steel." *Western Mail*, 10 December 1930.

— —. "Communists' Five-Year-Plan." *Western Mail*, 7 April 1931.

— —. "Russia's Future: Stupendous Plan of Communists." *Western Mail*, 8 April 1931.

— —. "Forces Behind Stalin's Dictatorship." *Western Mail*, 9 April 1931.

— —. "Mixture of Successes and Failures." *Western Mail*, 11 April 1931.

— —. "Preface," in *Experiences in Russia 1931—A Diary*. Pittsburgh: Alton Press, 1932.

— —. Correspondent. "The Peasant on the Farm: Increase and Its Cost." *The Times*, 14 October 1931.

— —. Correspondent. "The Outlook for the Plan: From the Farm to the Factory." *The Times*, 15 October 1931.

— —. Correspondent. "Youth and the Future: A Blessed Word." *The Times*, 16 October 1931.

— —. "Lenin's Widow Talks to a Welshman." *Western Mail*, 7 November 1932.

— —. "The World in 1931: A Retrospect of the Banking Crisis." *Western Mail*, 21 December 1931.

— —. "Land of Tragedy and Disillusion." *Western Mail*, 30 March 1932.

— —. "Amazing Poverty Amid Glut of Gold." *Western Mail*, 31 March 1932.

— —. "Mayor Walker's Secret." *Western Mail*, 10 September 1932.

— —. "Welshman's Bid for Presidency." *Western Mail*, 10 October 1932.

— —. "Will There Be Soup? Russia Dreads the Coming Winter." *Western Mail*, 15 October 1932.

——. "Russia Famished under the Five-Year Plan." *Western Mail*, 17 October 1932.

——. "Famine Rules Russia." *Evening Standard*, 31 March 1933.

——. "The Real Truth About Russia At Last." *Daily Express*, 3 April 1933.

——. "'We are Starving' cry from Russian Peasants." *Western Mail*, 3 April 1933.

——. "Starving Russians Seething with Discontent." *Western Mail*, 4 April 1933.

——. "'Bread! We Are Dying.'" *Daily Express*, 4 April 1933.

——. "O.G.P.U.'s Reign of Terror in Russia." *Western Mail*, 5 April 1933.

——. "Soviets Confiscate Part of Workers' Wages." *The Daily Express*, 5 April 1933.

——. "Nine to a Room in Slums of Russia." *The Daily Express*, 6 April 1933.

——. "15 Hours to Wait for the Shops to Open." *Daily Express*, 7 April 1933.

——. "My Thoughts on the Journey to Moscow." *Western Mail*, 7 April 1933.

——. "Why People are Dying of Starvation in Russia." *Daily Express*, 8 April 1933.

——. "Seizure of Land and Slaughter of Stock." *Western Mail*, 8 April 1933.

——. "Why There Is Unemployment in Russia." *Western Mail*, 10 April 1933.

——. "Good-Bye Russia." *Daily Express*, 11 April 1933.

——. "Soviet Ready for War." *Western Mail*, 11 April 1933.

——. "Easter in Godless Russia." *Western Mail*, 12 April 1933.

——. "Balance-Sheet of the Five-Year Plan: I Industrialisation." *Financial News*, 11 April 1933.

——. "Balance-Sheet of the Five-Year Plan: II Financial Impressions." *Financial News*, 12 April 1933.

——. "Balance-Sheet of the Five-Year Plan: III Ruin of Russian Agriculture." *Financial News*, 13 April 1933.

——. "O.G.P.U.'s Blow to Trade." *Western Mail*, 20 April 1933.

——. "The Peasants in Russia: Exhausted Supplies" [Letter to the Editor]. *Manchester Guardian*, 3 May 1933.

——. "Mr. Jones Replies" [Letter to the Editor]. *New York Times*, 13 May 1933.

——. "Methods of Nazis, Fascists, and Bolsheviks." *Western Mail*, 10 June 1933.

— —. "Soviet Collective Farm Move Caused Famine in Russia, Says Gareth Jones." *Boston Sunday Advertiser*, 11 June 1933.

— —. "Britain's Policy before the World Economic Conference." *Western Mail*, 15 June 1933.

— —. "Tramping in Three Welsh Counties: Mining Town Brimming Over With Music." *Western Mail*, 13 September 1933.

— —. "Opening the Door to Soviet Literature." *Western Mail*, 20 September 1933.

— —. "Russia—Land of Starvation." *Los Angeles Examiner*, 12 January 1935.

— —. "'There Is No Bread.'" *Los Angeles Examiner*, 13 January 1935.

— —. "Fate of Thrifty in USSR: Gareth Jones Tells How Communists Seized All Land and Let Peasants Starve." *Los Angeles Examiner*, 14 January 1935.

— —. Speech Delivered at the Institute of World Affairs, Riverside, California. 14 December 1934. Gareth Vaughan Jones Papers, National Library of Wales. File 47.

Knickerbocker, H. R. "Famine Grips Russia, Millions Dying. Idle on Rise, Says Briton." *New York Evening Post*, 29 March 1933.

— —. *The Soviet Five-Year Plan and Its Effect on World Trade*. London: John Lane, 1931.

Lee, Ivy Ledbetter. *USSR: A World Enigma*. New York: Privately Printed, 1927.

Letter from Ambassador Ivan Maiskii to Comrade Neiman, Press Department of NKID, 25 January 1933, Arkhiv vneshnei politiki Rossiiskoi Federatsii (AVP RF) f. 056 (Otdel pechati), op. 18, pap. 38, d. 9, I. 27.

Letter from Brodovskii to Umanskii, 29 March 1933, AVP RF f. 056, op. 18, pap. 38, d. 9, I. 95.

Letter from M. Litvinov to the USSR Embassy in London, 16 April 1933, AVP RF f. 056, op. 18, pap. 38, d. 10, I. 19.

Letter from Neiman to I. M. Maiskii in London, 4 February 1933, (AVP RF) f. 056, op. 18, pap. 38, d. 9, I. 45.

Letter from S. J. [A.] Sylvester to His Excellency, the Ambassador of the USSR, 8 April 1933, [marked "copy] AVP RF f. 056, op. 18, pap. 38, d. 10, I. 5.

Lyons, Eugene. Dispatch 12152. Henry Shapiro Papers, Library of Congress, Washington, D.C. Folder 8, Box 28.

— —. *Assignment in Utopia*. New York: Harcourt, Brace and Company, 1937.

Menken, Professor Jules. Letter dated April 20, 1933. Gareth Vaughan Jones Papers, National Library of Wales. File B6/8.

Mowrer, Edgar Ansel. "Russian Famine Now as Great as Starvation of 1921, Says Secretary to Lloyd George." *Chicago Daily News*, 29 March 1933.

[Muggeridge, Malcolm]. "Russia's 'Plan.'" *Manchester Guardian*, 13 January 1933.

— —. Letter dated April 17, 1933. Gareth Vaughan Jones Papers, National Library of Wales. File B6/8.

— —. Letter dated April 26, 1933. Gareth Vaughan Jones Papers, National Library of Wales. File 47.

— —. Letter dated September 29, 1933. Gareth Vaughan Jones Papers, National Library of Wales. File B6/8.

— —. *Chronicles of Wasted Time*. New York: William Morrow & Company, 1973.

— —. *Like It Was: The Diaries of MM, Selected and Edited by John Bright-Holmes*. New York: William Morrow and Company, 1982.

"Mr. Jones' Lecture." *Manchester Guardian*, 24 January 1933.

"'New Deal' Need for Entire World, Says Visiting Author." *Denver Post*, 1 April 1933.

"Over 15,000 N.Y. Ukrainian Americans March in Protest Parade Marking Anniversary of Soviet Fostered 1932-33 Famine in Ukraine," *Svoboda--Ukrainian Weekly Section*, 26 September 1953, 1.

Our Correspondent. "Fascist Dictatorship for Germany Now Possibility." *New York American*, 29 November 1931.

Political Propaganda Posters from the Collection of Gareth Jones.

"Russia As It Is." *Evening Standard*, 30 March 1933.

[Schiller, Otto] An Expert Observer. "Famine's Return to Russia." *Daily Telegraph*, 25 August 1933.

Shaw, G. Bernard [and twenty others]. "Social Conditions in Russia." Letters to the Editor, *Manchester Guardian*, 2 March 1933.

"Soviet Food Scarcity." *New York Times*, 26 November 1932.

Stalin, J. V. "Bukharin's Group and the Right Wing Deviation in Our Party," *Works*, Vol. 11 Moscow: Foreign Languages Publishing House, 1954

— —. "Concerning Questions of Leninism." In *Works*, Vol. 8 Moscow: Foreign Languages Publishing House, 1954.

— —. "Concerning Questions of Agrarian Policy in the USSR." In *Works*, Vol. 12 Moscow: Foreign Languages Publishing House, 1954.

— —. "Dizzy with Success: Concerning Questions of the Collective-Farm Movement." In *Works*, Vol. 12 Moscow: Foreign Languages Publishing House, 1954.

— —. "New Conditions—New Tasks in Economic Construction: Speech Delivered at a Conference of Business Executives." In *Works*, Vol. 13 Moscow: Foreign Languages Publishing House, 1954.

——. "Our Work in the Countryside." In *Works*, Vol. 13 Moscow: Foreign Languages Publishers, 1954.

——. "Political Report of the Central Committee to the Sixteenth Congress of the C.P.S.U." In *Works*, Vol. 12. Moscow: Foreign Languages Publishing House, 1954.

——. *The Stalin-Kaganovich Correspondence 1931-1936* compiled by R. W. Davies, Oleg V. Khlevniuk, E. A. Rees, Liudmila P. Kosheleva, and Larisa A. Rogovaya. Trans. By Steven Shabad. (New Haven: Yale University Press, 2003.

Statement of the Resolution of the NKID Collegium, 2 April 1933, AVP RF f. 056, op. 18, pap. 39, d. 15, I. 28.

Strong, Anna Louise. *The Soviets Conquer Wheat*. New York: Henry Holt and Company, 1931.

"The Five-Year Plan." *New York Times*, 1 January 1933, E4.

"The Famine in Russia." *Western Mail*, 30 August 1933.

Walker, Thomas. "6,000,000 Starve to Death in Russia." *New York Evening Journal*, 18 February 1935.

Wells, Carveth. *Kapoot*. New York: Robert M. McBride & Company, 1933.

Secondary Sources

Ammende, Ewald. *Human Life in Russia*. Cleveland: John T. Zubal, 1984.

Arendt, Hannah. *Responsibility and Judgment*. New York: Schocken Books, 2003.

Awad, Isabel. "Journalists and Their Sources: Lessons from Anthropology." *Journalism Studies* 7.6 (2006): 922-939.

Bartoshevitch, Alexsey. "The Fortunes of Russian Hamlet." Accessed on 23 September 2012 from http://eng.1september.ru/2001/16/2.htm.

Bassow, Whitman. *The Moscow Correspondents: Reporting on Russia from the Revolution to Glasnost*. New York: Morrow, 1988.

Bogdenko, M. L. "About the History of the Initial Phase of Massive Collectivization of the Rural Economy of the USSR." *Problems of History of the Communist Party of the Soviet Union* 5 (1963): 19-35.

Carey, George. "Hitler, Stalin & Mr. Jones." BBC Four Storyville Series. 5 July 2012.

Carynnyk, Marco. "Making the News Fit to Print: Walter Duranty, the New York Times and the Ukrainian Famine of 1933." In *Famine in Ukraine 1932-1933*, edited by Roman Serbyn and Bohdan Krawchenko, 67-96. Edmonton, Alberta: Canadian Institute of Ukrainian Studies, 1986.

Carynnyk, Marco, Lubomyr Y. Luciuk and Bohdan S. Kordan, eds. *The Foreign Office and the Famine: British Documents on Ukraine and the Great Famine of 1932-1933*. Kingston, Ontario: The Limestone Press, 1988.

Chalk, Frank and Kurt Jonassohn. "Conceptualizations of Genocide and Ethnocide." In *Famine in Ukraine 1932-1933*, edited by Roman Serbyn and Bohdan Krawchenko, 179-190. Edmonton, Alberta: Canadian Institute of Ukrainian Studies, 1986.

Cherfas, Teresa. "Reporting Stalin's Famine: Jones and Muggeridege: A Case Study in Forgetting and Rediscovery." *Kritika: Explorations in Russian and Eurasian History*, 14:4 (Fall 2013), 775-804.

Colley, Dr. Margaret Siriol. *More Than a Grain of Truth: The Biography of Gareth Richard Vaughan Jones*. Newark, Nottinghamshire: N. L. Colley, Margaret Colley, 2005.

Colley, Nigel Linsan. Footnote 4, RE: 'See Hamlet.' Accessed on 23 September 2012 from http://www.garethjones.org/published_articles/st_patricks/litvinov_famine_denial2.htm.

Colley, Nigel Linsan. Paper Delivered at the James Mace Memorial Panel, IAUs Congress, Donetsk, Ukraine, 19 June 2005.

Conquest, Robert. *Harvest of Sorrow: Soviet Collectivization and the Terror-Famine*. New York: Oxford University Press, 1986.

Cottle, Simon. "Journalists Witnessing Disaster: From the Calculus of Death to the Injunction to Care." *Journalism Studies*, Vol. 14, No. 2 (2013), 232-248.

Crowl, James William. *Angels in Stalin's Paradise*. Lanham, Maryland: University Press of America, 1982.

Davies, R. W., M. B. Tauger, and S. G. Wheatcroft. "Stalin, Grain Stocks and the Famine of 1932-1933." *Slavic Review* 54.3 (Fall 1995): 642-657.

Davies, R. W., and Stephen G. Wheatcroft. *The Years of Hunger: Soviet Agriculture, 1931-1933*. New York: Palgrave Macmillan, 2004.

de Certeau, Michel. *The Writing of History*. New York: Columbia University Press, 1978.

Delaney, Joan. "The Origins of Soviet Antireligious Organizations." In *Aspects of Religion in the Soviet Union 1917-1967*, edited by Richard H. Marshall, Jr., 103-129. Chicago: The University of Chicago Press, 1971.

Ellman, Michael. "Stalin and the Soviet Famine of 1932-33 Revisited." *Europe-Asia Studies* 59.4 (June 2007), 663-693.

Engerman, David C. "Modernization from the Other Shore: American Observers and the Costs of Soviet Economic Development," *The American Historical Review* 105.2 (April 2000): 383-416.

Grigorenko, Petro. *Memoirs*. New York: Norton, 1982.

Greenblatt, Stephen. *Learning to Curse: Essays in Early Modern Culture*. London: Routledge, 1990.

Gregorovich, Andrew. "Genocide in Ukraine 1933." Speech delivered at City Hall, Hamilton, Ontario, 14 November 1998. Accessed on 13 August 2012 from http://faminegenocide.com/resources/genocide/genocide-speech.html.

Grossman, Vasily. *Everything Flows*. Translated by Robert Chandler, Elizabeth Chandler, and Anna Aslanyan. New York: New York Review of Books, 2009.

Hampton, Mark. "Defining Journalists in Late-Nineteenth Century Britain." *Critical Studies in Media Communication* 22.2 (June 2005): 138-155.

"The Heinz Family," John Heinz: A Western Pennsylvania Legacy. Accessed December 23, 2011, from http://www.johnheinzlegacy.org/heinz/heinzfamily.html.

Herman, Edward S., and Noam Chomsky. *Manufacturing Consent: The Political Economy of the Media*. New York: Pantheon, 2002.

Himmelstein, Hal, and E. Perry Faithorn. "Eyewitness to Disaster: How Journalists Cope with the Psychological Stress Inherent in Reporting Traumatic Events." *Journalism Studies* 3.4 (November 2002): 537-555.

Höijer, Birgitta. "The Discourse of Global Compassion: The Audience and Media Reporting of Human Suffering. *Media, Culture & Society*, Vol. 26, No. 4 (2004), 513-531.

Ifversen, Jan. "Text, Discourse, Concept: Approaches to Textual Analysis." *Kontur* 7 (2003): 60-69.

Kansteiner, Wulf. "Finding Meaning in Memory: A Methodological Critique of Collective Memory Studies." *History and Theory* 41 (May 2002): 179-197.

Kieran, Matthew. *Media Ethics: A Philosophical Approach*. London: Praeger, 1997.

Killenberg, G. Michael, and Rob Anderson. "What Is a Quote? Practical, Rhetorical and Ethical concerns for Journalists." *Journal of Mass Media Ethics* 8.1 (1993): 37-54.

Kirkpatrick, David D. "Pulitzer Board Won't Void '32 Award to *Times* Writer." *New York Times*, 22 November 2003.

Kramer, Mark. "Breakable Rules for Literary Journalists." In *Literary Journalism*, edited by Norman Sims and Mark Kramer, 21-34. New York: Ballantine Books, 1995.

Levi-Strauss, Claude. *The Savage Mind*. Chicago: University of Chicago Press, 1966.

Lewin, Moshe. *Russian Peasants and Soviet Power: A Study of*

Collectivization. Translated by George Allen & Unwin Ltd. New York: Norton and Company, 1968.

Liber, George O. *Soviet Nationality Policy, Urban Growth, and Identity Change in the Ukrainian SSR 1923-1934*. Cambridge: Cambridge University Press, 1992.

Luciuk, Y. Lubomyr. "Not Worthy?" In *Not Worthy: Walter Duranty's Pulitzer Prize and the* New York Times, edited by Lubomyr Luciuk, v-x. Kingston, Ontario: Kashtan Press, 2004.

Mace, James E. "The Politics of Famine: American Government and Press Response to the Ukrainian Famine, 1932-1933." *Holocaust and Genocide Studies* 3.1 (1988): 75-94.

Mace, James E. "A Tale of Two Journalists: Walter Duranty, Gareth Jones, and the Pulitzer Prize." In *Not Worthy: Walter Duranty's Pulitzer Prize and the* New York Times, edited by Lubomyr Luciuk, 118-129. Kingston, Ontario: The Kashtan Press, 2004.

Mahoney, Barbara S. *Dispatches and Dictators: Ralph Barnes for the* Herald Tribune. Corvallis: Oregon State University Press, 2002.

Martin, Terry. *The Affirmative Action Empire: Nations and Nationalism in the Soviet Union, 1923-1939*. Ithaca: Cornell University Press, 2001.

Moeller, Susan D. *Compassion Fatigue: How the Media Sell Disease, Famine, War and Death*. New York: Routledge, 1999.

Morrell, Gordon W. *Britain Confronts the Stalin Revolution: Anglo-Soviet Relations and the Metro-Vickers Crisis*. Waterloo, Ontario: Wilfrid Laurier University Press, 1995.

Morris, Paul D. *Representation and the Twentieth Century Novel: Studies in Gorky, Joyce and Pynchon*. Wurzburg, Germany: Königshausen & Neumann, 2005.

Neiman, Susan. *Evil in Modern Thought: An Alternative History of Philosophy*. Princeton: Princeton University Press, 2002.

"New York Times Statement About 1932 Pulitzer Prize Awarded to Walter Duranty." Accessed from http://www.nytco.com/company/awards/statement.html.

Peris, Daniel. *Storming the Heavens: The Soviet League of the Militant Godless*. Ithaca: Cornell University Press, 1998.

Rappaport, Helen. *Joseph Stalin: A Biographical Companion*. Santa Barbara, Calif.: ABC-CLIO, 1999.

Regnery, Henry. "Paul Scheffer: At the Eye of the Storm." In *Perfect Sowing: Reflections of a Bookman*, edited by Jeffery O. Nelson, 232-248. Wilmington, Delaware: ISI Books, 1999.

Serbyn, Roman. "The Last Stand of the Famine-Genocide Deniers," *The Ukrainian Canadian*. February 1989.

Shapoval, Yurii. "Understanding the Causes and Consequences of the Famine-Genocide of 1932-1933 in Ukraine: The Significance of

Newly Discovered Archival Documents," in *Famine in Ukraine, 1932-1933: Genocide by Other Means*, ed. Taras Hunczak and Roman Serbyn, 84-97. New York: Shevchenko Scientific Society, 2007.

Sieff, Martin. "Commentary: Gareth Jones, Hero of Ukraine." United Press International website, 12 June 2003. Accessed from http://www.upi.com/Odd_News/2003/06/12/Commentary-Gareth-Jones-hero-of-Ukraine/UPI-42551055458838/.

Siegelbaum, Lewis H. *Soviet State and Society between Revolutions, 1918–1929*. Cambridge: Cambridge University Press, 1992.

Shklar, Judith. "The Liberalism of Fear," in *Liberalism and the Moral Life* ed. Nancy L. Rosenblum. (ambridge: Harvard University Press, 1989.

Snyder, Timothy. *Bloodlands: Europe between Hitler and Stalin*. New York: Basic Books, 2010.

Steiner, Linda and Okrusch, Chad. "Care as a Virtue for Journalists." *Journal of Mass Media Ethics*, Vol. 21, Nos. 2 & 3 (2006), 102-122.

Sutton, Antony C. *Western Technology and Soviet Economic Development*, Volume 2. Stanford: Hoover Institution Press, 1971.

Tauger, Mark B. "The 1932 Harvest and the Famine of 1933." *Slavic Review* 50.1 (Spring 1991): 70-89.

— —. "Natural Disaster and Human Actions in the Soviet Famine 1931-1933." *The Carl Beck Papers in Russian & East European Studies*, Number 1506, 1-65. Pittsburgh: Center for Russian and East European Studies, 2001.

Taylor, Sally J. *Stalin's Apologist: Walter Duranty—The New York Times's Man in Moscow*. New York: Oxford University Press, 1990.

Teer-Tomaselli, Ruth. "Memory and Markers: Collective Memory and Newsworthiness." In *News in Public Memory: An International Study of Media Memories across Generations*, edited by Ingrid Volkmer, 225-250. New York, Peter Lang, 2006.

Tester, Keith. *Compassion, Morality and the Media*. Buckingham: Open University Press, 2001.

Thevenin, Étienne. "France, Germany and Austria: Facing the Famine of 1932-1933 in Ukraine." Paper presented at the James Mace Memorial Panel, IAUS Congress, Donetsk, Ukraine, 29 June 2005.

Tottle, Douglas. *Fraud, Famine and Fascism*. Toronto: Progress Books, 1987.

Tzouliadis, Tim. *The Forsaken: An American Tragedy in Stalin's Russia*. New York: Penguin Books, 2008.

"Ukraine Honour for Welsh Reporter." BBC News. 22 November 2008. Accessed from http://news.bbc.co.uk/go/pr/fr/-/2/hi/uk_news/wales/south_east/7742330.stm.

Viola, Lynne. *Peasant Rebels Under Stalin: Collectivization and the Culture of Peasant Resistance*. New York: Oxford University Press, 1996.

Ward, Stephen J. A. "Ethics in a Nutshell." Center for Journalism Ethics. Accessed from http://ethics.journalism.wisc.edu/resources/ethics-in-a-nutshell/.

Zelizer, Barbie. "Journalists as Interpretive Communities." *Critical Studies in Mass Communication* 10 (1993): 219-237.

——. "Reading the Past Against the Grain: The Shape of Memory Studies." *Critical Studies in Mass Communication* 12.2 (June 1995): 214-239.

——. "On 'Having Been There': 'Eyewitnessing' as a Journalistic Key Word." *Critical Studies in Media Communication*, Vol. 24, No. 5 (2007), 408-428.

Index

Lightning Source UK Ltd.
Milton Keynes UK
UKHW02f1452250218
318454UK00003B/8/P